The Death Penalty in Dickens and Derrida

The Death Penalty in Dickens and Derrida

The Last Sentence of the Law

Jeremy Tambling

BLOOMSBURY ACADEMIC
LONDON • NEW YORK • OXFORD • NEW DELHI • SYDNEY

BLOOMSBURY ACADEMIC
Bloomsbury Publishing Plc
50 Bedford Square, London, WC1B 3DP, UK
1385 Broadway, New York, NY 10018, USA
29 Earlsfort Terrace, Dublin 2, Ireland

BLOOMSBURY, BLOOMSBURY ACADEMIC and the Diana logo are trademarks of
Bloomsbury Publishing Plc

First published in Great Britain 2023
Paperback edition published 2024

Copyright © Jeremy Tambling, 2023, 2025

Jeremy Tambling has asserted his right under the Copyright, Designs and Patents Act, 1988, to be identified as Author of this work.

For legal purposes the Acknowledgements on pp. x–xv constitute an extension of this copyright page.

Cover image: Grandville (Jean-Ignace-Isidore Gérard, 1803–1847), 'Dream of Crime and Punishment' (1847) © History and Art Collection / Alamy Stock Photo

All rights reserved. No part of this publication may be reproduced or transmitted in any form or by any means, electronic or mechanical, including photocopying, recording, or any information storage or retrieval system, without prior permission in writing from the publishers.

Bloomsbury Publishing Plc does not have any control over, or responsibility for, any third-party websites referred to or in this book. All internet addresses given in this book were correct at the time of going to press. The author and publisher regret any inconvenience caused if addresses have changed or sites have ceased to exist, but can accept no responsibility for any such changes.

A catalogue record for this book is available from the British Library.

A catalog record for this book is available from the Library of Congress.

ISBN: HB: 978-1-3503-5455-5
PB: 978-1-3503-5457-9
ePDF: 978-1-3503-5458-6
eBook: 978-1-3503-5456-2

Typeset by RefineCatch Limited, Bungay, Suffolk

To find out more about our authors and books visit www.bloomsbury.com and sign up for our newsletters.

Contents

Frequently Cited Texts and Abbreviations	vii
Preface and Acknowledgements	x
Introduction: Growing Up to Be Hanged	1
Lamb	1
The pale criminals and the great criminals	4
The first part: Dickens	10
The second part: Derrida	14

Part One Dickens – and the Eighteenth Century

1	Abolitionism and Dickens	27
	Dickens's letters	34
	The Mannings	41
2	Fielding, Hogarth and Dickens	49
	'Four Stages of Cruelty'	55
	Fielding and murder	63
3	*Barnaby Rudge*, Poe and *Caleb Williams*	67
	Poe, Godwin and *Caleb Williams*: 'An epoch in the mind'	76
	'The Man of the Crowd' and the criminality of great cities	84
	Dickens, Poe and secrecy	94

Part Two Derrida – The French Revolution Onwards

4	Deconstruction and Justice	101
	'Force of Law'	104
	The Beast and the Sovereign	108
5	The Death Penalty Seminars	113
	On fascination	115
	Simone de Beauvoir and Hannah Arendt	119
	On the guillotine: Hugo and Turgenev	125
	'The instant of my death'	132

	Shakespeare and blood	135
	The Death Penalty 2: Confession	142
	Robespierre	147
6	Decapitation and *A Tale of Two Cities*	153
	Secrecy	156
	Violence and fascism	160
	'I can devour thee'	163
7	On the USA: Violence and Terrorism	173
	In Cold Blood and *The Executioner's Song*	174
	Timothy McVeigh	181
	Terror and suicide	183
In Conclusion		191
	'New cruelty'	191
Index		199

Frequently Cited Texts and Abbreviations

Benjamin

Arcades Project, trans. Howard Eiland and Kevin McLaughlin (Cambridge, MA: Harvard University Press 1999).
'Critique of Violence': *Selected Writings Vol. 1: 1913–1926* (Cambridge, MA: Harvard University Press 1996), 236–52. (*CV* plus page number)
Selected Writing 4: 1938–1940, ed. Howard Eiland and Michael W. Jennings (Cambridge, MA: Harvard University Press 2003).

Carlyle

The French Revolution: A History in Three Volumes, ed. Mark Cumming and David R. Sorensen, text edited Mark Engel and Brent E. Kinser (Oxford: Oxford University Press 2020).

Derrida

The Beast and the Sovereign, 2 vols., trans. Geoffrey Bennington (Chicago: University of Chicago Press 2008, 2011). (*BS* plus volume and page number)
The Death Penalty, 2 vols., ed. Geoffrey Bennington and Marc Crépon (Chicago: University of Chicago Press, 2014, 2017). (*DP* plus volume and page number)
'Force of Law: The "Mystical Foundation of Authority"' (1994), in Jacques Derrida, *Acts of Religion*, ed. Gil Anidjar (London: Routledge 2002), 228–98.
Glas, trans. John P. Leavey, Jr., and Richard Rand (Lincoln, NE: University of Nebraska Press 1986).

Dickens

Dickens's Letters to the *Daily News* are most accessible online: https://www.bl.uk/collection-items/letters-from-charles-dickens-on-capital-punishment-23-february---16-march-1846.

Penguin editions:
Bleak House, ed. Nichola Bradbury (2003).
Christmas Books 1, ed. Michael Slater (1971).
David Copperfield, ed. Jeremy Tambling (2004).
Great Expectations, ed. David Trotter (2003).
Little Dorrit, ed. Stephen Wall and Helen Small (2003).
Martin Chuzzlewit, ed. Patricia Ingham (1999).
The Old Curiosity Shop, ed. Norman Page (2003).
Oliver Twist, ed. Philip Horne (2003).
Our Mutual Friend, ed. Adrian Poole (1997).

Other editions:
American Notes and Pictures from Italy, ed. F. S. Schwarzbach and Leonee Ormond (London: Dent 1997).
Barnaby Rudge, ed. Clive Hurst, introduction by Iain McCalman and Jon Mee (Oxford: Oxford University Press 2003).
Christmas Stories, ed. Ruth Clancey (London: Everyman 1997).
Dickens's Journalism, 4 vols, ed. Michael Slater (Vol. 4 co-edited with John Drew) (London: Dent 1994–2000).
Letters. The Letters of Charles Dickens, 12 vols., ed. Madeline House and Graham Storey, The Pilgrim edition (Oxford: Oxford University Press 1965–2002).
A Tale of Two Cities, ed. Andrew Sanders (Oxford: Oxford University Press 1998).

Foucault

Discipline and Punish: The Birth of the Prison, trans. Alan Sheridan (London: Penguin 1979). (*DandP* plus page numbers)

Freud

The Standard Edition of the Complete Psychologial Works of Sigmund Freud, ed. James Strachey, 24 vols. (London: Hogarth Press 1953–77). (*SE* plus volume and page-number)

Godwin

Caleb Williams, ed. David McCracken (Oxford: Oxford University Press 1970). (*CW* in text)

Lacan

Ecrits, trans. Bruce Fink (New York: W.W. Norton & Co. 2002).

Nietzsche

Thus Spoke Zarathustra, trans. Graham Parkes (Oxford: Oxford University Press 2005). (*Zarathustra*)
On the Genealogy of Morals, trans. Douglas Smith (Oxford: Oxford University Press 1996).

Poe

The Fall of the House of Usher and Other Writings, ed. David Galloway (London: Penguin 2003). (P plus page number)

Shakespeare

The Riverside Shakespeare, ed. G. Blakemore Evans (Boston, MA: Houghton-Mifflin 1974).

DSA – *Dickens Studies Annual*.
ODNB – *Oxford Dictionary of National Biography*.
OED – *Oxford English Dictionary*.

Preface and Acknowledgements

This Preface outlines the book's plan, and the issues preoccupying it – crime, punishment, law, cruelty, violence and blood, and the last sentence of the law, the death penalty. It tells how it developed this way, and the book's strategy: to put literature and a ring of writers around Dickens in the first half, and the philosophy of Derrida and his others in the second, and to compare these bodies of writing, both of which are primarily abolitionist.

I start with Dickens, witness of hangings, and, when travelling in Italy, of guillotining. Both, plus death by firing squad, are the subjects for this book; however, I omit the fantasy of being impaled on a spike, evoked at the start of *The Mystery of Edwin Drood*. Dickens's engagement with the death penalty appears throughout his writings; however, I concentrate first on five public letters he wrote, the first on Monday, 23 February 1846, appearing in the London-based *Daily News*, the newly founded liberal newspaper. Others, equally abolitionist, followed on Saturday, 28 February, Monday, 5 March, Friday, 9 March, and Monday, 16 March the same year. They comprise a body of writing of about 12,000 words, temperate, good-humoured, occasionally witty, and sustained in their rationalism. Not often studied, they motivate and enrich the novels. The Dickens novel I give fullest attention to in the first half is the much-underestimated *Barnaby Rudge*, while four other figures encircle Dickens: Hogarth, Fielding, William Godwin in *Caleb Williams*, and Edgar Allan Poe, whose criticism of *Barnaby Rudge* is exemplary for opening up the relationship of capital punishment to crime and the city, and detection of crime. This became a chief interest for Dickens, as in *Bleak House*, and discussion of that novel closes Part One.

Part Two derives from the late twentieth century, centring on the Algerian-born Jewish Jacques Derrida (1930–2004), one of the most significant of French intellectuals since his work, informed by an astonishing wide reading, began appearing in the 1960s. His seminars on the death penalty, delivered at the École des hautes études en sciences sociales in Paris between 8 December 1999 and 22 March 2000, and then, for the second of two volumes, between 6 December 2000 and 28 March 2001, appeared posthumously. What the novelist writes may be compared with the philosopher's seminars. Derrida will always divide opinion – too extreme, difficult or inbred for some, or not Marxist enough, even frustrating a 'left' politics – but the seminars, which take him out of his comfort zone, make the case against the death penalty richly, supporting it by a circle comprising Nietzsche, Freud, Walter Benjamin, Foucault, Maurice Blanchot and others. As Derrida is implicit in Part One, Dickens is not forgotten in Part Two, which studies his other historical novel, *A Tale of Two Cities*. This in turn enables discussion of terrorism, in being the novel of the French Revolution and the 'Reign of Terror'. Terrorism is part of the logic of crime and punishment, questioning both because it inverts these relationships; the suicide terrorist punishes, but punishes himself at the same time. Modern terrorism appears in the last chapter, and in the Conclusion.

I began research on Dickens formally at Nottingham, beginning in 1969, supervised by Sheila Smith and John Lucas. The external examiner, Philip Collins, was author of *Dickens and Crime* (1964) which painstakingly goes through materials much easier now for a researcher to access. It remains an impressive pioneer study, which I often use, though I think it limits Dickens intellectually, a then familiar position which Dickens criticism has slowly moved away from doing, as the letters and journalism have affirmed his width of reading, and his relevance to the European and American novel. I diverged from Dickens into other research after that, but a continuous thread of writing makes this book continue and develop from previously published books and articles. Concentrating on Dickens's response to capital punishment has been inseparable from thinking about Dickens and the prison, a topic of fascination since studying *Little Dorrit* for A Level, and reading Lionel Trilling thereon. I wanted to call my first book on Dickens *Dickens and the Dream of the Scaffold*, which of course quotes Baudelaire: 'Il rêve échafauds en fumant son houka' ('He dreams of scaffolds while smoking his hookah' from 'Au Lecteur' in *Les Fleurs du mal*). The publishers were against this, but *Dreams of the Scaffold* stayed as the subtitle to *Dickens, Violence and the Modern State* (1995). I briefly considered *Dickens and the Dead Body* as a title, but decided that was too restricted. Both draft titles registered my sense that Dickens is at his most crisis-ridden when confronted with the last sentence of the law, and this leitmotif accompanies much I have written on Dickens since, whether considering him on American penal systems and solitary confinement, in *Lost in the American City: Dickens, James, Kafka* (2002), or as the novelist of London, or when reading his novels as poetry, or when engaging with that neglected novel, *Nicholas Nickleby*. These are topics of various books. I mark my reading of Dickens through the abiding influence of F. R. Leavis at York in the 1960s, and in the 1970s, as an essential reader of Dickens, and then, later, through Foucault's *Discipline and Punish*.

Foucault brings us to Derrida, both of whom I engaged with when involved in further research in the early 1980s at Essex. Some Dickens readers may query the relevance of Derrida for this book, partly because there remains in Britain, if it has not increased, a hostility to 'theory', though many literature degrees, and film courses, run introductory courses on it. Some theory has been absorbed, some has been transmuted, or displaced by cultural studies which, however essential, are less text-based, less relevant to literature. It is also true that French theory has less obvious relevance to English literature; indeed theory demands a comparative literature approach, which is more important than simply engaging with a single national literature, or with being a 'Victorianist'. Deconstruction especially has been critiqued, from those hostile to 'theory' and by those who find it ultimately negative, lacking political purchase, which was in part the basis of the split between Derrida and Foucault. Confronting these issues, I approach Derrida's work at the beginning of Part Two, introducing it for whoever feels they need it.

In 2001, when teaching at Hong Kong University, I was invited to the Chinese University of Hong Kong where Derrida was speaking one afternoon, and to join a reception and meal afterwards. It was just after the 9/11 attacks in New York. His topic was capital punishment, arguing that philosophers had to date not supported abolition. It was the third time I had heard Derrida, and it gave the chance afterwards to ask him about the 'great criminal', as Benjamin writes of him in 'Critique of Violence'. He remembered and quoted the passage without hesitation. It was a conversation I wanted to continue, but small talk intervened, breaking it up; however, I have tried continuing it here.

Immediate impulse to write started from reading on holiday, in early 2018, the Paraguayan novelist Augusto Roa Bastos's *I the Supreme* (1974). One of the many novels about dictatorship in Latin America – not as many as the dictators are and have been – *I the Supreme* uses Joycean and Borgesian modes of writing to probe José Gaspar Rodriguez de Francia (1766–1840), the highly ambiguous Enlightenment and Robespierre-inspired revolutionary who secured Paraguay as an independent nation, at the cost of his own reign of terror. Francia was greatly admired by Carlyle, whose essay, 'Dr Francia', appeared in the *Foreign Quarterly Review* in 1843 (it is reprinted in Volume 7 of Carlyle's *Critical and Miscellaneous Essays*). Roa Bastos, who treats Francia from the standpoint of the twentieth century, from the impact that Francia has had, including leading to novels whose subject is the dictator, quotes Carlyle in it. Unprepared for this, it was fascinating to find his presence there, and, when I got back to England and could check his essay, to see how Carlyle treats talk of abolition as 'twaddle', and regards Francia as another of the heroes about whom he wrote in *On Heroes and Hero Worship* (1840), and was to continue to write, with Frederick the Great, as a truly heterogeneous force in a country truly different from anything Carlyle could know. Anything connecting the nineteenth-century context with the Latin American novel, which has some of the most exciting writing of the twentieth century, and helped form critical theory such as Derrida's, as well as being informed by it, was immediately exciting. Carlyle appears in this book because of *The French Revolution*, source material for *A Tale of Two Cities*, and much else in Dickens. I was speculating on what Dickens might have thought of Carlyle's essay; it set me to reading Dickens's public letters to the *Daily News*. The book has grown from this, begun sometime in 2019, and intensified in the Covid-19 lockdowns of 2020 and 2021.

One publisher's reader for a draft of this book thought that it should have more address to Dostoevsky. I wanted to preserve the initial duality of Dickens and Derrida in the book, which would have excluded Dostoevsky necessarily. Dostoevsky, whose reception of Dickens connects him with European culture, is nonetheless an essential figure, demanding another, and weighty, consideration. I have approached him in previous work, in my *Confession: Sexuality, Sin, the Subject*, in *Dickens, Violence and the Modern State* for *The Idiot*, or, with *The Brothers Karamazov*, in my *Histories of the Devil*. I hope I may try one day to go back to writing on Dostoevsky, though in translation. The Dostoevskian witness works in France: in 2010 I saw the Musée d'Orsay in Paris exhibition, *Crime et châtiment* (curator Jean Clair). Its first room contained a guillotine, perhaps too obscene to reproduce in the excellent catalogue (Gallimard 2010) which opens with an essay by Robert Badinter, whom Derrida discusses. Seeing the guillotine was so unnerving, I had to return to it at the end, swimming against the tide of visitors coming the other way, to adjust to its awfulness.

Another consideration, making the writing of this book seem an endless process – a point reflected in the Conclusion – is the Russian invasion of Ukraine, starting on 24 February 2022. It has produced accusations of war crimes, including the treatment of war criminals, and threats to execute prisoners, which may indeed have happened, and almost certainly will. This book was finished in a week when the dictatorship in Myanmar recommenced capital punishment, to add to a huge tally of violence in that country (see Editorial, *Guardian*, 27 July 2022). The Ukrainian war has meant resuming older modes of violence which terrorism had apparently temporarily replaced; now war possesses the spirit of state terrorism. I have wanted to say something about this acceleration of violence and execution in wartime, with a sense of inadequacy about what a book such as this could say, and what can be thought in the face of the renewal of aggression apparently uncontainable except by worse.

I should add that whenever the word 'criminal' appears in the text, it should be understood as being in quotation marks: I do not want to pre-empt the question of whether any of the people discussed as criminals should be considered so or not. I am not denying, in any Panglossian spirit, that the word is often appropriate, but I leave open the question of where and to whom it is applicable, and the same might be said about the word 'terrorist'.

I have accumulated many debts. I have referenced everything I have read for the book, I hope, but earlier writings on Dickens should indicate many other books and articles I have worked with, and which extend their influence here. Even so, no one can read everything. However, I owe thanks to friends who have been helpful and resourceful, some by recording disagreements, which were helpful: Michael Hollington, Pam Morris, Dennis Walder, all authors of studies of Dickens. Malcolm Andrews was unfailingly helpful. He published an early short version of Chapter 1: 'Dickens and the Last Sentence of the Law' in *The Dickensian* (116 (2020), 121–31). Michael Slater then invited me to speak to the London Dickens Fellowship, also in 2020, on the same material. Raj Kamal Jha, author of *The City and the Sea* (Penguin Random House India 2019), an interesting novel-treatment of the Delhi rape case discussed in the Conclusion, talked to me about it when I met him in Nepal, when I was privileged to be a judge for the DSC Prize for South Asian Literature, in late 2019. Near the end of the writing of this book I lectured on *Oliver Twist* at the University of Vechta; thanks to the students who helped refine the ideas I had about that book, and Norbert Lennartz for the invitation. Many ex-students have been indispensable, such as Tristan Burke and Ben Moore. One, Dan Bristow, now a psychoanalyst, sent me an email confirming a conversation we had in Hampstead:

> I recall my father telling me a story from the time he worked in construction in Saudi Arabia in the 1970s. At their building site, it had been got wind of that a public execution was to take place and a colleague of my father's was eager to attend the spectacle, and tried to convince him too, which he refused, on point of principle. When this Englishman turned up to the event, seen as a tourist, he was pushed to the front of the crowd, and witnessed the execution to the extent that from this proximity he was spattered with the blood of the beheaded. By my father's account, he came back completely blanched, and a changed man.

It was Dan who also got me to read Simone de Beauvoir. Thanks also to Tadeuz Rachwał, Jonathan Hall, always excellent for insightful conversation; Nick and

Cicely Havely. My son Felix has kept me thinking about criminal law, and my daughter Kirsten about Hogarth, on the strength of her University of London PhD on Watteau and Hogarth. Thanks above all to Pauline, who apart from a hundred other helps given every day, got me to look at the Iranian Mohammad Rasoulof's film, *There is No Evil* (2020), four narratives about people who are designated to be executioners, and very interesting and thought-provoking. I dedicate the book to her.

Introduction: Growing Up to Be Hanged

Lamb

On 9 January 1824, John Thurtell, born in 1794 in Norwich, England, an amateur prize boxer, was hanged outside Hertford gaol for murdering the gambler William Weare in Gill's Hill Lane, Radlett in Hertfordshire, on 24 October 1823.[1] Of his two accomplices, Joseph Hunt, aged 26, an itinerant singer, was sent to the hulks and to Botany Bay in New South Wales, which had become a colony for transports since 1787, because he had turned King's evidence. The other, William Probert, born 1789, was hanged in 1825, ostensibly for horse stealing, or because of his involvement in this murder. Thurtell was sentenced to have his body dissected in the state it was after being cut down; but the corpse lingered in public view, and did not arrive intact at the Surgeons' Hall because part of a finger had been amputated; a reminder, to be developed later, that there was a lingering sense of the criminal's body having a sacral quality, parallel to that of the murdered corpse. Thurtell had fired two pistols at Weare, cut his throat, and brained him. The hanging judge at the Hertford winter assizes was Sir James Park (1763–1838).[1] On that hanging day, Charles Lamb (1775–1834), generous writer and critic, and a casualty of life in many respects, writes to Bernard Barton, a Quaker friend and minor poet, and a banker, living in Woodbridge, Suffolk (the two maintained friendship by post and hardly met), saying that he has succumbed to 'an insurmountable daymare – a whoreson lethargy, Falstaff calls it'. In this state of 'apathy':

> I have not a thing to say – nothing is of more importance than another – I am flatter than a denial or a pancake – emptier than Judge Park's wig when the head is in it – duller than a country stage when the actors are off it . . .

---

[1] Eric R. Watson (ed.), *The Trial of Thurtell and Hunt* (Edinburgh: William Hode 1920); this indicates Park's foolish vanity (16–18,31). See Albert Borowitz, *The Thurtell-Hunt Murder Case* (London: Robson Books 1988).

The hint that it is Thurtell's hanging which is giving him such melancholia expands when he writes: 'tis 12 o'clock and Thurtell is just now coming out upon the New Drop – Jack Ketch alertly tucking up his greasy sleeves to do the last office of mortality, yet cannot I elicit a groan or a moral reflection.' He finishes with:

> It is fifteen minutes after 12. Thurtell is by this time a good way on his journey, baiting at Scorpio perhaps, Ketch is bargaining for his cast coat and waistcoat . . .[2]

Thurtell's reputation lasted: in his essay 'On Murder Considered as one of the Fine Arts' (*Blackwood's Magazine* February 1827), Thomas De Quincey decides that in terms of ranking murderers according to the aesthetic pleasingness of how they presented what they had done, there was something '*falsetto* in the style of Thurtell' – punning: meaning 'false' and 'strained, unnatural', as if Thurtell forced himself on public consciousness, overacting.[3]

Thurtell became Thornton in Bulwer's 'fashionable' novel, *Pelham, Or The Adventures of a Gentleman* (1828), written a year after De Quincey. Thornton kills Sir John Tyrrell – whose name is borrowed from William Godwin's novel *Caleb Williams* (1794), a novel we shall consider. *Pelham* makes the dandy the detective, tracking down the killer so helping his friend, Sir Richard Glanville, the chief suspect. In Lamb's letter, Jack Ketch, the public executioner (1663–86), was, of course, the generic name for the hangman, with a right to the clothes of the hanged. While Lamb's wit, range of reference and neatness of expression show in this letter, other things are noteworthy. Lamb recognizes Thurtell's nastiness (the human scorpion – remembering Shakespeare's most famous murderer: 'O full of scorpions is my mind, dear wife' – (*Macbeth* 3.2.37) – 'baiting at Scorpio' as he moves through the celestial spheres, on his way to his last judgment), and reacts violently, somatically, against capital punishment.

The idea of violence upon another is troubling, whether as a means to an end, or as an end; it places the beholder in a strange position: how is it possible to witness the pain of others? It challenges by asking how to react to it – sympathizing, turning away or looking on? Lamb, not witnessing the hanging, follows it mentally, for violence cannot be done to others, without impacting on others, forcing a new response. Nor was this hanging the ending for Lamb. On 30 November 1824, Henry Fauntleroy, aged 40, the manager of Berners Street

---

[2] Charles Lamb, *The Letters of Charles Lamb*, ed. E. V. Lucas and Guy Pocock, 2 vols (London: Dent 1945), 2.107–8.
[3] Thomas De Quincey, *The English Mail-Coach and Other Essays* (London: Everyman 1912), 72.

Bank in London was hanged at Newgate for forgery and buried in Bunhill Fields on 2 December. On 1 December, Lamb writes again to Barton:

> And now my dear Sir, trifling apart, the gloomy catastrophe of yesterday morning prompts a sadder vein. The fate of the unfortunate Fauntleroy makes me, whether I will or no, to cast reflecting eyes around on such of my friends as by a parity of situation are exposed to a similarity of temptation ... Your hands as yet, I am most willing to believe, have never deviated into others' property. You think it impossible that you could ever commit so heinous an offence. But so thought Fauntleroy once; so have thought many besides him, who at last have expiated, as he hath done. You are as yet upright. But you are a Banker, at least the next thing to it ... I tremble, I am sure, at myself, when I think that so many poor victims of the Law at one time of their life made as sure of never being hanged as I in my presumption am too ready to do myself. What are we better than they? Do we come into the world with different necks? Is there any distinctive mark under our left ears? Are we unstrangulable? I ask you. Think of these things. I am shocked sometimes at the shape of my own fingers, not for their resemblance to the ape tribe (which is something) but for the exquisite adaptation of them to the purposes of picking, fingering, etc. No-one that is so framed, I maintain it, but should tremble.[4]

Fauntleroy's biographer notes him succeeding his father, original manager of a private bank (Marsh and Sibbald) which opened in 1792. He casts him as a 'great criminal', meaning that Fauntleroy identified with Napoleon his contemporary, like many others, real and imaginary, (Eugene Onegin, Julian Sorel or Raskolnikov). Even the eighteenth-century Jonathan Wild in W. H. Ainsworth's novel *Jack Sheppard* (1839) was called by his author 'the Napoleon of knavery'.[5] Fauntleroy, though married, domiciled at 7 Berners Street, north of Oxford Street, had a 'villa in the suburbs' – in Hampton-on-Thames; and later an apartment in Brighton where he kept a mistress. He forged signatures to finance that lifestyle.[6] Arrested on 10 September 1824, his trial at the Old Bailey lasted only five hours. Put alongside the trial of Thurtell and Hunt, it could be called an

---

[4] Charles Lamb, *Letters* 2. 132.
[5] W. H. Ainsworth, *Jack Sheppard*, ed. Edward Jacobs and Manuela Mourão (Peterborough, ON: Broadview Press 2007), 240. See George J. Worth, *William Harrison Ainsworth* (New York: Twayne 1972).
[6] Horace Bleackley, *Some Distinguished Victims of the Scaffold* (London: Kegan Paul 1905), quotation from Preface, no page reference, and 180–1 for Fauntleroy as Napoleonic, and for the villa. His private life is described in terms of the then contemporary Pierce Egan exploring all aspects of the metropolis in *Life in London* (1820).

early example of 'trial by newspaper'.[7] It had reverberations: Bulwer used it in plotting *The Disowned* (1828), his third novel.

Lamb found something to think about with Fauntleroy. In an essay of April 1825, 'The Last Peach' (*London Magazine*) he says he 'lives in constant fear of one day coming to the gallows', and records the temptation of wanting to pluck forbidden fruit (a peach), moved by 'a demon of contradiction'. He does so, though he does not want the fruit. The essay imagines Fauntleroy's privileged birth, and his life's 'very different exit'. E. V. Lucas notes the Quaker Caroline Fox (1819–71) writing, from Penjerrick near Falmouth, a diary entry for 25 October 1839:

> G. Wightwick [architect: 1802–72] and others dined with us. He talked agreeably about capital punishment, greatly doubting their having any effect in preventing crime. Soon after Fauntleroy was hanged, an advertisement appeared, 'To all good Christians! Pray for the soul of Fauntleroy'. This created a good deal of speculation as to whether he was a Catholic, and at one of Coleridge's soirées it was discussed for a considerable time; at length Coleridge, turning to Lamb, asked, 'Do you know anything about this affair?'; 'I should think I d-d-did', said Elia, 'for I paid s-s-s-seven and sixpence for it!'
>
> 133

Lamb was evidently haunted by Fauntleroy's fate, as by Thurtell's, who was also a figure Dickens remembered, an example of an anxiety produced by fear of punishment; as if the deterrence effect of capital punishment has reached and plagued the wrong person. It excites a sense that he could be the criminal; that there is an affinity between his neck and the hangman's rope. The death penalty has the wrong influence. It does not touch the person it is intended for, only disturbing and worrying someone with Lamb's sensitivity. He wrote when the death penalty had become a new subject of debate. He fits into the scope of the first part of this book, which addresses the hundred years onwards from 1764, when Beccaria published his abolitionist treatise *Dei delitti e delle pene* (*Of Crimes and Punishments*) to 1868, when Britain moved hanging to the inside of jails.

The pale criminals and the great criminals

In Lamb's day, the question was which offences – obviously not just murder – should incur the death penalty. Lamb was distinctive in identifying with

---

[7] Horace Bleackley, *The Trial of Henry Fauntleroy and Other Famous Trials for Forgery* (Edinburgh: William Hodge 1924), Preface, no page reference. See Keith Hollingsworth, *The Newgate Novel 1830–1847: Bulwer, Ainsworth, Dickens, and Thackeray* (Detroit: Wayne State University Press 1963), 41–7.

criminals, feeling he could be like them. How this sense of guilt was constructed is discussed in non-specific terms by Freud, in a short piece, 'Criminals from a Sense of Guilt' (1916), one of three with the umbrella title, 'Some Character-types Met with in Psychoanalytic Work' (1916). This third essay deals with respectable people who in their youth transgressed doing so 'principally because they were forbidden'. The execution gave mental relief, for the transgressor 'was suffering from an oppressive feeling of guilt of which he did not know the origin, and after he had committed a misdeed this oppression was mitigated. His sense of guilt was at least attached to something' (Freud, *SE* 14.332).

How much this helps with Lamb must be discussed, and needs expanding upon. Continuing, therefore, with Freud: he says of the reasons for guilt, that 'parricide and incest with the mother are the two great human crimes' (333). We need not disagree when recalling that *Hamlet* locates the primal crime in fratricide, for the family sets brothers against each other. When the King tells Hamlet to cease mourning his father, he alludes to 'the first corse' (1.2.100) – i.e. that of Abel. It may be a Freudian slip, since he is talking about his own brother, making himself Cain. In his soliloquy, he feels his guilt:

> O my offence is rank, it smells to heaven,
> It hath the primal eldest curse upon't,
> A brother's murder . . .
>   What if this cursed hand
> Were thicker than itself with brother's blood
> Is there not rain enough in the sweet heaven
> To wash it white as snow?
>
> 3.3.36–8, 43–6

He has the curse of Cain, whom Hamlet incidentally names when commenting on the gravedigger with skulls: 'how the knave jowls it to the ground, as if 'twere Cain's jawbone, that did the first murder' (5.1.77–8).[8] In the King's soliloquy, blood, though he has not shed it literally, takes over his mind, evoking God's words to Cain:

> the voice of thy brother's blood crieth unto me from the ground, and now art thou cursed from the earth, which hath opened her mouth to receive thy brother's blood from thy hand.
>
> Genesis 4:10–11

---

[8] On the richness of this language, and symbolism, the puns on jowl, and on whose jawbone it is, see Cherrell Guilfoyle, 'The Staging of the First Murder in the Mystery Plays in England', *Comparative Drama* 25 (1991), 42–51.

Claudius's speech recalls, however negatively, Isaiah 1:18 – 'though your sins be as scarlet [Luther's Bible: 'blutrot'], they shall be white as snow'. The *Hamlet* reference makes blood integral to this study, wherein punishment and murder are braided together, while Lamb's 'expiate', because of its Latin source *piare*, 'to seek to appease (by sacrifice), from *pius*, "devout"' (so *OED*), recalls the point that capital punishment has a religious sense from which it gets its justification. No wonder the King thinks his hand is cursed by God.

With that reminder of blood and guilt going together, we return to Freud's argument that children want to provoke punishment, and are quiet and contented afterwards. Among adult criminals, some 'have either developed no moral inhibitions, or … in their conflict with society, [they] consider themselves justified in their action'.

> But as regards the majority of other criminals, those for whom punitive measures are really designed, such a motivation for crime might very well be taken into consideration; it might throw light on some obscure points in the psychology of the criminal, and furnish punishment with a new psychological basis.

Irony shows in 'those for whom punitive measures are devised'. They are melancholics like Lamb, anxiety-ridden by the death penalty. Law deters from crime those already predisposed to obey the law; the others, criminals, or 'great criminals', if they exist, are not really the object of the reach of the law. They include those featuring in literature, who, Freud writes in 'On Narcissism: An Introduction' (1914), 'compel our interest by the narcissistic consistency with which they manage to keep away from their ego anything that would diminish it' (*SE* 14.89). Law only increases anxiety in those it can frighten or make feel a compulsion to confess by threatening punitive measures. It speaks to an homogeneous group, to which the 'hardened' criminal is heterogeneous. Lamb feared that Fauntleroy was no different from himself or Barton.

Concluding 'Criminals from a Sense of Guilt', Freud makes a slightly embarrassed allusion to Nietzsche, whose huge influence on him was not always acknowledged:

> A friend has since called my attention to the fact that the 'criminal from a sense of guilt' was known to Nietzsche too. The pre-existence of the feeling of guilt and the utilization of a deed in order to rationalise this feeling, glimmer before us in Zarathustra's sayings 'On the Pale Criminal'. Let us leave it to future research to decide how many criminals are to be reckoned among those 'pale' ones.
>
> *SE* 14.333[9]

---

[9] Freud's editors compare *SE* 10.42 and 17.28, the latter passage adding in 'the complicating factor of masochism'.

That references Part One, chapter 6 from *Thus Spake Zarathustra* (1883–5), which has that title. Why is the criminal there pale? Nietzsche's complex argument – reflection and narrative – works backwards, since the chapter starts with the end, the death sentence by the 'scarlet judge', who is 'red' because he is licensing violence. The beginning is a person's impulse to murder: the pale criminal starts as a disturbed soul – 'a heap of sicknesses . . . a ball of snakes that are seldom at peace with each other'. The 'poor body' interpreted these conflictual 'sufferings and desires' as 'murderous pleasure and greed for the joy of the knife'. The man 'wants to hurt with that which hurts him'. The murder which follows is misinterpreted, by the judge and by the criminal himself, as a Utilitarian desire for gain:

> Thus speaks the scarlet [*rothe*] judge. 'But why did this criminal murder? He wanted to rob'. But I say to you all, his soul wanted blood, not loot; he was thirsting for the joy of the knife!
> But his meagre reason was unable to grasp this madness, and won him over. 'What is the point of blood!' it said. 'Do you not at least want to steal something too? Or to take revenge?'
> And he listened to his meagre reason . . . and so he robbed when he murdered. He did not want to be ashamed of his madness.

Hence, 'an image made this pale man pale. Equal to his deed was he when he did it: but its image he could not endure when it was done' (*Zarathustra* 34).

Following Nietzsche, the criminal must (mis-)self-interpret his desire for blood as only the desire to steal. He cannot admit the madness which wants blood; he was equal to doing murder, not to living with it. He accepts the court's, and society's description of himself as a criminal – and in the quotation, the judge assumes that he was a criminal *before* he murdered: he murdered because that was his character type. Guilt is immanent before the crime happens. The violence tearing him apart inwardly (Nietzsche wrote before the word 'schizophrenia' was devised) must be allayed by a violent act; Nietzsche, like Derrida, and Dickens, is fascinated by this desire for blood, and how it brings crime, and punishment, as both desiring blood, together. The King in *Hamlet*, who has not literally shed blood, fantasizes having blood on his hands. He resembles Lady Macbeth saying 'here's the smell of the blood still' (*Macbeth* 5.1.50) while continuing, sleep-walking, to wash her hands in an obsessive compulsive disorder.

A 'sense of guilt' makes Freud consider a 'need for punishment', which produces two forms of masochism. One comes from obedience to the superego, the internalized power of the father, the moral policeman with the power of aggressive criticism over the ego. In this book, dealing with the law's ultimate penalty, we can start with a Freud quotation, when he says the super-ego 'rages with merciless violence' within 'a pure culture of the death drive', succeeding 'in driving the ego into death, if the latter does not fend off its tyrant in time by the change round into mania' ('The Ego and the Id', *SE* 19.53). Such is the law's power: maddening, suicide-inducing. Then there is 'moral masochism', the other form, coming from the ego which seeks punishment, 'either from the superego, or the parental powers outside' – stirring up the law against it ('The Economic Problem of Masochism', *SE* 19.169). It relates to the death-drive, subject of 'Beyond the Pleasure Principle' (*SE* 18.3–64), as an almost primary desire within life; it may move via crime towards desire for punishment.

Lamb identified with guilt, while fascinated by the criminal, and almost terrorized by capital punishment. In an essay, 'Critique of Violence' (1921), the cultural critic Walter Benjamin (1892–1940) contends that the law wants not to preserve legal ends, but to preserve itself, and its privileges. Law conceals the violence which established it, siding with power, not justice. As the Artful Dodger says of his trial at Bow-Street, 'this ain't the shop for justice' (*OT* 3.6.368). In Benjamin's example, classically, law turns its fire against a woman, Niobe, (249–50). In opposition to the violence of law:

> violence, when not in the hands of the law, threatens it not by the ends that it may pursue but by its mere existence outside the law. The same may be more drastically suggested, for one reflects how often the figure of the *'great' criminal*, however repellent his ends may have been, has aroused the secret admiration of the public.
>
> This can result not from his deed, but from the violence to which it bears witness.
>
> CV 239[10]

We can associate that with Freud:

> The charm of a child lies to a great extent in his narcissism, his self-contentment and inaccessibility, just as does the charm of certain animals which seem not to concern themselves about us, such as cats and the large beasts of prey. Indeed, even *great criminals* and humorists, as they are represented in literature, compel

---

[10] On Benjamin, see Peter Fenves and Julia Ng, *Walter Benjamin: Toward the Critique of Violence: A Critical Edition* (Stanford: Stanford University Press 2021). Benjamin's essay is discussed by Derrida in 'Force of Law: The "Mystical Foundation of Authority"' (1994). A revision in 2001 added a prolegomena and postscript to that second half of the essay (see pp. 258–62, 293–8; 262–93) where Derrida is more critical of Benjamin. See Robert Zacharias, '"And Yet": Derrida on Benjamin's Divine Violence', *Mosaic* 40 (2007), 103–16.

our interest by the narcissistic tendency with which they manage to keep away from their ego anything that would diminish its enigmatic nature...

'On Narcissism', *SE* 14.89, my emphasis

In literature, and in popular culture, criminals associate with narcissism, while the cult of the serial killer shows fascination with 'great criminals'. Shakespeare produced some of these – Richard the Third, Macbeth and Lady Macbeth – though the last does not, possibly could not, actually kill anyone. De Quincey's 'On Murder Considered as One of the Fine Arts' concentrates on John Williams, who killed, bloodily, the members of two separate households in the Radcliffe Highway in East London, apparently with no motive. He hanged himself in his cell (27 December 1811). His body was publicly paraded through the streets by the order of the Home Secretary, Richard Ryder, a reactionary valetudinarian opposed to Samuel Romilly's attempts to reform capital punishment.[11] De Quincey (133) says Williams was buried at the conflux of four streets with a stake driven through his heart, 'and over him drives for ever the uproar of unresting London'. Ryder must have been infuriated that Williams's suicide allowed him to void the state's power to assert the length of life, and to enforce it. Even committing suicide recognizes life as 'other', and as not calculable; hanging Williams would have made his life something controlled by state calculation (a Derridean point). The state must demonstrate that power, and to lengthen out life in order to destroy it; hence the parading, as if attempting to maintain power over life, though the person is dead.[12]

Benjamin, in the *Arcades Project*, chronicling nineteenth-century Paris, notes one 'great criminal': Pierre François Lacenaire (1800–36) – 'it was at 271 Rue Sainte-Martin, in the Passage du Cheval Rouge, that Lacenaire committed his murders'. Lacenaire, who appears in Marcel Carné's film *Les Enfants du Paradis* (1945), is remembered for his beautiful handwriting, and for writing before his execution an 'Ode à la guillotine', 'in which the criminal is celebrated in the allegorical form of a woman, of whom it is said, "This woman laughed with horrible glee / As a crowd tearing down a throne will laugh"' (*Arcades* 52, 703, 713). Criminality becomes inseparable from sexual ambiguity or deviancy. The attraction of people towards the 'great criminal', careless of guilt, gallows-marked,

---

[11] See Leon Radzinowicz, 'The Radcliffe Murders', *Cambridge Law Journal* 14 (1956), 39–56. On De Quincey's on Williams, described by De Quincey in the 'Postscript' to 'On Murder Considered as One of the Fine Arts', see Joel Black, *The Aesthetics of Murder: A Study in Romantic Literature and Contemporary Culture* (Baltimore: Johns Hopkins University Press 1991), 56–103.

[12] Miriam Jerade, '*Mors Certa, Hora incerta*: Derrida on Finitude and the Death Penalty', trans. Felipe Quinteros, *CR: The New Centennial Review* 17 (2017), 103–21.

is matched by that attraction punishment possesses. Foucault noted a popular dual response towards law, wanting it to maintain itself in punishment, and also, like the great criminal, wanting to show the law up as empty. Derrida, too, as we shall see, considers the 'great criminal', following Benjamin and Foucault (*DP* 2.44–7).

The first part: Dickens

> His neck was so twisted, that the knotted ends of his white cravat usually dangled under one ear; his natural acerbity and energy, always contending with a second nature of habitual repression gave his features a swollen and suffused look; and altogether, he had a weird appearance of having hanged himself at one time or other, and of having gone about ever since halter and all, exactly as if some timely hand had cut him down.
>
> *LD* 52

Domestic crime stirred the prejudices and journalistic interests of the nineteenth-century middle class.[13] Dickens was different. His interest in crime, criminals and hanging was virtually obsessional, and near-identificatory, and as with the portrait of Jeremiah Flintwinch in *Little Dorrit*, the language silently recalling Oliver Twist's name (twisting on a rope's end – 'that boy will be hung' (*OT* 15)) – it included capital punishment within other parts of his writing. It filled his novels with the sense of the hanged man being inside life in its most casual aspects, the grotesque reality undermining a sense of life and death as separate. Magwitch in *Great Expectations* is as if walking towards a gibbet on the coastline with chains dangling from it which had once held a pirate: 'The man was limping on towards this latter, as if he were the pirate come to life, and come down, and going back to hook himself up again' (*GE* 7). That perception, of capital punishment as inside life, not the last sentence of the law, but an ongoing episode in a relationship with the law, is this book's subject. Crime, murder, punishment, and the lack of rational explanation covering these, filled Dickens's sense of narrative, in confronting motives and actions which do not know themselves and which turn awry any presumption of behaviour as following Utilitarian,

---

[13] Richard D. Altick, *Victorian Studies in Scarlet* (New York: W.W. Norton & Co. 1970) and Judith Flanders, *The Invention of Murder: How the Victorians Revelled in Death and Detection and Created Modern Crime* (London: Harper Press 2011) give representative popular (non-theorized) accounts of the popularity of crime.

self-interested and self-aware principles. The death penalty sends the 'criminal' into a state where nothing else can be said, where it is pretended that all uncertainties have been resolved. What Dickens writes about capital punishment goes beyond the public letters, engaging with his novels, two discussed in detail here – *Barnaby Rudge* and *A Tale of Two Cities*. The choice follows from Edgar Allan Poe, himself profoundly interested in crime, who finds something missing in Dickens, which he calls a sense of mystery, translatable, as here, into considering Dickens unable to follow through on his own deepest insights into crime and criminality, including their unknowability, because of a commitment he has to law and to an ameliorative approach to society. That split was detected by Edmund Wilson in his 1941 essay, 'Dickens: The Two Scrooges', still an indispensable critique.[14] Poe was partially right, as we shall see, but wrong in underestimating the power of fantasy in Dickens.

Dickens started, virtually, with 'A Visit to Newgate' (*Sketches by Boz*), describing a visit on 5 November 1835, to see three men: one, Robert Swan, a guardsman convicted of robbery with menaces (reprieved), and two others hanged on 27 November 1835: John Smith and John Pratt, for homosexual offences (*Journalism* 1.198–200). *Oliver Twist* includes two hangings, astonishingly varied in how they are encompassed, and moves through pantomime comedy about being 'scragged' (1.17.150) to the last night in the condemned cell, whose effect is intensified by Cruikshank's illustration of Fagin. 'Scragged' is explicable from the 'scrag-end' of dead meat. The anthropologist Talal Asad notes that the neck is the weakest part of the body, taking this from how the body becomes pieces in suicide bombings.[15] Jokes and allusions to the noose are omnipresent. Fagin fantasizes about his comrades being hanged ('what a fine thing capital punishment is . . .' – 1.9.68); Nancy remembers men in their last twelve hours in the condemned cell (1.16.125), this being prelusive for the final concentration on Fagin in the condemned cell, thinking 'with what a rattling noise the drop went down and how suddenly they changed from strong and sturdy men to dangling heaps of clothes' (*OT* 445). The traumatic event, the chiasmic moment, becomes traumatic in *David Copperfield* where, as troubled as Lamb, the mad Mr Dick, flying his kite inscribed with his autobiographical 'memorial' to the Lord Chancellor written on it, cannot complete this because of King Charles I's head. He says of this: 'how could the people about him have made that mistake of putting some of the trouble out of *his* head, after it was taken off, into *mine*'?

---

[14] Edmund Wilson, *The Wound and the Bow* (London: Methuen 1961), 1–93.
[15] Talal Asad, *On Suicide Bombing* (New York: Columbia University Press 2007), 69.

(*DC* 212). *OED* gives a first citation for 'off one's head' – 'crazy' – from Thomas Hood in 1842. The colloquial meaning and literal sense of having lost the head unite in someone obviously traumatized by cruelty, and feeling that decapitation is not a final act; and the statue of Charles I in Whitehall is seen to be prominent, a warning sign in the novel. A change of status has occurred; the head of sovereign power, however unjust, cannot, finally, be cut off. It remains to menace and punish, as part of an unforgettable, trauma-inducing event. Lastly, in *Great Expectations*, Pip and Wemmick visit Newgate, seeing the 'Colonel', due for execution on Monday for coining (*GE* 262-4).

The selective references given here set aside Dickens's detailed writing about prisons, and their effects in American and London prisons.[16] Further, he was fascinated with murderers, who bear witness to an opacity, unknowability within any narrative. One instance is William Palmer (1824 – hanged at Stafford gaol on 14 June 1856). An essay for *Household Words* (14 June 1856), 'The Demeanour of Murderers', discusses his composure in the dock, and invokes Thurtel, who had been another man of the turf, and so a gambler, for parallels (*Journalism* 3.377-83). For Dickens, Palmer's composure proved his guilt, indicating that Palmer had the coolness to poison perhaps three people (the count of murders might even have reached sixteen). Poisoning requires – unlike throat-cutting – coolness and hypocrisy, especially since Palmer was a surgeon, and attended the bedside of the third person killed, his friend John Cook, another man of the turf. Palmer was a complex case for there was only highly novelistic circumstantial evidence against him. The trial was accordingly deeply prejudiced against him, like the witnesses, wanting to secure a conviction; and Palmer might have hanged in error.[17]

Dickens apparently finds Palmer guilty because Thurtell was. His writing tries to close the gap between wanting something to be so, and it being so, while definite knowledge eludes everybody. Writing becomes rhetorical, possibly revealing an anxiety, that it may be impossible to prove murder, which would mean the failure of writing which wants to prove it, and which in any case thinks it has the public role which allows it to make a difference. As if playing the policeman, like the one who investigated Palmer, Inspector Field, a friend of Dickens, Dickens detected a restlessness in Palmer's putting a glove on and off, passing his hand over his face, and in his incessant note writing while he was in

---

[16] See my 'New Prisons, New Criminals, New Masculinity: Dickens and Reade', in Jan Alber and Frank Lauterbach (eds.), *Stones of Law, Bricks of Shame: Narrating Imprisonment in the Victorian Age* (Toronto: University of Toronto Press 2009), 46–69.

[17] John Sutherland, 'Wilkie Collins and the Origin of the Sensation Novel', *DSA* 20 (1991), 243–58.

the dock. Yet these parapraxes, as Freud would call them, may mean nothing, and suggest that the article's severity – it is not his best – indicates what it is that makes a crux of the death penalty: it requires closing a gap between certain calculable knowledge that may (though unjustifiably) be acted on, and the mystery within identity – the opacity discussed earlier – which defies analysis. What was the secret of Palmer's coolness, which impelled the law to resort to trickery to convict him?

The novelist, unlike the journalist, probes in a way disallowing distance from the criminal. There is a more vulnerable case of criminality, where Dickens's writing is strong: that of the pauper turned schoolmaster, Bradley Headstone in *Our Mutual Friend*. Headstone feels his inferiority before the more privileged lawyer Eugene Wrayburn, and hates school teaching – 'watching and repressing himself daily to discharge [his duties] well', as he says, and while 'white with passion'; speaking of himself in the third person (289), so that he has plural superegos with sadistic power over his ego, one incentivizing him to action, one trying to objectify him making him appear as rational as what he teaches. When Lizzie Hexam refuses him as a suitor, he suspects it is in favour of Eugene Wrayburn:

> 'Then', said he ... bringing his clenched hand down upon the stone with a force that laid the knuckles raw and bleeding, 'then I hope I may never kill him!'
>
> OMF 390

Violent aggression turned outwards has a masochistic effect on his body. The hand is to double business bound: clenched in repression *and* ready to punch. After being, later, further taunted by Wrayburn, whom he has been stalking, Dickens speculates:

> The state of the man was murderous, and he knew it. More; he irritated it, with a kind of perverse pleasure akin to that which a sick man sometimes has in irritating a wound upon his body. Tied up all day with his disciplined show upon him, subdued to the performance of his routine of educational tricks encircled by a gabbling crowd, he broke loose at night like an ill-tamed wild animal. Under his daily restraint, it was his compensation, not his trouble, to give a glance towards his state at night and to the freedom of its being indulged. If *great criminals* told the truth – which, being great criminals, they do not – they would very rarely tell of their struggles against the crime. Their struggles are towards it. They buffet with opposing waves, to gain the bloody shore, not to recede from it.
>
> OMF 535–6, my emphasis

Dickens allows no separation from this man. Headstone is not a 'great' criminal, like those Oliver Twist must read about (*OT* 164), being a pauper schoolmaster trying to keep himself decent, while becoming wildly heterogeneous. He demands the reader's understanding attention. His death-drive is announced in his last wrestling with Rogue Riderhood, who says he cannot be drowned. He answers 'in a desperate clenched voice': 'I can be . . . I am resolved to be. I'll hold you living and I'll hold you dead. Come down!' (*OMF* 781). They fall backwards into the ooze, Riderhood 'girdled with Bradley's strong ring': that being the power of the 'clench', a word now quoted twice about Headstone. Is Headstone murdering or committing suicide? Which comes first in fantasy? The question may be asked of the suicide terrorist. In both, is it that the life and the environment are alike insufferable, creating the resolution to die? Or is there the intention to murder? Are these the same? Ironically, the man Headstone murders is not the man he meant to murder.

The image of the sick man scratching at a wound separates Headstone from the more spontaneous 'great criminal' of popular culture. His onanistic self-irritations, self-stimulations, are sadistic and masochistic together, torturing his body as he would torture Wrayburn's, making the fantasy of murder sexual. Wrayburn is the fantasized superego which he would destroy, and his self-inflicted violence internalizes his perception of Wrayburn's violence of manner and speech. His destructiveness works against his own body and ego, like Freud's or Nietzsche's 'pale criminal'. Freud argues that 'masochism is actually sadism turned round upon the subject's own ego' ('Instincts and their Vicissitudes', *SE* 14.127). This is the area wherein Dickens works. That the same act is sadistic *and* masochistic destroys concepts of a single subject with knowable motivations, since a sadistic or masochistic act cannot necessarily know what produces it, nor the meaning within it; that the masochism shows itself in sadism, and that sadism is also masochistic.

The second part: Derrida

Derrida writes in our present, when neither EU countries nor Britain have the death penalty. In the United States, twenty-nine states retain the death penalty, leaving twenty-one without.[18] Further, the Federal government has the right of

---

[18] Those states without are: Alaska, Connecticut, Delaware, Hawaii, Illinois (thanks to Governor George Ryan in 2003), Iowa, Maine, Maryland, Massachusetts, Michigan, Minnesota, New Hampshire, New Jersey, New Mexico, New York, North Dakota, Rhode Island, Vermont, Washington, West Virginia, Wisconsin, plus, effectively, California, Colorado, Oregon and Pennsylvania (Website of the Death Penalty Information Center).

execution.[19] The states which have it, Derrida shows may be mapped onto the southern states in the Civil War, and the states with the largest black populations (*DP* 1.74). They are also the states comprising what H. L.Mencken called the 'Bible Belt'. Derrida notes that 'the most militant opponents of abortion are most often ... especially in the United States, advocates of the death penalty' (2.14). The situation in the USA is worse than when Derrida was writing. Other countries practising the death penalty are, in alphabetical order, Bangladesh, China, Egypt, Ethiopia, India, Indonesia, Iran, Japan, Nigeria, Saudi Arabia, South Korea, Sri Lanka and Taiwan. That list is not all-inclusive, and it only speaks for 'official' executions, and does not account for what are deemed exceptional circumstances – occasions when, as Derrida says, a country exercises its sovereignty by killing people. (An example appears in the Conclusion.) Amnesty International has a higher number of countries which have recently carried out the death penalty. It adds, for 2018 (going alphabetically), Afghanistan, Belarus, Botswana, North Korea, Singapore, Somalia, South Sudan, Sudan, Thailand, Vietnam, Yemen.[20]

Though the USA adheres to capital punishment, Derrida notes an 'other' America: Michigan, in 1846, was the first state anywhere to abolish the death penalty (1.181). Pennsylvania, in 1787, following Beccaria, who influenced Thomas Jefferson, attempted to abolish the death penalty (1.212). To Michigan could be added Rhode Island (1851) and Wisconsin (1853). Antebellum America had abolitionist writings, as with the jurist and statesman Edward Livingston (1764–1836), the lawyer and journalist John L. O'Sullivan (1813–95), and the Charleston-born novelist William Gilmore Simms (1806–70), in *Martin Faber* (1933) and *Guy Rivers: A Tale of Georgia* (1834) and *Confession, Or the Blind Heart* (1841). Yet, ironically, Simms remained throughout his life pro-slavery.[21] In contrast was Lydia Maria Child (1802–80), who was an abolitionist, and feminist, and anti-slavery since 1830. She had contact with Dickens in his American visit (see *Letters* 3.403–4), and may have influenced his views on capital punishment, being an instance of the intellectual stimulus America could give Dickens. Her letters may be seen pondering the death of Mary Rogers who almost certainly died after a botched abortion (the case which Poe – who incidentally admired her – attempted solving in *The Mystery of Marie Roget*). Her journalism takes up

---

[19] 'US Government to execute a woman for first time since 1953', *Guardian*, 19 October 2020 – i.e. Lisa Montgomery, killed on 12 January 2021. The last state execution of a woman was Kelly Renee Gissandaner in 2015, for murdering her husband in 1997.
[20] Amnesty International Global report: Death Sentences and Executions 2018, accessed online.
[21] See John Cyril Barton, 'William Gilmore Simms and the Literary Aesthetics of Crime and Capital Punishment', *Law and Literature* 22 (2010), 220–43.

capital punishment, and urban crime, becoming the book *Letters from New York* (1843).[22] And further short stories: 'The Juryman' and 'Elizabeth Wilson' and 'Hilda Silfverling' approached the problem of infanticide.[23]

Is capital punishment on the way out, as Roger Hood thinks?[24] The state still regularly kills its citizens; Russia by poisoning its critics, Saudi Arabia by strangling and chopping into pieces. The state kills on a broad scale: in Myanmar; or with the Chinese government's destruction of the Uighur population in Xinjiang province; and before that, in 1989, in the Tiananmen Square massacre, which left relations unable to grieve because to acknowledge who was killed was too dangerous. That account omits Nazi atrocities, genocide practised in secret.[25] At this writing, a war of aggression against Ukraine has left thousands dead. Though the EU has formally abolished the death penalty, Britain quitting the EU for its own nationalism permits British reactionariness to make noises about reviving it. Anecdotally, the present writer was discussing this book project with a benign member of the British Conservative Party and Parliamentary candidate, who said that how to deal with party members' demands that the death penalty be resumed was a sticking point for candidates hoping for adoption by a particular constituency. He said that the defence that innocent people had undoubtedly been hung (Timothy Evans, for instance) had been his own line in constituency adoption meetings.[26] However, another Tory MP from the shires, he said, had rounded on this argument, contending that though innocent people had undoubtedly been hanged in error, nonetheless, if murderers were not hanged, how many more murders would happen which would otherwise have been prevented … A justificatory Utilitarianism. And capital punishment remains in force in some African countries, and in much of Asia including Japan, another democracy supporting it.[27]

---

[22] Carolyn L. Karcher, *The First Woman in the Republic: A Cultural Biography of Lydia Maria Child* (Durham, NC: Duke University Press 1994), 274, 299–310.

[23] On Simms and Lydia Maria Child, see John Cyril Barton, *Literary Executions: Capital Punishment and American Culture 1820-1925* (Baltimore: Johns Hopkins University Press 2014), 59–95.

[24] Roger Hood, *The Death Penalty: A Worldwide Perspective* (Oxford: Oxford University Press 2015).

[25] For a comparison of the Terror and the death camps, see Daniel Gordon, 'The Theater of Terror: The Jacobin Execution in Comparative and Theoretical Perspective', *Historical Reflections* 29 (2003), 251–73.

[26] For Evans, see my *Confession: Sexuality, Sin, the Subject* (Manchester: Manchester University Press 1990), 206–13.

[27] See Austin Sarat and Christian Boulanger (eds.), *The Cultural Lives of Capital Punishment: Comparative Perspectives* (Stanford: Stanford University Press 2005), and for the pressures imposed internationally since the Universal Declaration of Human Rights (10 December 1948) which proclaimed the right to life, see William A. Schabas, *The Abolition of the Death Penalty in International Law* (Cambridge: Cambridge University Press 1997): a study mentioned by Derrida, 1.80–3: Austin Sarat, *When the State Kills: Capital Punishment and the American Condition* (Princeton: Princeton University Press 2001), 33–59. In Sarat and Boulanger, Judith Randle, 'Capital Punishment in the United States', 107, notes the number of non-lethal felonies punishable by death in the US (the state killing the most being Texas).

Yet capital punishment is obviously neither an adequate nor even minimal deterrent to future possible murderers. Being open to mistakes and misidentifications, it produces feelings in those who participate which may be cruel, sadistic or masochistic, and is maintained by reasons which exceed utilitarian justifications. It remains a source of fascination, of attraction as well as repulsion, which carries into the prison the accompaniment to, or the substitute for, capital punishment, and the jumping-off point for so many hangings and suicides, as the source of despair. It raises the question whether life imprisonment is more subtly cruel than capital punishment. The range of questions covered by capital punishment takes in the criminal, including the 'great criminal', assuming the latter exists beyond popular culture. There is, further, the relationship of punishment – notionally at least, in many jurisdictions, the death penalty – to justice, and revenge, and to victims' "rights". Are these last two reconcilable with the first term, 'justice'?

The concept of victimhood is currently absorbed into the discourse of trauma, which, however, poses its own problems in erasing distinctions between different experiences of victimhood. It reinvents good and bad victims aligned along political – or sheer Western – lines, and in covering both discernible physical and more subjective effects, may legitimate some people as victims, while not recognizing others.[28] 'Victimology', unlike psychoanalysis, is unwilling to find commonality between the criminal and the victim, whereas psychoanalysis shows how these may work together, even confusing the boundaries as to who is victim and who is victimized. Psychoanalysis seems essential, in probing guilt and transgression and law, and in its citing law as producing crime. Does a murderer desire to be found out? We know about returning to the scene of the crime, and the cat-and-mouse game between the detective and the criminal. The presence of law asks about priority: which comes first – crime, or law waiting, incentivizing crime; or reacting to it? Lamb thought that his neck might be pre-marked, that occasions to crime presented themselves too easily, that the agents of the law were already at work prompting transgression, making crime too easy, law playing a double game.

Derrida says that the abolitionist cause has been served better by writers and poets than by philosophers and politicians, and that women's writing, and feminism, has been more spontaneously and more frequently abolitionist than men (2.232). The point might include Sarah Kofman, Hélène Cixous, Julia

---

[28] Didier Fassin and Richard Rechtman, *The Empire of Trauma: An Inquiry into the Condition of Victimhood*, trans. Rachel Gomme (Princeton: Princeton University Press 2009).

Kristeva and Marguerite Duras. Women's writing may expose issues of masculinity which surface with the death penalty. From America, he might have added Angela Davis, as essays on the Seminars from primarily American scholars indicate, showing that Derrida's range of literary examples is primarily European, preventing him from consolidating the links between American slavery and racism, in relation to black lives and capital punishment.[29] The fear that issues of racism colour justice in present-day America is only one practical reason for discontinuing the death penalty. But the contestation of capital punishment which has been 'uneven, heterogeneous, discontinuous', though irreversible, shows itself in such discourses as 'literature and death', and 'literature and the right to death' (Maurice Blanchot's theme, discussed in Part Two) 'literature and rights' and in 'the right to literature' (1.30). Literary history has shown a greater pushing for rights, and for the right to speak in literature in non-censorable ways. Women's writing is inseparable from this. Contrastedly, says Derrida, there is 'no philosophy against the death penalty' (1.17).

We have seen that the great criminal, according to *Our Mutual Friend*, hardly struggles against the crime. That would be attempting to calculate, to rationalize. In an excellent essay on *Oliver Twist* as critiquing Benthamite Utilitarianism, and its calculators (those who built workhouses in the new Poor Law), K. J. Fielding quotes Hazlitt's *Spirit of the Age*: '[L]egislators are philosophers, and governed by their reason; criminals are a set of desperadoes, governed only by their passions ... Criminals are not to be influenced by reason; for it is the very essence of crime to disregard consequences both to ourselves and others.'[30] If legislators are philosophers, is that why philosophy has not opposed the death penalty? If so, does that align literature with crime? (Hazlitt's slippage from 'themselves' to 'ourselves' is intriguing – his statement is confession.) The criminal struggles towards the crime – that is, s/he is held by a non-rational compulsion. Only literature, which must be anti-Benthamite, not accepting the greatest happiness of the greatest number, since it knows that 'happiness' may take the form of what is heterogeneous to the majority, can work with those arguments. If literature means 'ceding the initiative to words' (so Mallarmé), it must criticize absolute statements. Contrastedly, the death sentence is paradigmatic for enacting a violent closure on speech by its use of calculation. Literature exceeds the social

---

[29] Kelly Oliver and Stephanie M. Straub (eds.), *Deconstructing the Death Penalty: Derrida's Seminars and the New Abolitionism* (New York: Fordham University Press 2018). See the essays by Sarah Tyson (225–38) and Lisa Guenther (239–57).
[30] K. J. Fielding, 'Benthamite Utilitarianism and *Oliver Twist*: A Novel of Ideas', *Dickens Quarterly* 4 (1987), 49–65, quotation 59.

sciences or philosophy, in being created by the instabilities of language, meanings exceeding conscious intentions, drawing on the double nature of thoughts and motivations. Verbal ambiguity – Freud notes 'the antithetical meaning of primal words' (*SE* 11.153–61), and ambivalence, explored in 'Instincts and their Vicissitudes' (*SE* 14.131), and implying that actions contain the shadow of their opposite in them – are older than psychoanalysis, but basic to literature. They let a text move consciously towards a contrary position from that which its language asserts, and in that, literature can only be liberatory. Resistance to meaning is inherent to poetry, even when stating or letting a meaning emerge.

Derrida, though never mentioning Dickens, comments so much on Shakespeare – an essential figure within Dickens – in his later writings that it seems that he might have afforded him a sustained treatise. From literature, Derrida's Seminars cite Shelley, and Victor Hugo, which leads him to the French Revolution, that crucial event for this book, and Camus, whose abolitionist arguments are the nearest, in Derrida's use of him, to Dickens. Derrida works in the shadow of Michel Foucault on the marginalized, and mad, and prison, and prisoners – outstandingly in *Discipline and Punish; The Birth of the Prison* (*Surveiller et punir: Naissance de la prison*, 1975). The book's Second Part discusses Derrida's relationship with Foucault's work. *Discipline and Punish* has often been critically attacked, especially by historians more assured of the facts. A work of theory dressed up as empiricism, its speculations are always in excess of what could be empirically validated, but they work.[31] They are meditations; the subject is the body, and the state's increasing policing of that, and the eroticizing of relations of authority and power within the domain of the prisoner's body. This, as Suzanne Gearhart says, 'undercuts authority by disrupting the process of desexualisation which is [authority's] foundation.'[32] Foucault begins with the tortures (*supplices* – the word has a religious ring) within France preceding the French Revolution. Such spectacles could turn carnivalesque, making the criminal a hero, creating solidarity between the criminal and the spectator, and mocking authority (*DandP* 61, 63). After the Revolution, in France, the new prison regime meant avoiding touching the body. In the *supplice*, however, the body had been prominent, the subject of punishment. There is a greater degree of sadomasochism now, in the Panoptical conditions of

---

[31] See Michael Meranze, 'Michel Foucault, the Death Penalty, and the Crisis of Historical Understanding', *Historical Reflections* 29 (2003), 191–209.
[32] Suzanne Gearhart, 'The Taming of Michel Foucault: New Historicism, Psychoanalysis, and the Subversion of Power', *New Literary History* 28 (1997), 457–80 (p. 464).

modern incarceration. The prisoner is kept visible, and exposed to endless introspection and compulsions to confess:

> a 'soul' inhabits him and brings him to existence, which is itself a factor in the mastery that power exercises over the body. The soul is the effect and instrument of a political anatomy; the soul is the prison of the body.
>
> *DandP* 30

Foucault inverts the Christian trope whereby the soul is imprisoned in the body till death. Rather, a soul comprising the self-consciousness, which is imposed by the superego, imprisons the body, the locus of spontaneous impulses. Modern disciplining and punishing sets itself against the body, repressing it or enforcing its expressiveness. Spectacular torture had sexualized what the state (specifically the King) commanded; the prison now makes the criminal more the agent of his or her sadomasochism. Bradley Headstone, never literally imprisoned, exemplifies just how much his body is imprisoned by his 'soul'. When he is 'encircled' by a 'gabbling crowd', he is in Panoptical conditions.

Foucault's major debt is to Nietzsche.[33] That includes *The Genealogy of Morals* (1887), whose three essays pursue, not the sources of a moral sense, but a 'genealogy' of how the moral senses have been imposed on people. Here some summary may be helpful. The first essay, '"Good and Evil", "Good and Bad"', explains how *ressentiment* works. Here, the disempowered – e.g. slaves who adopted Christianity with its acceptance of weakness, which they made to signify inner strength and the power of forgiveness – have by that achieved the status permitting the statement: 'We good men – *we are the just*':

> They do not call what they demand retaliation, but 'the triumph of justice'; they do not hate their enemy, no! they hate - '*injustice*', 'godlessness'; their belief and hope is not the hope of revenge, the intoxication of sweet revenge (– 'sweeter than honey', as Homer described it, already in his day), but the triumph of God, of the just God over the godless.
>
> *Genealogy* 32

Desire for revenge ceases to be pagan/classical spontaneous heroism. It translates into belief that universal justice must prevail, favouring the 'weak', the powerless,

---

[33] Michel Foucault, 'Nietzsche, Genealogy, History', *Language, Counter-Memory, Practice*, ed. Donald Bouchard (Ithaca: Cornell University Press 1977), 139–64. See also James Miller, 'Carnivals of Atrocity: Foucault, Nietzsche, Cruelty', *Political Theory* 18 (1990), 470–91. On Nietzsche, see David B. Allison, *Reading the New Nietzsche* (London: Rowman & Littlefield 2001); and see the Cambridge translation by Carol Diethe of the text, ed. Keith Ansell-Pearson (1994).

whose character perforce becomes an envying of those they feel are doing better than themselves. *Ressentiment*, to be Englished as 'rancour' or 'resentment', is reactive; its primary impulse is negative, saying no. It creates the mutual surveillance exhibited in tabloid journalism, outstandingly in Britain the *Daily Mail*, in America Fox News, encouraging suspicion that some people, perhaps those doing just a little better than ourselves, get a ticket to ride: hence Foucault notes the shift in perception running from 'a criminality of blood to a criminality of fraud' (*DandP* 77).

'"Guilt", "Bad Conscience" and Related Matters' stresses the painful disciplining – for example, in education – which means to create a memory which will make people keep promises, i.e. pay debts. This second essay connects debt (*Schulden*) with guilt (*Schuld*), and with the creation of a 'bad conscience' (2.4.44) perpetually monitoring the self. Christianity prays about forgiving our debts as we forgive those indebted to us, so keeping guilt and owing money silently side by side. 'Genealogy' is explained when showing that the reasons for something coming into existence and its uses are not identical. Uses are subject to interpretations, and reinterpretations, lacking consistency with each other. Origins are invented for what exists at any time, in a retro-formation, so that we think that if something exists with a present use (not necessarily usefulness) it must have had a reason for coming into being (2.12.57–9). Bad conscience comes from consciousness, forced into self-examination and remembering by the power of disciplinarity. Forgetfulness, a more spontaneous condition, unaffected by the discipline which enforces memory, becomes impossible. Further, 'Every instinct which does not vent itself outwardly, *turns inwards*' (2.16.65). Reactiveness enforces a conscience-laden spirit, careful, discreet, self-protective and judgmental of the other, becoming *ressentiment*, systematized envy of an imaginary other.

The third essay, 'What is the meaning of ascetic ideals?', asks how it is that a 'will to truth' dominates in philosophy as in theology. Truth, counted as single and as accessible, and its pursuit – in the will to possess a sure knowledge of other people's behaviour and morality, which is claimed to be disinterested (3.24) – conceals a will to domination. That pursuit is belied by *The Genealogy of Morals* Preface: 'we are unknown to ourselves, we seekers after knowledge' (3); the agency that would know is itself unknowable, and that uncertainty skews all its knowledge.

It is that truth which is supposed to emerge in the law courts. A fascination was exerted in France by the lawyer Jacques Vergès (1925–2013) 'who defended the most unsustainable causes by practising what he calls "the strategy of rupture" – that is, the radical contestation of the given order of the law ... and of the state that summons his clients to appear' ('Force of Law' 267). Like the 'great criminal', Vergès exposed something empty or corrupt within the law; his defences took the form of, effectively, putting the court on trial. Derrida's citation of lawyers is provocative, as when he mentions Robert Badinter, who was influential in causing the cessation of capital punishment in France in 1981, when François Mitterand was president. Derrida makes these barristers sound like psychoanalysts, their subject the law. Dickens does something analogous with the criminal lawyer, Mr Jaggers, in *Great Expectations*, who attempts to shake existing justice however he can – on never-revealed principles – yet admires Bentley Drummle, 'the Spider', criminal, and a sadist, whom he calls 'one of the true sort'.[34] Dickens the novelist and Derrida the (anti-) philosopher here are comparable. Jaggers's ambiguity, which is secured by using Wemmick as his agent, his 'subordinate' (2.31.263), includes a violence which makes him bully the lawmakers, and control known criminals. He defends the latter, while cool about the point that the evidence against may be too strong and that people will be hanged. In this he repeats a schizoid tendency even more obvious in his clerk Wemmick, with the antithesis he shows between his home and his office behaviour. At his first appearance Jaggers, with great condescension, yet still meaning it, attacks Mr Wopsle for agreeing with the newspaper reports of a trial for murder which have pre-condemned the defendant. Popular journalism in its *ressentiment* creates popular opinion which identifies with the law against the criminal (*GE* 133–6). Jaggers practises his own private justice at one degree further than the criminals and the law. When, surprisingly, he is nearly outwitted by Pip, who has worked out that Estella is the daughter of Molly, a murderer, and of Magwitch, he 'puts the case' about a putative criminal lawyer who

> lived in an atmosphere of evil, and that all he saw of children was, their being generated in great numbers for certain destruction ... He often saw children solemnly tried at a criminal bar, where they were held up to be seen ... he habitually knew of their being imprisoned, whipped, transported, neglected, cast out, qualified in all ways for the hangman, and growing up to be hanged.
>
> *GE* 413

He explains, indirectly, and non-self-incriminatingly, as if confessing to a weakness contrary to his sadism, why he abducted Estella from her mother, and gave her to Miss Havisham. He acts with the quasi-legal authority of what Lacan

---

[34] Q. D. Leavis calls Jaggers 'probably Dickens's greatest success in any novel' – F. R. and Q. D. Leavis, *Dickens the Novelist* (London: Chatto & Windus 1970), 311.

calls 'the name of the father', in a double relation to the law and its subjects, which relates to a horror of 'growing up to be hanged' as the inevitable lot of so many, who otherwise stand no chance.

These materials and their implications hold Dickens, and so, in comparable ways, Derrida, who theorizes them more openly, as the dual centres in the ellipsis of interests this book explores.

Part One

Dickens – and the Eighteenth Century

1

Abolitionism and Dickens

How was hanging practised in London in the eighteenth century? Its main theatre was at the village of Tyburn, where the Tyburn river flowed from Hampstead to Westminster through present-day Oxford Street. Tyburn is mentioned for execution in William Langland's fourteenth-century poem *Piers Plowman* (C text 6.368, 14.129). Until 1759, as shown in Hogarth's *Industry and Idleness*, it had a permanent triple gallows, and seating for people to watch; this was replaced by a portable gallows. The ending of the two- to three-hour procession to Tyburn in 1783, relocating hangings outside the walls of Newgate, began a process which would lead to hanging being carried out in semi-private.[1] The sheriffs of London and Middlesex, Thomas Skinner and Barnard Taylor, resolved on the change, partly out of nervousness caused by the Gordon Riots, partly because desiring more discipline, less carnival, and a more deterrent effect.[2] This 'innovation', as Boswell calls it in his *Life of Johnson* (1791), met Dr Johnson's disapproval:

> 'No, Sir, (said he, eagerly,) it is not an improvement: they object that the old method drew together a number of spectators. Sir, executions are intended to draw spectators. If they do not draw spectators they don't serve their purpose. The old method was most satisfactory to all parties: the publick was gratified by a procession; the criminal was supported in it. Why is all this to be swept away?' I perfectly agree with Dr Johnson upon this head, and am persuaded that executions now, the solemn procession being discontinued, have not nearly the effect which they formerly had. Magistrates both in London, and elsewhere, have, I am afraid, in this, had too much regard to their own ease.[3]

---

[1] So Peter Linebaugh, 'The Tyburn Riots Against the Surgeons' in Douglas Hay, Peter Linebaugh, John G. Rule, E. P. Thompson and Cal Winslow (eds.), *Albion's Fatal Tree: Crime and Society in Eighteenth-Century England* (London: Penguin 1977), 67.
[2] Simon Devereux, 'Recasting the Theatre of Execution: The Abolition of the Tyburn Ritual', *Past and Present* 202 (2009), 127–74.
[3] James Boswell, *Life of Johnson*, ed. R. W. Chapman, preface Pat Rogers (Oxford: Oxford University Press 1980), 1211–12.

Boswell speaks of visiting Johnson on Wednesday 23 June 1784, 'after having been present at the shocking sight of fifteen men executed before Newgate'. Further, thinking of the numbers here, Boswell adds a commendation of 'the Reverend Mr Vilette, who has been Ordinary of Newgate for no less than eighteen years, in the course of which he has attended many hundreds of wretched criminals, [and] his earnest and humane exhortations have been very effectual' (1318, 1319). Vilette was the Ordinary who attended on Dr William Dodd (hanged 27 June 1777), a writer, *bon viveur* and clergyman, and forger when pressed by want of money; forgery being, says Boswell, 'the most dangerous crime in a commercial country' (828). Johnson attempted to obtain a reprieve for Dodd, but failed.[4] Boswell shows how Johnson wrote for Dodd, writing as Dodd, appealing for a royal pardon, exclaiming against 'the spectacle of a clergyman dragged through the streets, to a death of infamy, amidst the derision of the profligate and profane', saying 'that justice may be satisfied with irrevocable exile, perpetual disgrace, and hopeless penury ... Permit me to hide my guilt in some obscure corner of a foreign country, where, if I can ever attain confidence to hope that my prayers will be heard, they shall be poured with all the fervour of gratitude for the life and happiness of your Majesty' (831–2).

Johnson defended the procession to Tyburn as a way of supporting the criminal, and showing how homogenous the society was: the criminal was not the exception, but rather, part of the crowd. Yet in 1769, in conversation with Boswell:

> I mentioned to him that I had seen the execution of several convicts at Tyburn, two days before, and that none of them seemed to be under any concern. JOHNSON: 'Most of them, Sir, have never thought at all.' BOSWELL. 'But is not the fear of death natural to man?' JOHNSON. 'So much so, Sir, that the whole of life is but keeping away the thoughts of it.' He then, in a low and earnest tone, talked of his meditating upon the awful hour of his own dissolution, and in what manner he should conduct himself upon that occasion: 'I know not (said he) whether I should wish to have a friend by me, or have it all between GOD and myself'.
>
> 416

In the context of the procession to Tyburn, Johnson's hesitation between privacy and companionship is powerful.

---

[4] See A. D. Barker, 'The Early Career of William Dodd', *Transactions of the Cambridge Bibliographical Society* 8 (1982), 217–35.

The change to Newgate for hangings accompanied a shift towards the courtroom, not the scaffold, as the scene of justice. For instance, in 1836 the Prisoner's Counsel Act ensured the right of the accused to be represented, and lawyers could cross-examine witnesses and make a closing argument for the prisoner.[5] Those who opposed the death penalty followed Bentham, writing against the death penalty in 1775, and again in 1831.[6] He followed Beccaria's treatise, *On Crimes and Punishments* (1764), which launched Utilitarian objections to capital punishment, in a single chapter arguing that law was part of the social contract (Rousseau) by which people came together to produce a commonwealth, since individual life was too dangerous (Hobbes). It affirmed the importance of freedom (Montesquieu) and that law should have no other motivation – nor other severity – than public utility.[7] We should note Beccaria's tone, and one of his emphases, that the death penalty was a spectacle for the majority:

> and for some others an object of compassion mixed with disdain; these two sentiments rather than the salutary fear which the laws pretend to inspire occupy the spirits of the spectators. But in moderate and prolonged punishments [such as penal servitude] the dominant sentiment is the latter, because it is the only one. The limit which the legislator ought to fix on the rigor of punishments would seem to be determined by the sentiment of compassion itself, when it begins to prevail over every other in the hearts of those who are the witnesses of punishment, inflicted for their sake rather than for the criminal's.[8]

Beccaria took much from Montesquieu (1689–1755), whose *L'Esprit des lois* (1748) urges moderation, and the spirit of liberty in carrying out law, though Montesquieu was not an abolitionist.[9]

---

[5] See Jonathan H. Grossman, *The Art of Alibi: English Law Courts and the Novel* (Baltimore: Johns Hopkins University Press 2002), 17–24 especially. On the nineteenth-century lawyer in Dickens, Trollope and George Eliot, see my *On Reading the Will: Law and Desire in Literature and Music* (Brighton: Sussex Academic Press 2012), 121–68.

[6] See Hugo Adam Bedau, 'Bentham's Utilitarian Critique of the Death Penalty', *Journal of Criminal Law and Criminology* 74 (1983), 1033–65.

[7] James E. Cummins, 'The Principles of Utilitarian Penal Law in Beccaria, Bentham, and J. S. Mill', in Peter Karl Koritansky (ed.), *The Philosophy of Punishment and the History of Political Thought* (Columbia, MO: University of Missouri Press 2011), 136–71.

[8] Cesare Beccaria, *On Crimes and Punishments*, trans. Henry Paolucci (Indianapolis: Bobbs-Merrill 1963), 47. Derrida notes this passage – 1.43.

[9] For Montesquieu's support for capital punishment, see *The Spirit of the Laws*, trans. and ed. Anne M. Cohler, Basia C. Miller and Harold S. Stone 12.4 (Cambridge: Cambridge University Press 1989), 191. See David W. Carrithers, 'Montesquieu's Philosophy of Punishment', *History of Political Thought* 10 (1998), 213–40.

The eighteenth century sentenced people to physical punishment and degradation (the pillory, the stocks, whipping), to transportation, or to hanging. The Hanoverian century was marked by repression: the Riot Act (1715), the Transportation Act (1710), the Combination Act (1721), the Workhouse Act (1723), and the Black Act (1723) which, legislating against poaching, protected property and the 'rights' of the country gentleman. It was expanded to create 200 capital offences.[10] The reactionary years which accompanied the English government's take on the French Revolution and the wars with France meant that the main years for reducing the number of 'crimes' for which people could be publicly hanged came a century later than the Black Act, in the 1830s. Slave revolts in Barbados (1816), Demerara (1823) and Jamaica (1831) were put down with dozens of executions.[11] Nonetheless, by and after the 1830s, virtually the only crime punishable by death in Britain was murder: Henry Fauntleroy, Lamb's subject, would have got off for forgery, which was dropped as a capital offence in 1836, the last victim of the rope for forgery being in 1829. (Mr Merdle in *Little Dorrit*, set in 1825, would have been hanged for his forgeries; he pre-empted that through suicide.) From reformist pressures, under a new sense of encouraging middle-class tastes and rational amusements, and a new desire to create a culture defining violence more closely, a Royal Commission on Criminal Law (1833–6) led to the reduction of crimes punishable by death. William Ewart (1798–1869), the Radical MP for, successively, Liverpool, Wigan and Dumfries, had in 1834 moved to end the hanging of bodies in chains, then in 1836 to have felons defended by counsel, and in 1837 for abolition of the death penalty for all crimes save murder. On 3 March 1840, he introduced a motion in Parliament to abolish capital punishment altogether.

One Ewart supporter was Richard Monckton Milnes (1809–85), MP and poet, an early editor of Keats, and a Germanist (a friend of Heine) who invited Thackeray to witness with him the hanging of Benjamin Courvoisier (a valet who had murdered his employer, Sir William Russell), to check the crowd's reactions to a public hanging.[12] Thackeray wrote two letters about it, one to his mother, begun that 6 July:

---

[10] E. P. Thompson, *Whigs and Hunters: The Origin of the Black Act* (London: Penguin 1977); on law in the eighteenth century, using *Caleb Williams*, see David Punter, 'Fictional Representations of the Law in the Eighteenth Century', *Eighteenth Century Studies* 16 (1984), 47–74. For a listing of penal laws, see Leon Radzinowicz, *The History of English Criminal Law* (5 vols., 1948–86): Vol 1: *The Movement for Reform* (London: Stevens and Sons 1948), 49–79 for the Black Act.

[11] Claire Anderson, 'Execution and its Aftermath in the Nineteenth-Century British Empire', in Richard Ward (ed.), *A Global History of Execution and the Criminal Corpse* (London: Palgrave Macmillan 2015), 174.

[12] James Pope-Hennessy, *Monckton Milnes: The Years of Promise 1809–1851* (London: Constable 1949), 128–30.

I have been to see Courvoisier hanged & am miserable ever since. I can't do my work and yet work must be done for the poor babbies' sake. It is most curious the effect his death has had on me, and I am trying to work it off in a paper on the subject. Meanwhile it weighs upon the mind, like cold plum pudding on the stomach, & as soon as I begin to write, I get melancholy.[13]

To a friend, Mrs Procter, on 7 July, he explains:

The greatest poet in the House of Commons came here [Great Coram Street: Thackeray's home] yesterday morning at half past three, and we drove together in his famous fly (which had been sitting up all night) to Newgate to see Courvoisier hanged. It was a horrible sight indeed and I can't help mentioning it for the poor wretch's face will keep itself before my eyes, and the scene mixes itself up with all my occupations.

Ray 454

The essay 'Going to See a Man Hanged', written for *Fraser's Magazine*, ends:

I fully confess that I came away down Snow Hill that morning with a disgust for murder, but it was for the murder I saw done.[14]

'Murder' must refer either to a crime which an individual, or group of individuals, performs, or be the work of the state, whether with its endorsement, or in those acts of killing which the police or vigilante groups carry out on the state's behalf.[15] Murder seems to be a dual act; that of someone who gets called a murderer, and an act of revenge: action and reaction. It shows a willing disposition towards violence where the greater capacity is in the state, and as seen from Fauntleroy and from many others, it customarily committed murder for lesser offences than murder. And the individual's act of murder must be less than that reciprocal power which hangs over the person, or which creates such anxiety in Lamb.

Courvoisier claimed that reading W. H. Ainsworth's *Jack Sheppard* had led him into crime.[16] What is more likely is that the murder in *Barnaby Rudge* (see below) is based on the Courvoisier case.[17] Ainsworth was accused of having romanticized

---

[13] Gordon Ray (ed.), *The Letters and Private Papers of William Makepeace Thackeray*, Vol. 1: 1817–1840 (Oxford: Oxford University Press 1945), 453.

[14] Thackeray, 'Going to See a Man Hanged', 125 in William Makepeace Thackeray, *A Shabby Genteel Story and Other Writings*, ed. D. J. Taylor (London: Everyman 1993), 110–25.

[15] For Thackeray's continued abolitionism, see Deborah A. Thomas, 'Thackeray, Capital Punishment, and the Demise of Jos Sedley', *Victorian Literature and Culture* 33 (2005), 1–20.

[16] Kathyrn Chittick, *Dickens and the 1830s* (Cambridge: Cambridge University Press 1990), 162. See Elizabeth Stearns, 'A "darling of the Mob": The Antidisciplinarity of the Jack Sheppard Texts', *Victorian Literature and Culture* 41 (2013), 435–61.

[17] Myron Magnet, *Dickens and the Social Order* (Philadelphia: University of Pennsylvania Press 1985), 81.

criminals, making them cultural heroes, as part of the 'Newgate novel' phase, which comprises, in particular, Bulwer's *Paul Clifford* (1830) and *Eugene Aram* (1832), and Ainsworth's *Rookwood* (1834), its subject Dick Turpin the highwayman hanged at York in 1739.[18] Further there was Dickens's *Oliver Twist* (serialized in *Bentley's Miscellany* from February 1837 to April 1839), *Jack Sheppard* (serialized in *Bentley's Miscellany* from January 1839 to February 1840) and Bulwer's *Lucretia: Or the Children of Night* (1846). This last was based on Thomas Wainewright (1794–1847), artist and journalist in the 1820s, who was transported for forgery, and suspected too of having poisoned his sister-in-law to collect the insurance.[19] Dickens, Forster and William Macready encountered Wainewright in prison on 27 June 1837 (see *Letters* 1.277), and something of him informs Julius Slinkton, the murderer in *Hunted Down* (*All the Year Round*, 4 and 11 April 1860).

Dickens, asked to write for the *Edinburgh Review*, may refer indirectly to Ainsworth when saying that he could write something on the 'Punishment of Death and sympathy with Great Criminals; instancing the gross and depraved curiosity that exists in reference to them, by some of the outrageous things that were written, done, and said, in recent times'.[20] Arguing for abolition, Dickens is careful not to say anything about the criminal; indeed, he holds that the criminal is 'already mercifully and sparingly treated' – even though he is hanged. The ability to hold the criminal at a distance from the reasons he has for abolition of the death penalty is intriguing. While it is partly real, and partly a wish not to be thought to be a sentimentalist, it may also be a desire not to be like Ainsworth. Unquestionably, Dickens's interest in criminality was neither Romantic, nor of the Newgate type; it was not sensationalist, nor did it make a hero of the criminal, relating more to the question: which comes first, the punishment or the crime: and what is the fascination which murder holds?

Dickens was not exceptional in wanting abolition. In April 1846, at a meeting in London's Exeter Hall, the Society for the Abolition of Capital Punishment was formed, with Dickens's support, though not his involvement, and with the support of Douglas Jerrold.[21] Its inspiration had come from the Quaker radical

---

[18] For eighteenth-century highwaymen, see Lincoln B. Faller, *Turned to Account: The Forms and Functions of Criminal Biography in Late Seventeenth- and Early Eighteenth- Century England* (Cambridge: Cambridge Univerity Press 1987), 174–93, and for Claude Duval, Macheath, Turpin and *Rookwood*, see Erin Mackie, *Rakes, Highwayman, and Pirates: The Making of the Modern Gentleman in the Eighteenth Century* (Baltimore: Johns Hopkins University Press 2009), 71–113.

[19] See *ODNB* entry by Annette Peach for the most accurate details, which are hard to ascertain.

[20] To Macvey Napier, 28 July 1846, *Letters* 4.340.

[21] See Dickens, *Letters* 4.520, 542, to Charles Gilpin (1815–74). On abolition, see James Gregory, *Victorians Against the Gallows: Capital Punishment and the Abolitionist Movement in Nineteenth-Century Britain* (London: I.B. Tauris 2012), chapters 1 and 3.

Charles Gilpin (1815–74), MP for Northampton after 1857. Nor was this the first such movement. William Godwin (1756–1836), in 'Of Crimes and Punishment', Book 7 of his *Enquiry Concerning Political Justice* (1793), presented a case which was wholly anti-punishment, and inherently, therefore, against capital punishment; drawing, here, upon Beccaria. (Discussion of Godwin follows in Chapter III.) There had also been the partly Quaker Society for the Diffusion of Knowledge Respecting the Punishment of Death and the Improvement of Prison Discipline (1808) which had advocated abolition of hanging for all offences save premeditated murder. This was led by the Quaker William Allen (1770–1843) and Basil Montagu (1770–1851), friend of Wordsworth, and Sir Samuel Romilly (1757–1818). Romilly had been successful in 1808 in repealing the 1565 Act which had made pickpocketing, important for *Oliver Twist*, a capital offence, though over the course of ten years (1808–18) he was unable to move the House of Lords to support abolition of the death penalty for shoplifting where goods of five shillings' worth were involved. His major opposition came from Lord Ellenborough (i.e. Edward Law, 1750–1818), who in 1803 had introduced a statute creating ten new capital offences, and had taken the view that a hanged man could be dissected without that sentence having been specifically passed (*ODNB*). Romilly notes the 'dread of innovation' in Parliament, and 'the savage spirit' which he attributes to reaction to the French Revolution, when narrating how the brother of a peer told him 'I am against your bill, I am for hanging all', adding, 'there is no good done by mercy. They only get worse. I would hang them all up at once.'[22] Another organization, the Society for the Diffusion of Information on the Subject of Capital Punishment, followed in 1828. The context of this pressure was the sheer familiarity to so many of the death penalty. V. A. C. Gatrell estimates that some 35,000 people were sentenced to death between 1770 and 1830: in 1765 it was estimated that 165 'crimes' could be punished by the hanging-tree. In the years mentioned, most were reprieved, and sent to prison hulks, or transported. About 7,000 were hanged, throughout England, before crowds of 3,000 to 7,000.[23] Dissection of hanged bodies for medical purposes had been

---

[22] Quoted Patrick Medd, *Romilly: A Life of Sir Samuel Romilly, Lawyer and Reformer* (London: Collins 1968), 215, and 204–46 for Romilly's attempts at reform, and the opposition. For reform, see also Medd on William Eden (1744–1814 – later Baron Auckland), in *Principles of Penal Law* (1771). Eden, influenced by Blackstone and by Beccaria, attempted to have regulated the housing of convicts on the hulks, and to allow for their employment in projects such as clearing the Thames (law in 1776); he also tried to create penitentiaries (1779) (*ODNB*), though these were frustrated by the availability of transportation to New South Wales.

[23] V. A. C. Gatrell, *The Hanging Tree: Execution and the English People 1770–1868* (Oxford: Oxford University Press 1994), 7. On the history of capital punishment in Britain, see Harry Potter, *Hanging in Judgment* (London: SCM Press 1993).

passed into law in 1752, adding further humiliation, and attacking the sanctity of the body, whose value could be seen in what happened to Thurtell after his execution.

Gatrell (558) singles out the Tory Home Secretary, Sir Robert Peel, as (in the 1820s) insistently reactionary in carrying out the death penalty, saying 'it was right for the sake of example to let the law take its course'. Gatrell argues that in the end, squeamishness, not sympathy with the prisoner, led to the passing of the Capital Punishment within Prisons Bill in 1868 which put capital punishment inside prison walls. According to the sociologist of criminology Pieter Spierenburg, tracing a history of the 'repression' of public execution, taking examples especially in the Netherlands, the first execution inside a prison was at Maidstone Jail, 13 August 1868.[24] Spierenburg thought such 'repression' was part of a change in sensibility, or mentality, in the history of a 'civilizing process' for which he quotes Norbert Elias writing in 1939.[25] This 'repression' meant a decline in the homicide rate from the early modern period onwards. Spierenburg's data are interesting, but it is worth wondering about what 'repression' means when it appears outside its use in psychoanalysis, which means that it has nothing of the sense of something going on more in the civilizing process than appears on the surface, the subject of Freud's 'Civilisation and its Discontents', which posits guilt as the price paid for civilization (*SE* 21.134).

Dickens's letters

Dickens, then, was neither original nor in the vanguard. His first public letter announces that he is not part of a 'morbid and odious sentimentality' sympathetic to murderers – 'ruffians' as he calls them. He is, however, alive to people being hanged in error; while claiming that punishment must have reform as its intention, he disputes that there could be religious 'reformation' in the condemned cell in 'the dreadful hurry of the time'. In the second letter, his subject is the criminal, as when he quotes from a report of 1841 to the State Assembly of New York on the question, asking

---

[24] Pieter Spierenburg, *The Spectacle of Suffering: Executions and the Evolution of Repression: From a Preindustrial Metropolis to the European Experience* (Cambridge: Cambridge University Press 1984), 198.
[25] Norbert Elias, *The Civilizing Process: Sociogenetic and Psychogenetic Investigations* (rev. ed., Oxford: Blackwell 2000). See Pieter Spierenburg, 'Violence and the Civilizing Process: Does it Work?', *Crime, History, and Societies* 5 (2001), 87–105, and 'Punishment, Power, and History: Foucault and Elias', *Social Science History* 28 (2004), 607–36.

whether there sleep within the breast of man, certain dark and mysterious sympathies with the thought of that death and that futurity which await his nature, tending to invest any act expressly forbidden by that penalty, with an unconscious and inexplicable fascination, that attracts his thoughts to it, in spite of their very shuddering dread, and bids his imagination brood over its idea, 'till out of those dark depths in his own nature comes gradually forth a monstrous birth of Temptation.

That use of 'sleeping' suggests the power of unconscious thought. Dickens adds to this characterization of the person who is on the way to committing a crime, that he has found a 'metaphysical truth' at work, this 'truth' being the idea that there is 'a horrible fascination' in the idea of crime, which makes a criminal under sentence of death to be 'the subject of a morbid interest and curiosity' which he calls 'irresistible', part of an 'attraction of repulsion' which is 'a law of our moral nature'.[26] The phrase 'attraction of repulsion' appears frequently in Dickens. This 'law' is in the criminal, and those who see the criminal, and comprise the audience to his hanging. Dickens makes clear that forgery or coining (as a hanging offence) does not have a similar appeal for an 'audience' watching a forger being executed; nor does transportation capture the imagination, but murder holds an infinite 'fascination'. This implies that murder is begotten as an idea by the gallows, and it extends its appeal to those who read about murderers, or see capital punishment. The 'repulsive' has the power of 'attraction' in a way which the positive power of capital-punishment-as-deterrence cannot. At that point he mentions that he saw the execution of Courvoisier (8 July 1840), which he calls an 'obscene spectacle'.

Another strand of the same (second) letter discusses the reluctance of juries to convict. Juries are unwilling to argue that a suicide could be other than mad, and as 'grave doctors have said all men are more or less mad', juries are more likely to find a murderer mad than to convict in a way which would bring on 'public execution, with all its depraving and hardening influences'. This itself relates back to the case of Courvoisier, who was defended by Charles Phillips (1787–1859) in a way which had made Dickens (under the pseudonym 'Manlius') write to the *Morning Chronicle* (21 June 1840), complaining how his defence had imputed guilt to other, innocent parties. Phillips's challenge to the jury – that they would be haunted in the future by returning a 'Guilty' verdict – appears to

---

[26] Philip Collins, *Dickens and Crime* (London: Macmillan, 1964), discussing these letters sympathetically in his chapter X, says this is the first letter, rather than the second (248); see also his bibliographical note 16 (343).

have rattled Dickens, and to extend to this second *Daily News* letter. It makes him say, as 'Manlius', 'a plain man', and a 'practical', that in the light of this, 'I never would stretch out my hand to arrest a murderer, with these pains and penalties before me' (*Letters*, 21 June 1840, 2.86-9). He has come to the conclusion maintained in the second letter, that he could take no part in convicting a prisoner to death.

The third *Daily News* letter asks about 'the effect of capital punishment on the commission of murder', proposing that 'some murders are committed in hot blood and furious rage; some, in deliberate revenge; some, in terrible despair; some (but not many) for mere gain; some for the removal of an object dangerous to the murderer's peace or good name; some, to win a monstrous notoriety'. He gives examples; one being murder for gain, where he instances Courvoisier, and a woman who murdered in Westminster for a banknote (having 'little calculation beyond the absorbing greed of the money to be got'), so that this sort of murder becomes in this case like a crime of passion, not premeditated. In considering murders as revenge, Dickens asks: '[I]s there reason to suppose that the punishment of death has the direct effect of an incentive and an impulse?' Here, the *lex talionis* seems to be invoked, in the idea of a murderer who has killed for revenge expecting therefore to die (indeed, sometimes giving himself up). This idea not only establishes an idea of 'strict justice and fair reparation', it also, more perversely, produces a 'stubborn and dogged fortitude and foresight', creating a mentality of tit for tat; 'he wouldn't mind killing her, though he should be hanged for it' (in the case of killing a detested object – perhaps Dickens is suspecting, or imagining, a sexual motive for murder). The idea of 'life for life' and other 'balanced jingles' incentivizes murder, then, and the repeated words 'though I should die for it' become a 'common avowal' made by the murderer. Dickens begins to speculate that the 'jingle' works negatively – perversely – against the object of the man's anger, i.e. the person (say a woman) who is liable to be killed. At its simplest, the man does not consider his own best interests. At every new temptation to violence (after a quarrel, or a contemplation of 'the continuance of this life in his path'), he thinks that the gallows is there, stronger and blacker yet, trying to terrify him. When she defies or threatens him, the scaffold seems to be her strength and vantage ground. But let her not be too sure of that, 'though he should die for it'.

Dickens sums up the way in which the likelihood of capital punishment (note: not life imprisonment) incentivizes murder by saying:

> Thus, he begins to raise up, in the contemplation of this death by hanging, a new and violent enemy to brave. The prospect of a slow and solitary expiation would

have no congeniality with his wicked thoughts, but this throttling and strangling has. There is always before him, an ugly, bloody, scarecrow phantom, that champions her, as it were, and yet shows him, in a ghostly way, the example of murder. [There is] a presence always about her, darkly menacing him with that penalty whose murky secret has a fascination for all secret and unwholesome thoughts. And when he struggles with his victim at the last, 'though he should be hanged for it', it is a merciless wrestle, not with one weak life only, but with that ever-haunting, ever- beckoning shadow of the gallows, too, and with a fierce defiance to it, after their long survey of each other, to come on and do its worst.

Present this black idea of violence to a bad mind contemplating violence; hold up before a man remotely compassing the death of another person, the spectacle of his own ghastly and untimely death by man's hands; and out of the depths of his own nature you shall assuredly raise up that which lures and tempts him on. The laws which regulate those mysteries have not been studied or cared for, by the maintainers of this law; but they are paramount, and will always assert their power.

The 'throttling and strangling' describes a murderous act, that committed by the law: it means hanging. These paragraphs are at the heart of Dickens's case against capital punishment; it is a novelist's or a psychoanalyst's interest. He has discovered 'laws' which are the opposite of those which lawmakers and law enforcers try to 'maintain'. These 'laws' associate with Freud's sense of the unconscious power of the death-drive: they spur on the desire to murder because they attract the man towards his own death. Dickens argues that the effect of trying to keep to the law produces the reverse effect: temptation *increases* with the prospect of punishment. The gallows is not separable in the mind of the potential murderer from the person who is to be killed, who sounds like, judging from the context of the letter, a long-married wife, or partner (like Stephen Blackpool's wife in *Hard Times*), or a mother, or an older woman. This person to be murdered merges with the menace of capital punishment, which is to be challenged as an equal obstacle, or as a challenge in itself. Dickens has passed from the fascination of murder to the crowd, to the fascination of the gallows to a person contemplating a murder, and in considering the negativity of the impact of the gallows, and indeed the absurdity of thinking it a deterrence: Dickens gives a statistic: of sixty-seven condemned people questioned by a clergyman, only three had not been to a hanging.

The argument is furthered by talking of those who murder for the sake of notoriety – the notoriety being that of being hanged; here, the punishment *creates* the crime. Dickens gives an instance of Thomas Hocker, playing novelistically with the life of a real-life murderer (see *Letters* 4.341). It is a case of 'mad self-deceit', and 'self-complacency'; the story of the son of a working shoemaker, a Hogarthian idle apprentice, his vanity making him want to get 'that head of hair into the print-shops'. Dickens follows and imagines his reasoning; for example, he hypothesizes a 'Victim Friend' – presumably male – and the letter from the woman to the Victim Friend which causes the murder; he imagines the man saying that hanging would be to 'die game' (as people 'die game' at the Minor Theatres and the Saloons). The phrase to 'die game' comes from the mid-eighteenth century, deriving from gamecocks fighting. Thus Mr Wopsle, acting out *The London Merchant* and *Richard the Third* and *King John*, 'died amiably at Camberwell, and exceedingly game on Bosworth Field, and in the greatest agonies at Glastonbury' (*GE* 119).

In considering this imagined Thomas Hocker, Dickens gives also the example of John Thurtell, whose execution had such a traumatizing effect on Lamb. Dickens works out the narrative, giving the man's 'dancing-master airs', seeing life as a playbill advertising him; being the 'first gentleman in Europe' (so being a dandy, like 'Beau' Brummell); and being in the condemned cell, where his life is divided between 'telling lies and writing them'. And 'his last proceeding of all (not less characteristic, but the only true one) is to swoon away miserably, in the arms of the attendants, and to be hanged up like a craven dog'. We may think in that context of the word 'hangdog', applying both to an executioner (and to the status of the one being hanged), and to a human, or a dog, being hanged. As a parallel to this imagined and partly 'real' case, Dickens passes to the insane Edward Oxford (1822–1900), who fired at Victoria in 1840, and finds him 'brimful of conceit'. The Letter, then, has turned on the numerous incentives given to crime by hanging and it seems that one of the most effective is the idea of having one's vanity flattered by being hanged. Narcissism seems to align itself with a death-drive, as in the case of Narcissus himself.

The fourth letter asks whether capital punishment prevents crime in those who attend executions; here Dickens notes the guillotining he witnessed in Rome, which is described in *Pictures from Italy* (418–22). Here, too, he quotes from *Facts Relating to the Punishment of Death* by Edward Gibbon Wakefield (1796–1862), the abolitionist pamphleteer. Wakefield had noted in the crowd 'sympathy for the crowd [i.e. sympathy inside the crowd for anarchist tendencies] and hatred of the law' (obviously an inappropriate response!); and had found that execution was not frightening to the people, who replied instead: 'No – *why should it?*', while 'I thought it was a – Shame' was another reaction. Incidentally, Sir Samuel Romilly, thirty years back, had argued that crowds at an execution would be unaware of the nature of the crime, or of the evidence which had produced a conviction.[27] The reaction also includes the crowd's aversion from the hangman (historically, then, William Calcraft, 1800–79); and since Dickens thinks this aversion to be unavoidable, he finds in that another sign that capital punishment can deliver no good lesson. It is a point reinforced from another abolitionist, Lord Nugent (1788–1850), showing that the number of crimes diminishes in inverse relation to the number of executions.[28]

Dickens finishes with satire directed against the highly reactionary Lord Eldon (1751–1838, Lord Chancellor 1801–28), for opposing the ending of capital punishment for forgery. Eldon had been followed in this by the Tory Law Lords Lyndhurst (1772–1863, several times Lord Chancellor after Eldon), Wynford (1767–1845) and Tenderden (1762–1832). All that leads Dickens to a point which he resumes within the last letter, that 'a criminal judge is an excellent witness against the Punishment of Death, but a bad witness in its favour', because he is too much of an actor in the drama, and clearly enjoys playing his part. The tone, as said, is satirical. The unreliability of judges associates with examples of miscarriages of justice; Dickens mentions a New York report of 1841 which found 100 cases of miscarriage of justice recorded in England; examples are also given from the USA, and Ireland, where Mr O'Connell defended three brothers who were hanged in error.

He concludes with neat assorted points. A youth now under sentence at Newgate had seen the last three public executions. He says that Robespierre, before being 'in blood stept in so far' (*Macbeth* 3.4.136) opposed capital punishment. The point was available to him from Carlyle's *The French Revolution*, and will be essential for Part Two. He gives favourable instances of places such as Bombay where capital punishment had been stayed; he says that biblical authority for executions cannot be evoked, otherwise Christians would still be justifying slavery and polygamy. He also resists Macaulay (1800–59) who in the House of Commons 'last Tuesday night' found an 'effeminacy of feeling' in abolitionists. His reply to that accusation asks what is manly and heroic in advocating the gallows, suggesting that on this basis Mr Calcraft must be 'one of the most manly specimens now in existence'. He argues that there was a more gracious spirit in the abolitionists who asked for mercy in the case of the Quaker John Tawell (1784–1845), executed as a poisoner, while recognizing how abhorrent his case was.

---

[27] Medd, 220.
[28] For George Nugent Grenville, second Baron Nugent of Carlanstown, see Gregory, 60–1.

The gender reference is opportune for noting how much the death penalty affected women. From 1843, the first year that records were kept, to 1901, the figures indicate that women accounted for 15 per cent of those hanged, this happening at the rate of one a year. Murder seems to have been the only case where the arrest rates for women had any comparability with those for men (40 per cent in the years 1855–74).[29] Wilkie Collins's final novel, *The Legacy of Cain* (1889), opens in a prison in the late 1850s, and shows a women condemned for murder. Coolly, she asks the doctor, who is no sentimentalist about women, about the pain to be expected in her execution, and he tells the more sympathetic prison governor that she fulfils an idea he has, that

> the worst murders – I mean murders deliberately planned – are committed by persons absolutely deficient in that part of the moral organization which *feels*. The night before they are hanged they sleep. On their last morning they eat a breakfast. Incapable of realising the horror of murder, they are incapable of realising the horror of death. Do you remember the last murderer who was hanged here – a gentleman's coachman who killed his wife? He had but two anxieties while he was waiting for execution. One was to get his allowance of beer doubled, and the other was to be hanged in his coachman's livery. No! no! these wretches are all alike; they are human creatures born with the temperament of tigers. Take my word for it, we need feel no anxiety about tomorrow. The Prisoner will face the crowd round the scaffold with composure; and the people will say, 'She died game'.[30]

The doctor lacks a sense of gender difference; and even the Governor speaks of 'righteous retribution', saying afterwards that 'the one self-possessed person among us was the miserable woman who suffered the penalty of death' (26), as if that justified the proceedings, and meaning that sympathy ought to go to those who executed her. Commenting on Ruth Ellis's hanging, Jacqueline Rose notes hanging as being regarded, perhaps unconsciously, as a female death.[31]

---

[29] Virginia B. Morris, *Double Jeopardy: Women who Kill in Victorian Fiction* (Knoxville: University of Kentucky Press 1990), 30. Morris discusses cases of infanticide, though indicating that this, however widespread, tended not to draw on the death penalty (compare *Adam Bede*). Abortion was criminalized in 1861 (Morris, 28), infanticide was differentiated from murder in 1922.

[30] Wilkie Collins, *The Legacy of Cain: A Novel* (London: Chatto & Windus 1889), 25–6.

[31] Jacqueline Rose, 'Margaret Thatcher and Ruth Ellis', in *Why War?: Psychoanalysis, Politics, and the Return to Melanie Klein* (Oxford: Blackwell 1993), 41–86. She references Eva Cantarella, 'Dangling Virgins: Myth, Ritual, and the Place of Women in Ancient Greece', in Susan Robin Suleiman (ed.), *The Female Body in Western Culture* (Cambridge, MA: Harvard University Press 1986), 57–67. Jocasta in Sophocles' *Oedipus* remains an image of the mother hanging herself. Richard Clark, *Women and the Noose: A History of Female Execution* (Stroud: Tempus 2007) discusses female hangings – with no suggestion of supporting abolition.

The Mannings

Before analysing these arguments, and noting Philip Collins admitting that the theme of capital punishment in the letters stimulated Dickens 'to a more sustained exploration of unconscious motives than is common in his novels of this period',[32] it seems that the primary marker of Dickens's opposition lay in noting the 'attraction of repulsion' – for the criminal, for the crowd, for the courts – in the death penalty, an attraction exceeding rational statements against – or for – capital punishment. In this light we must consider what happens in 1849. On 1 May 1849, Sir George Grey (1799–1882), the Home Secretary, opposed Ewart's bill to abolish hanging. He implied a willingness to consider hangings in private, a course of action which what follows shows was a diversion, and a successful one.

On 13 November 1849, Frederick Manning and his wife Maria (born in Lausanne in 1821) were hanged outside Horsemonger Gaol in south London for murdering Patrick O'Connor for his money in their house in Bermondsey on 9 August 1849. As part of the fall-out of this sensational event, they seem to have helped create the Italian Count Fosco and Mme Fosco in *The Woman in White*.[33] Maria Manning, who had been a lady's maid, working at Stafford House (present-day Lancaster House in the West End), becomes Hortense, Lady Dedlock's maid, in *Bleak House*. Maria Manning and Hortense both reference, for the popular mind, feminist anti-patriarchy in the French Revolution, mutating into Mme Defarge in *A Tale of Two Cities*, and adding the symbolic power of the Lady Macbeth who kills herself. Mme Fosco indeed used to speak for women's rights (before she was 'tamed' by her husband – he is killed in a private vendetta by the end of the book). In a well-crafted scene discussing how crime does not cause its own detection, that murder will *not* out, how wise criminals – as opposed to 'foolish' – need not be caught, Count Fosco pronounces 'the hiding of a crime or the detection of crime' to be 'a trial of skill between the police on one side and the individual on the other' (*Woman in White* 236). Collins slips, probably unconsciously, from 'criminal' to 'individual'. Criminality, and indeed feminism, are expressions of individuality, with which the reader must identify; indeed the reader has no choice. (Collins doubtless has the case of William Palmer in mind in this dialogue, which will recall Dickens's irritation in reporting it: Dickens is both pro-justice and pro the criminal, and that shows in how he writes.)

---

[32] Collins, *Dickens and Crime*, 232.
[33] Wilkie Collins, *The Woman in White*, ed. John Sutherland (Oxford: Oxford University Press 1996), 220.

Dickens attended the Mannings' hanging with John Leech and 30,000 others, and it induced two letters to *The Times* (13 and 17 November 1849). The first came immediately after the hanging, hating the levity of the crowd: '[their] upturned faces, so inexpressibly odious in their brutal mirth, or callousness, that a man had cause to feel ashamed of the shape he wore, and to shrink from himself, as fashioned in the image of the Devil' (*Letters* 5.644–5).

This compares with *Punch*'s threefold commentary on the Mannings' hanging. *Punch* first published a sketch of the crowd at the jail, and included a poem underneath, where one man talks to another, 'Bill' who has asked him to come to the 'hanging match', where the place is 'just like a fair', and commenting on 'Jack Ketch':

Quick, JACK's about it. There he's got the first beneath the beam,
And now the other! Not a stare, a tremble or a scream!
All's ready. There they stand alone. The rest have gone below,
Look at him – look – he's at the bolt! Now for it! Down they go!

'Twas over. Well, a sight like that afore these eyes of mine
I never had – no sort of mill, cockfighting or canine.
Hurrah! you dogs, for hangin, the feelings to excite,
I could have throttled BILL almost, that moment, with delight.

But after all, what is t? A tumble and a kick!
But anyway, 'tis seemingly over precious quick
And shows that some, no matter for what they've done, dies game!
Ho ho! if ever my time comes, I hope to do the same!

Punch 1849, 210

The 'fair' is also a 'mill' (*OED* noun 6: '*slang*. A fist fight; (hence) a boxing match. Also more generally: a fight, a scrap') – the first citation being Piers Egan in 1812; a rowdy fight alongside dogfighting and cockfighting.

Second, *Punch* noted how quickly the Mannings appeared at Madame Tussaud's, and compared the image of Mrs Manning with Mrs Siddons playing Lady Macbeth, her head covered with old point lace. Third, in the article, 'The Proper Time for Public Executions', it instanced proprietors of *The Sunday Drop, The Scaffold Weekly News, The Old Bailey Enquirer* and *Life in Newgate*, 'newspapers published on the morning of the Sabbath', petitioning the government that hangings be moved to Saturdays for them to cover the stories. 'And as it is right that executions should be public, it is clear that they should be as public as possible – to make them so public it is evident that the agency of the public prints is necessary, hence the statesman will see that the more newspapers that are sold the better.' Below this satire appeared a picture of a house near a jail, with a notice 'An eligible investment' – 'This house, conveniently overlooking County Gaol, to be let' (*Punch* 214). *Punch* declares itself a 'mortal enemy of JACK KETCH' (220).

The *Times* editorial the following day (14 November) dissented from Dickens's plea for *public* hanging to be abolished, for 'were it otherwise, the mass of the people would never be sure that great offenders were really executed, or that the humbler class of criminals were not executed in greater numbers than the State chose to confess'. Nor did *The Times* think Dickens could gauge the 'real feelings'; and the 'abiding impression' of the crowd (*Letters* 5.645, note). Clearly, *Punch*, on the basis of the poem, would have disagreed; the affair was an entertainment, making 'dying game' seem an entirely plausible activity. However, on 15 November 1849, Dickens writes to Gilpin regretting that he cannot attend a meeting of the Society which was held at the Bridge House hotel in Southwark, with 300 present, and with supporting letters from Richard Cobden, John Bright and Douglas Jerrold:

> I believe that the enormous crimes which have been committed within the last year or two, and are fresh, unhappily, in the public memory, have indisposed many good people to share in the responsibility of abandoning the last punishment of the Law. And I know there are many such who would lend their utmost aid to an effort for the suppression of *public* executions for evermore, though they cannot conscientiously abrogate capital punishment in extreme cases.

Perhaps he includes himself in this last sentence, but where he stands in relation to the first is unclear. It seems, however, that his anxiety is not to be out of step with 'public memory': we can make of that what we will. While rejecting the idea of a Public Meeting to uphold total abolition, perhaps because he thought it would be impolitic, 'the other vast improvement could be compassed in a very short time, and ... it would save a prodigious amount of harm, indecency, and horror' (from public executions) (*Letters* 5. 647–8).

Jerrold, in contrast, supporting what Dickens called 'the Platform people', i.e. the abolitionists, deprecated 'the mystery of private hanging'. Dickens reproached him for this on the basis that all moves towards improving and altering public punishments involved a mystery, and asked him to remember when there was 'no mystery connected with these things, and all was as open as Bridewell when

Ned Ward went to see the women whipped'.[34] His second long letter to *The Times* (*Letters* 5.651–4) responded to a correspondent claiming that though Dickens had said public executions were 'the leading cause of the depravities he describes ... in fact they only afford exhibitions of it'. Dickens in reply urged again the character of the crowd he had witnessed, saying 'the mirth was not hysterical, the shoutings and fightings were not the efforts of a strained excitement seeking to vent itself in any relief'. He instanced a woman arrested for trying to murder another woman in the multitude, 'proclaiming that she had a knife about her, and would have her heart's blood, and be hanged on the same gibbet with her namesake Mrs Manning, whose death she had come to see – as she had her evil passions excited to the utmost by the scene, so had all the crowd'. Further, he cites Henry Fielding's article, *Enquiry into the Causes of the Late Increase of Robbers etc With Some Proposals for Remedying this Growing Evil: In the Which. The Present Reigning vices are Impartially exposed; and the Laws that Relate to the Provision for the Poor, and to the Punishment of Felons are largely and freely examined* (January 1751), on the benefit of private executions. This pamphlet of Fielding's will be discussed below. For now, it is enough to note how Dickens uses Fielding. Offstage murders, e.g. Duncan's in *Macbeth*, carry more 'terror' 'than by all the blood which hath been spilt upon the stage', he says, using an example from Fielding. He adds that he would have a condemned murderer sequestered so that no news of him or her should emerge: certainly not from the loquacious William Calcraft. The execution would be carried out in front of selected witnesses, 'and during the hour of the body's hanging I would have the bells of all the churches in that town or city tolled, and all the shops shut up, so that all might be reminded of what was being done'. The 'mystery' thus introduced into the proceedings would solemnize this 'last sentence of the law'. He concludes with talking of the abolitionists, finding them, 'however good and pure in intention', 'unreasonable', partly because they will not take the step of making capital punishment private.

Dickens was criticized for this apparent going back on himself, though it is also true and relevant to say that the abolitionists continued to use him into the 1860s to support their arguments, and he did not dissociate himself from that use. The criticism was expressed by Jerrold, writing to him on 20 November 1849:

---

[34] *Letters* 5. 650. Edward Ward (1667–1731) wrote about this in *The London Spy*, 1698–9: see the reprint, ed. Ralph Straus (London: Casanova Society 1924), 136–44.

Grant private hanging, and you perpetuate the punishment... As to the folly and wickedness of the infliction of death as a punishment, possibly I may consider them from a too transcendental point. I believe, notwithstanding, that society will rise to it. In the meantime my Tom Thumb voice must be raised against any compromise that, in the sincerity of my opinion, shall tend to continue the hangman amongst us, whether in the Old Bailey street, or in the prison press-yard.[35]

Clearly, Jerrold felt that Dennis the hangman in *Barnaby Rudge* had been the final word on the subject: for a society to tolerate a Dennis was an obscenity.

More damagingly, John Bright accused Dickens of having 'a mere longing to put someone to death', while Cobden said that Dickens was of the Calcraft party. They in turn were criticized in *The Times* for saying that 'Dickens was possessing a homicidal disposition and sort of monomania to take somebody's life'.[36] Abolitionists had made the evils of public hanging (the degradation, the encouragement to riotous behaviour, the danger of sympathy with the prisoner) their strongest suit, and so they were forced into arguments which said that if the punishment was not public, it should not happen at all. That in turn produced the argument that execution in private would be like assassination, not the exercise of justice. Not seeing justice done publicly was against the spirit of English liberties. The abolitionists sided with those who thought that the privileged prisoner would, after all, not be hanged, but would bribe his way out of prison, so that they were noting the class issues which would be involved in making hanging real, and private.

Dickens seems exceptional, to the degree to which he objected to the behaviour of the crowds, for there were plenty – like *The Times*'s editorials – who argued that their levity concealed a more grim awareness of death, and that Dickens could not *know* what the crowds were thinking under their carnival show. Dickens's point, however, was that *The Times* could not know either; that it could not see 'the attraction of repulsion' which overtook those who watched, and which incited them to further crime. His anxiety to make capital punishment a 'mystery', as he was accused of doing, produces some very improbable attempts by him to almost sacralize the proceedings, the solemnity (bells ringing, etc.) being the only marker of what had taken place. The craziness of these attempts to heighten the secrecy and mystery, and create a serious public, undo themselves,

---

[35] Quoted, Michael Slater, *Douglas Jerrold 1803–1857* (London: Duckworth 2002), 181.
[36] David D. Cooper, *The Lesson of the Scaffold* (London: Allen Lane 1974), 85. See the discussion of Dickens, 72–97.

and expose his argument as highly problematic. For in asking for capital punishment to take place outside public scrutiny, Dickens damages his own ideas. He is in danger of diminishing its deterrence value, however slight that might have been. He encourages a new secrecy and creates a new potential for state oppression of the criminal – a point which is one of those inherent in Foucault's *Discipline and Punish* (1975). And, recalling Bright and Cobden's objections to him, he is open to the accusation that since he had argued that executions should end because their public character ruined everything of order and deterrence, his new idea of private executions inevitably makes him appear to want to have *more* hangings, only more efficient ones. The charge made that he *wanted* more punishment becomes valid; for in his solemn proposals for streamlining executions in private he concedes something to the dilemma which the abolitionists wrestled with, and which justified – and justifies – their position: if we agree that punishment should be exemplary, and on display, because society is showing that it approves of the offender being taken from its midst, then it should be public. If arguing, however, that capital punishment degrades the spectators, making them voyeurs, and worse, incites them to crime – then there is a reason for discontinuing capital punishment, not for putting it out of sight. If it continues out of sight, its very continuance becomes signs of the 'monomania' Dickens was accused of: wanting to kill criminals when any justification for this is gone.

The point holds with imprisonment itself for lesser offences. Dickens has asserted that the public is not interested in people being transported, removed from sight in that way. Putting people out of sight only represses a problem to which Dickens is alive when he shows, in his letters to the *Daily News*, that people are not put off murder by the thought of punishment. And if they are not put off by capital punishment, they certainly will not be deterred by life imprisonment. Punishment cannot be carried out in a way which makes sense; and Dickens's letters show it to be an empty way of trying to solve a problem which it creates. Punishment exposes what a public is, and shows – to return to an earlier point – what 'laws' of behaviour are occluded by the exercise of law. Yet the nature of the public, who are sadistic and attracted to crime itself, and to hunting down the weak, and the victim – a subject which keeps Dickens's interest from its appearance as a subject in *Oliver Twist*, and so throughout – renders private execution a mockery, as a way of dealing with the consequences of what the public is, and how it and the criminal are alike incited to violence by it. It is unsurprising that *The Times* was unwilling – or unable – to engage Dickens in the question of what the crowd at a hanging actually was like. Capital punishment in private represses the way that the public is more implicated in crime than lawmakers would like to recognize, and how, if the 'attraction of repulsion' means anything, it implies that punishment attracts 'Temptation'. If we cannot abide the consequences of what is done in public hanging, we had better not do it in secret.

In saying Dickens suffered from monomania, it seems that the total abolitionists had a point. Dickens could not have been so voyeur-like in considering how capital punishment could be carried on in private if there was not some attraction within it to him; one making it likely that there was some form of autobiographical impulse in how his letters had defined the attraction of the gallows in leading to crime, or the added attraction that crime gained from punishment. As Derrida says, 'the death penalty can seduce' (*DP* 1.94).

We can conclude this section by returning to the point *Punch* made – that capital punishment sold newspapers – to see how the attraction that people feel towards seeing someone hanged, and the impetus it gives to crime, is furthered in the nineteenth century by a press able to exploit, indeed create, a voyeur-like interest. Such an interest would only be furthered if it took place in secret, a point which would frustrate Dickens's thinking of it happening under such conditions. If hanging sells, and, through the waxworks, gains an afterlife, it becomes part of the capitalist arrangements of society, making the criminal essential in creating a cohesive consumerist public.

We have noted Fielding (1707–54) and must divert to him in the following chapter because Dickens so patently brings him in; hence what follows unpacks Fielding's influence on Dickens's arguments. After Fielding, and Hogarth, we can return to Dickens's most abolitionist novel of the period, *Barnaby Rudge*, which will show what was interesting, and what questionable in Dickens's analysis of crime and the criminal.

2

Fielding, Hogarth and Dickens

Even without Dickens's deliberate nodding to Fielding on capital punishment, the latter would still need attention, as one of the most significant forces discernibly influencing and working inside Dickens. The author of plays in the 1730s, and of *Shamela* (1741), *Joseph Andrews* (1742) and *The History of Tom Jones, a Foundling* (1749), Fielding had become an advocate in 1740, and made a deliberate career change by becoming a magistrate for Middlesex, with offices in Bow Street, in the winter of 1748–9. *Tom Jones* has an interest in criminality, for the 'foundling' is pronounced 'certainly born to be hanged', which Dickens borrows for his foundling in *Oliver Twist*.[1] Alexander Welsh, discussing the rise of circumstantial evidence, and this being rated alongside witness statements in trials, quotes John Preston saying that the novel is making assessments all the time, and asking the reader to do the same: 'The book is *about* judgment. It focusses attention not only on events, but on the mind which perceives and judges them.'[2] Reader-response criticism, which Preston is here writing, joins with a sense that the novel is being written for readers to sit in judgment, and in a way which condemns the criminal. Wilkie Collins similarly imagines the reader as a judge, and that may be a point of differentiation from Dickens, who is more uncomfortable with that position.[3] Welsh (63) says that Fielding 'specialises in the management of evidence'. Judge, advocate for the prosecution, and jury are aligned.

Effectively, Fielding was responsible for everything in the area north of the river in London, with the exception of the City of London. He stayed in post until early 1754, when ill health made him to try to regain health in warmer

---

[1] Fielding, *Tom Jones*, ed. Thomas Keymer and Alice Wakely (London: Penguin 2005), 109, *Oliver Twist* 17.
[2] Alexander Welsh, *Strong Representations: Narrative and Circumstantial Evidence in England* (Baltimore: Johns Hopkins University Press 1992), 49, quoting John Preston, *The Created Self: The Reader's Role in Eighteenth-Century Fiction* (London: Heinemann 1970), 117.
[3] Wilkie Collins, *The Moonstone*, ed. Anthea Todd (Oxford: Oxford University Press 1982), 213. Cp. *The Woman in White*, 5.

climes – in Lisbon, where, however, he died, leaving his magistrate's work to be continued by his half-brother Sir John Fielding (1721–80 – his death preceded the Gordon Riots of that year). Another legacy the Fielding brothers left was the Bow Street Runners, who continued until 1839. These, for their last ten years, worked alongside the new Metropolitan Police.[4] Not simply because he was a magistrate, rather impelled by being one, Fielding wanted to write about crime by the end of 1750, as he did, supporting capital punishment (this being some thirteen years before Beccaria). *An Enquiry into the Late Increase of Robbers* (1751) discusses increased tendencies to crime in a 'trading' society, and probes drunkenness and gin-drinking in tones paralleling Hogarth's *Gin Lane* (1751).[5] It is a conservative, essentially Utilitarian, document directed against the poor, whom Fielding wants to have controlled, and so not wandering, not vagrants (a new Vagrancy Act had come into law in 1744). Hence its criticisms of the temptations to 'voluptuousness' which, along with 'vanity' – more prevalent with the rich – lead to 'luxury', which is like Idleness for Fielding, something at the root of crime. He criticizes, therefore, the numbers of places of diversion in the town, the drunkenness, and the gaming. Finding present conditions giving encouragements to theft, which are the subject of section 5 of the *Enquiry* onwards, lends several points which feed into Dickens, who must have noted Fielding discussing how easy it was to be undetected in London.

The point holds for *Barnaby Rudge*, for Rudge has been hiding out in London since the double murder he committed in 1753:

> Whoever indeed considers the Cities of *London* and *Westminster*, with the vast Addition of their Suburbs; the great Irregularity of their Buildings, the immense Number of Lanes, Alleys, Courts, and Bye-places; must think, that, had they been intended for the very Purpose of Concealment, they could scarce have been better contrived. Upon such a View, the whole appears as a vast Wood or Forest, in which a Thief may harbour with as great Security, as wild Beasts do in the Desarts of *Africa* or *Arabia*. For by wandering from one Part to another, and often shifting his quarters, he may almost avoid the Possibility of being discovered.
>
> *Enquiry* 131

The passages in *An Enquiry* giving most to Dickens succeed section 10, 'Of the Encouragement given to Robbers by Frequent Pardons', which contends against

---

[4] On the Bow Street Runners, see Gilbert Armitage, *The History of the Bow Street Runners 1729–1829* (London: Wishart and Co. 1952), J. M. Beattie, *The First English Detectives: The Bow Street Runners 1750–1840* (Oxford: Oxford University Press 2012).

[5] Henry Fielding, *An Enquiry into the Causes of the Late Increase of Robbers and Related Writings*, ed. Malvin R. Zirker (Oxford: Clarendon Press 1988), lii–lxxii and 61–172; see 90 for gin-drinking.

'ill-grounded clemency' with regard to the death penalty – 'Pardons have brought many more Men to the Gallows than they have saved from it' (166). Section 11, 'On the Manner of Executions', which contains the material which Dickens quoted in 1849, argues:

> the Day appointed by Law for the Thief's Shame is the Day of Glory in his own Opinion. His Procession to *Tyburn* and his last moments there, are all triumphant, attended with the Compassion of the meek and tender-hearted, and with the Applause, Admiration, and Envy of all the bold and hardened.
>
> 167

Foucault cites this, and other passages from Fielding, in discussing 'The Spectacle of the Scaffold' (*DandP* 60). The 'Example' is far from being 'an Object of Terror', and we should note the pre-Revolutionary sense of that word, since Terror is what the state creates, for deterrence purposes (terror and deterrence share a common etymology: Latin *terrere*, to frighten). In other words, terror is not here what is exercised against the state. Fielding comments on why capital punishment fails to deter. One reason is, the frequency of executions, about one a week. Fielding's editors note that criminals were executed every six weeks, and cite Leon Radzinowicz, that of 389 capital convictions in London and Middlesex from 1749 to 1754, 285 offenders were executed, i.e. 5 or 6 each six weeks (167–8). Fielding concludes:

> the Thief who is hanged today hath learned his Intrepidity from the Example of his hanged Predecessors, as others are now taught to despise Death, and to bear it hereafter with Boldness from what they see today.
>
> 168

This frequency gives Fielding a dilemma, coupled with the point that the design of open capital punishment was 'to add the Punishment of Shame to that of Death, in order to make the Example an Object of greater Terror' (168). He concedes that this desire to create shame fails, and at that point, he turns to 'the Poets', citing Aristotle on tragedy as intending to arouse pity and terror. Fielding has the theatre in mind as a model for hanging, arguing 'that the Execution should be as soon as possible after the Commission and Conviction of the Crime'. Delay only focuses attention on the punishment, not the crime, 'and no good Mind can avoid compassionating a 'Set of Wretches, who are put to Death we know not why, unless, as it almost appears, to make a Holiday for, and to entertain the Mob' (169). He concedes that hangings are a spectacle – hence the question becomes how to make that effective on the stage – and he must go against the judge in himself in acknowledging pity as an important element, trumping, indeed, the sensation of terror.

Hence, executions should be 'in some degree private'. 1744 saw David Garrick playing Macbeth, and Fielding reverts to the play:

> the Poets will again assist us. Foreigners have found fault with the Cruelty of the *English* Drama, in representing frequent Murder upon the Stage. In fact this in not only cruel, but highly injudicious. A Murder behind the Scenes, if the Poet knows how to manage it, will affect the Audience with greater Terror than if it was acted before their Eyes. Of this we have an Instance in the Murder of the King in *Macbeth*, at which, when *Garrick* acts the Part, it is scarce an Hyperbole to say, I have seen the Hair of the Audience stand an End. Terror hath, I believe, been carried higher by this single Instance, than by all the Blood which hath been spilt on the stage.
>
> 169–70

Fielding thinks how more 'dreadful' punishment would be to the criminal if he died only in the presence of his 'Enemies', not of his friends in the procession to Tyburn. Yet Fielding's rhetoric betrays something, that is, his own complicity in cruelty, in using the word 'Enemies' – an important word for him in *An Enquiry*. It is impossible for justice to be impartial; impossible to 'truly and indifferently administer justice', as the Prayer Book puts it; indeed if it *was* objectively done, which is what Fielding wants, the inhumanity here which objectivizes, would be cruel; if it is done with a sense of being an enemy, then justice becomes both personal, and theatrical, in the sense that sympathies have been aroused as much as they are by watching Garrick – even if Garrick is playing not the judge, but Macbeth, the criminal. Nor can we forget that the word 'Murder', which has such an emotive effect when it is offstage, inevitably contaminates the idea of offstage execution, which is what Fielding wants; as though Fielding's unconscious recognizes that what he is talking about is indeed murder.

Hence for Fielding, 'the Execution should be in the highest degree solemn. It is not the Essence of the Thing itself, but the Dress and Apparatus of it, which make an Impression on the Mind' (170). We may pause over 'apparatus', which *OED* notes from 1728 as having the sense of 'the mechanical requisites employed in scientific experiments or investigations'. Dickens gives the word in the chapter on Fagin's last night alive, with 'the black stage, the cross-beam, the rope, and all the hideous apparatus of death' (*OT* 450). The desire for solemnity in this 'Image of Death' (171) – Fielding quotes Montaigne, but also Shakespeare's 'strange images of death' (*Macbeth* 1.3.97) – makes the gallows allegorical. It figures the dead person who is hanged on them, and it belongs to an aestheticizing argument, which wants performances to have a classical dignity, and immediacy, disliking the popular, carnival drama which, in the quotation following, is implied in the word 'Holiday':

> Suppose then, that the Court at the *Old Bailey* was, at the End of the Trials, to be adjourned during four Days' that, against the Adjournment-day, a Gallows was erected in the Area before the Court; that the Criminals were all brought down on that Day to receive Sentence, and that this was executed the very Moment after it was pronounced, in the Sight and Presence of the Judges.
>
> Nothing can, I think, be imagined ... more terrible than such an Execution; and I leave it to any Man to resolve himself upon Reflection, whether such a Day at the *Old Bailey*, or a Holiday at *Tyburn*, would make the strongest Impression on the Minds of every one.
>
> 171

The aestheticizing tendency makes capital punishment a matter of extreme cruelty, where, if it happened, the prospect of the judge watching the death penalty performed on the person would certainly influence the prior decision to pronounce sentence. It would personalize, if not sexualize, the issue. Kant's *Critique of Pure Reason* (1781) notes the philosopher A. G. Baumgarten (1714–62) first using the word 'aesthetic' to mean 'the critique of taste' in *Aesthetica* (1750).[6] Aesthetics, however it may have been unknown to Fielding as a word, informs what he is indulging in unconsciously, when wanting the execution of the sentence of the court to be the period of the actual pronouncing of the sentence, and wanting the audience to be an elite in a proper theatre, not a carnival mob. He wants to shame the criminal ('shame' is a keyword for *Tom Jones*), so that it is not just the performance of the rite which is important to him, but the idea that the man should feel himself disgraced, should find no friends, but enemies; a point Johnson considered differently. Fielding returned to the subject in *The Covent-Garden Journal*, a twice-weekly magazine he published (4 January–25 November 1752). Most of its pieces he wrote, as with no. 55 (18 July 1752) which opens: 'On Monday last eleven Wretches were executed at Tyburn, and the very next Night one of the most impudent Street-Robberies was committed near St James's Square; an instance of the little Force which such Examples have on the Minds of the Populace.'[7] It is the very spirit of Dickens's letters.

---

[6] Immanuel Kant, *Critique of Pure Reason*, trans. Norman Kemp Smith (London: Macmillan 1929), 66.
[7] Henry Fielding, *The Covent-Garden Journal and A Plan of the Universal Register-Office*, ed. Bertrand Goldgar (Oxford: Clarendon Press 1988), 447. See also no. 25 (28 March 1752), 161–6, reacting to the new 'Murder Act' which had received the Royal Assent on 26 March 1752 – Fielding felt it did not go far enough in bringing about execution in private.

It is almost impossible to look at the familiar arguments about the procession to Tyburn without them becoming romanticized or aestheticized: such, for example, has been the effect of popular histories drawing on Hogarth's images. Swift (1667–1745), visiting London in 1726 and 1727 (his last visit), writes 'Clever Tom Clinch going to be hanged' (1735), full of advice for those in the 'trade'. It recalls Jonathan Wild's fate, hanged in 1725:

> As clever *Tom Clinch*, while the Rabble was bawling,
> Ride stately through *Holbourn*, to die in his Calling;
> He stopt at the *George* for a Bottle of Sack,
> And promis'd to pay for it when he'd come back.
> His Waistcoat and Stockings and Breeches were white.
> His Cap had a new Cherry Ribon to ty't.
> The Maids to the Doors and the Balconies ran,
> And said, lack-a-day! He's a proper young Man.
> But, as from the Windows the Ladies he spy'd,
> Like a *Beau* in the Box, he bow'd low on each Side;
> And when his last Speech the loud Hawkers did cry,
> He swore from his Cart, it was all a damn'd Lye.
> The Hangman for Pardon fell down on his Knee;
> *Tom* gave him a Kick in the Guts for his Fee.
> Then said, I must speak to the People a little,
> But I'll see you all damn'd before I will *whittle*.
> My honest Friend *Wild*, may he long hold his Place,
> He lengthen'd my Life with a whole Year of Grace.
> Take courage, dear *Comrades*, and be not afraid,
> Nor slip this Occasion to follow your Trade.
> My Conscience is clear, and my spirits are calm,
> And thus I go off without Pray'r-Book or Psalm.
> Then follow the Practice of clever *Tom Clinch*,
> Who hung like a Hero, and never would flinch.[8]

The neat wit within the rhyming couplets (e.g. 'Like a *Beau* in the Box, he *bow'd low* on each Side') give this poem its 'clinch' (a clinch is a pun, and Clinch has been 'clinched', i.e. fastened, held tight (compare 'clenched'), finished off). It is an account of 'dying game', of not 'whittling', which is a variant of 'to whiddle' (*OED* 1725: 'to enter into a Parley, to compound with, or take off by a Bribe'; not

---

[8] Jonathan Swift, *Jonathan Swift: The Complete Poems*, ed. Pat Rogers (New Haven: Yale University Press 1983), 316.

impeaching anyone (cp. the name Peachum in *The Beggar's Opera* (1728)). Clinch's last speech is already available, as an alternative account of his life, competing with his own. Swift himself wrote *The Last Speech and Dying Words of Ebenezor Elliston, who was Executed the Second Day of May, 1722*; this fictitious account by a robber born in 1690 and executed in Dublin gives encouragement to what Fielding writes. The robber declares that 'nothing can be more unfortunate to the Public, than the Mercy of the Government in ever pardoning or transporting vice' (38). For there can never be any lasting repentance. Even those hanged and then 'wonderfully came to life and their Escapes, as sometimes happens' (38) are doomed to repeat their offences and be hanged at the last.[9]

'Four Stages of Cruelty'

> The British, avid for the cruelty of spectacles, are desirous of seeing murders and bloody bodies on stage.[10]

Fielding, then, was no abolitionist. His pessimism about crime in London shows in the *Enquiry*, and in the novel written at the same time, *Amelia*. It shows, too, in *A Voyage to Lisbon*, when he boards the ship at Redriffe (=Rotherhithe), carried in a chair because of his bad physical state, attended by sailors and watermen giving 'all manner of insults and jokes on my misery. No man who knows me will think I conceived any personal resentment at this behaviour; but it was a lively picture of that cruelty and inhumanity in the nature of man which I have often contemplated with concern, and which leads the mind into a train of very uncomfortable and melancholy thoughts.'[11] With cruelty, we re-enter territory associated with punishment, and relevant for all this study – specifically, at this moment, Hogarth.

Fielding had authored *The History of the Life of the Late Mr Jonathan Wild the Great* (published 1743, possibly written three years earlier, when it commented on the departing and corrupt Robert Walpole; it was revised in 1754). Jonathan

---

[9] Jonathan Swift, *The Prose Works of Jonathan Swift*, ed. Herbert Davis, 13 vols., Vol. IX: *Irish Tracts 1720-1723 and Sermons* (Oxford: Blackwell 1948), 35–41. Davis prints as Appendix E a rival account of Elliston (365–7), so that two at least rival versions were available of this life. The idea of the criminal being revived is used by Dickens, *Sketches by Boz*, 'The Black Veil'.
[10] Entry for 'Cruelty', *Dictionnaire de Trévoux* (1705), quoted James A. Steintrager, *Cruel Delight: Enlightenment Culture and the Inhuman* (Bloomington: Indiana University Press 2004), 5.
[11] Henry Fielding, *Jonathan Wild and A Voyage to Lisbon*, ed. A. R. Humphreys (London: Everyman 1973), 202. I quote from this edition of *Jonathan Wild*; the Penguin edition, ed. David Nokes (1982) reprints Defoe's account.

Wild, born in Wolverhampton probably in 1683, had been hanged at Tyburn (24 May 1725), and had passed into literature through a biography by Daniel Defoe, and then with *The Beggar's Opera* (1728). John Gay, the author, makes him into Peachum, though the latter is over-genial in relation to the thieves he shops. *The Beggar's Opera*, satirizing Walpole, opera and aristocratic speech, works best less by eroticizing the fate of the young men hanged, which is one of its preoccupations, than by commenting on the inequality, which shows the nihilism implicit in lawmaking and enforcement, for there is no justice in who gets to be hanged, as every lawyer knows. The rich get off, the poor are penalized, a point which holds with all legislation which wants to assert a new authority. So Air LXVII, sung to 'Greensleeves', shows:

> Since laws were made for ev'ry degres,
> To curb vice in others, as well as me,
> I wonder we han't better company,
>   Upon Tyburn tree!
> But gold, from law, can take out the sting:
> And if rich men like us were to swing
> 'Twould thin the land, such numbers to string
>   Upon Tyburn tree![12]

Wild styled himself 'Thief-Taker General', for he operated a cartel to which thieves had to belong and to pay, otherwise he shopped them to the authorities. As a fence, like Fagin, Wild owned 'lost property offices' around the Grub Street area of London, where victims could buy back what had been stolen.[13] In *The Beggar's Opera*, the valiant thief and prison-breaker whom he has sent to the gallows was a version of Jack Sheppard.

In *Jonathan Wild*, Fielding's rendering of Wild makes him most vicious towards Heartfree – his allegorical name derived from *The Pilgrim's Progress* – and his wife. Heartfree is sent to Newgate, and is within an ace of execution. *Jonathan Wild* indicates another contradiction within Fielding, which is that the novelist (the writer of 'romance') may believe in a Providence which does not sanction the innocent to die, while Heartfree believes strongly in an afterlife which will justify him if he was executed. Yet even in those terms, it is not

---

[12] John Gay, *The Beggar's Opera and Polly*, ed. Hal Gladfelder (Oxford: Oxford University Press 2013), 66. See its quotation in *Little Dorrit* 586.

[13] Gerald Howson, *Thief-taker General: The Rise and Fall of Jonathan Wild* (London: Hutchinson 1970), 111. See Sean Silver, *The Mind is a Collection: Case Studies in Eighteenth-Century Thought* (Philadelphia: Pennsylvania University Press 2015), 252–68.

inevitable that the innocent is not hanged: the plot could equally easily have gone in the other direction, as it is chance which also prevents Tom Jones from being hanged. The magistrate, author of the *Enquiry*, may believe in the virtue of hanging, yet the novel he writes will not support him. If Fielding had considered that, it would demonstrate the commonly respected argument against the death penalty: that the innocent may suffer – and have done so – with no possibility of reparation.

Cruelty relates to the idea of spectacle, insofar as it means having someone in one's power. *An Enquiry into the Causes of the late Increase of Robbers* appeared the same year as Hogarth's *The Four Stages of Cruelty*, whose subject Ronald Paulson argues developed out of the earlier *The Harlot's Progress* (1732). In the six plates comprising that narrative, Paulson singles out the fourth and fifth.[14] The fourth shows the Harlot, who is shown as giving herself airs, being guilty of affectation, enforced to beat hemp in the Bridewell Prison (the House of Correction in Tothill Fields, Westminster). Hemp would, of course, be used for the rope to hang people; and indeed, at the back of the shed where the labour is enforced, someone has scrawled an image of the magistrate hanging from a gallows. Plate 5 shows Molly Hackabout dying from a sexual disease, with two doctors in consultation, one of whom may also be a version of Walpole.

On Monday, 5 March 1733, Hogarth visited Newgate, making a likeness of Sarah Malcolm (Paulson no. 129). The sketch became a print on 10 March, as well as a picture showing the woman at a table, arms folded, a rosary before her.[15] Who was she? Born in Durham in 1710, she had been a laundress at the Temple in London, and was alleged to have strangled three women in Mitre Court: her mistress Lydia Duncomb, who lived with another old woman, and her maid (*ODNB*). She admitted having taken part in a robbery of these three, though claiming that others – Mary Tracy, James and Thomas Alexander – had done the murders. Her trial on 23 February 1733 condemned her, rejecting the story that she had accomplices. She was hanged in Fleet Street on 7 March, at the end of Fetter Lane, opposite Mitre Court, two clergymen, William Piddington and John Middleton, accompanying her, and a vast crowd watching. Her body was exhibited at an undertaker's in Snow Hill, before being dissected, 'and her skeleton presented to the Botanic Garden, Cambridge, in a glass case' (Paulson 86).

---

[14] Ronald Paulson, *Hogarth: Graphic Works*, 3rd ed. (London: British Museum 1989). *The Harlot's Progress* comprises Plates 121–6.
[15] Elizabeth Einberg, *William Hogarth: A Complete Catalogue of the Paintings* (New Haven and London: Paul Mellon Centre for Studies in British Art by Yale University Press 2016), 121–3.

Hogarth played on the 'before' and 'after' motif in pairs of paintings, in showing scenes of seduction of the woman (Plates 141–2). This is another 'before' picture, the caption for the print reading 'Sarah Malcolm Executed in Fleet Street, March the 7th 1732 [this is the old calendar] for Robbing the Chambers of Mrs Lydia Duncomb in the Temple, and Murdering Her, Eliz. Harrison & Ann Price'. This 'before', which is also a 'between' crime and hanging picture, cannot have an 'after' from Hogarth, that being its poignancy. Death is the force that seduces her, in a motif Hogarth would have known – Capulet tells Paris: 'the night before thy wedding day / Hath Death lain with thy wife' (*Romeo and Juliet* 4.5.35–6). Apart from the numerous images which were taken from Hogarth's sketch, following a tradition of Hogarth's father-in-law, Sir James Thornhill, sketching Jack Sheppard in 1724 (Dickens, like Ainsworth knew this, and Cruikshank used it for 'Fagin's Last Night Alive'), Sarah Malcolm was exhibited in plural ways. She was shown at the scaffold, and after her death. She met this spectacularization by dressing for execution in a crape mourning gown, a sarsenet hood and black gloves. John Ireland (d. 1808), who edited Hogarth for John Boydell, called her 'a Lady Macbeth in low-life'.[16] Paulson connects this episode with George Lillo's melodrama *The London Merchant* (1731), and if that permits thinking forward to *Great Expectations*, via Maria Manning's self-stylization on the scaffold, we may see, in the woman's muscular arms, something of Molly in that novel.[17]

The Four Stages of Cruelty may be approached via the series *Industry and Idleness* (1747), showing a London polarized between the worlds of Francis Goodchild and Tom Idle. That being so, it makes Hogarth's subject London, and the urban, in a wider sense than the specific locales intimate.[18] As often in Hogarth, the gallows remains in the unconscious of the image before being brought forward. In the fifth plate, 'The Idle 'Prentice Turned Away and Sent to Sea', the one which identifies him by name, Tom is being rowed down the Thames to join a ship, while a gallows is also in view with a body swinging from it. Its eleventh, penultimate plate shows 'The Idle 'Prentice Executed at Tyburn', and this ride to Tyburn, with Tom leaning on his own coffin (Paulson Plate 178), contrasts with one in the Lord Mayor's carriage, which concludes the series. Tom goes out towards the west of London, Goodchild rides in towards the east, to the Guildhall. The right–left contrast for the two contradicts traditional ascriptions

---

[16] See Jenny Uglow, *Hogarth: A Life and a World* (London: Faber & Faber 1997), 232.
[17] Ronald Paulson, *Hogarth Vol. 2: High Life and Low, 1732–1750* (New Brunswick: Rutgers University Press 1992), 7–11; for the painting, see fig. 6.
[18] Mark Hallett, *Hogarth* (London: Phaidon 2000), 199–234.

of which is right, which wrong. The pictures show Hogarth's interest in crowds, and recall Sarah Malcolm and the stands erected for people to witness her execution, some of which collapsed causing injury. Paulson notes the contrast between the Anglican clergyman, the ordinary of Newgate, in his covered coach (vs the Methodist preacher uncovered, helping Idle in his last moments) and Goodchild in his covered, closed coach, guarded by the sword of state (Paulson 1992, 299). The man holding this at the coach window is the Marshal of the City, for the magistrate 'beareth not the sword in vain' (Romans 13.4). Privilege protects itself both by its enclosure and the emblem of execution from the crowd, who are an element representing instability in both. On the far right, a pedlar holds a broadsheet, 'A full and true account of the Ghost of Thom. Idle. Which ...'. So a spectre haunts the procession, and marks Hogarth's sympathies.

Paulson discusses the *Four Stages of Cruelty* (1751, Plates 187–90), whose 'four', as in Hogarth's *Four Times of the Day*, connotes universality, comprehensiveness and something which is QED. 1751 also saw Hogarth's *Gin Lane*, and *Beer Street* (1750–1), pictures polarizing Industry (*Beer Street*) and Idleness (*Gin Lane*). One shows self-satisfaction, the other how idleness is enforced, and made something much worse, death-dealing. The violence that gin implies, as a deadening refuge for the poverty of those in St Giles's parish (beer was more expensive, and so more middle-class), contributes to the image of the barber who has hanged himself, visible in *Gin Lane*. There are plural signs of casual cruelty here, but Derrida connects cruelty with blood ('*cruor* is red blood, blood which flows') (*DP* 1.96), contending that cruel derives from *crudus*, i.e. blood (as well as that which is uncooked). Cruelty cannot be confined to actual letting of blood, but Derrida, for whom the subject of cruelty is a leitmotif in his later writings, says it points to a 'radical evil', a term from Kant's *Religion within the Limits of Reason Alone* (1794). 'Radical evil', for Kant, means a power at the base of human motivations, which can corrupt these, and produces the human's adoption of evil maxims.[19] For Derrida, less theologically, it implies the ability to abstract, to work in abstraction, so ignoring the alterity of 'the other'.[20] Cruelty, which Derrida calls 'cold' (1.61) and connects with the guillotine's hardness and heartlessness, is a 'suffering inflicted so as to make suffer' (1.96). Hogarth's title does not imply any *lex talionis*, any law of retribution: it is not so moralistic. It rather implies a progression; punishment is a continuation of the crimes of the

---

[19] Peter Dews, *The Idea of Evil* (Oxford: Blackwell 2006), 19–21.
[20] On radical evil in Derrida, see his 'Faith and Knowledge' in Jacques Derrida, *Acts of Religion*, ed. Gil Anidjar (London: Routledge 2002), 43.

beginning, with images of torturing animals for fun; another Tom Idle, this time Tom Nero, the parish-boy of the series, has his fate chalked up on the wall in this urban setting (also St Giles's parish): he will be hanged. This image means we need not see the actual hanging. Some scientific experiments, anticipating the fourth picture, are being practised as a cat is launched from a window, to see if it can fly on the mock wings given it. The second stage continues the association with animals, for Tom beats the horse which has collapsed under the weight of pulling a coach containing four fat lawyers, going from Thavie's Inn in Fetter Lane to Westminster Hall. The third plate, 'Cruelty in Perfection', shows Tom being apprehended having cut the throat of his pregnant mistress who lies at his feet in a country churchyard, having robbed on his behalf. She is the only woman in the series, perhaps contributing to the sense, though of course women are hanged, that the death penalty is a thoroughly masculine problem.[21]

The setting is night-time, and the weapons (e.g. a pitchfork) of those who arrest him, imply that cruelty goes both ways, for the capture of Tom includes features of the arrest of Christ in Gethsemane. 'The Reward of Cruelty' shows the dissection of Tom's body after he has been hanged. Here, the male body replaces the female whom has murdered, and he is in the hands of the Surgeons, whose dissecting theatre near Newgate has a presidential chair with the arms of the Royal College of Physicians above the magisterial and judgmental Physician, enthroned in baroque state. 'Physician' (to use Dickens's language) is flanked by two niches containing skeletons. In the third version, one is that of James Field, a pugilist hanged on 11 February 1751; the other, James MacCleane, a highwayman hanged at Tyburn on 3 October 1750. They will recall Sarah Malcolm's fate. Skeletons, also visible on either side of the Tyburn picture in 'Industry and Idleness', suggest the Dance of Death – death inside life. Their pointing gives them a strange automaton quality, and they may have been remembered by Dickens for the two casts of hanged criminals in Mr Jaggers's office in Little Britain in *Great Expectations* (chapter 24).[22] Gouging out the eye, a feature of these plates, and having the logic of castration, recalls Gloucester's blinding in *King Lear*, cruelty intended to make the man indistinguishable from

---

[21] See Scott J. Juengel, 'Of Beauty, Cruelty, and Animal Life: Hogarth's Baroque', *differences* 16 (2005), 24–62.
[22] David Paroissien, *The Companion to Great Expectations* (London: Helm Information 2000), 222–3.

the animal ('let him smell his way towards Dover' – *King Lear* 3.7.91–2). As Paulson says, it recalls the *lex talionis* of 'an eye for an eye'.[23]

The rope is still round Tom's neck, preserving his identity as a criminal, and he may even be still alive, for the Surgeons have evidently made off with his body after hanging, as fast as they could, whether he was dead or alive.[24] While dissection of criminals' bodies was not officially provided for until a 'Murder Act' of 1752, which allowed for two days between sentencing and execution, Jonathan Wild's presumed skeleton, from what happened to him in 1726, is at the Hunterian Museum in London (Silver, 261). Cruelty seems equally the province of lawyers/barristers and physicians as of parish-boys, and functionally attempts to separate the human from the animal, by exploiting the latter, though the animal returns to consume the body of the man murdered by the state in Plate 4. And what of the apparatus within the picture, the revolving table, the pulleys, the weapons used for the autopsy, which supplements the industriousness? Three people work separately on the body, giving another sense to the word 'industrious'. We have entered another regime, scopic and technological and industrial, which makes the body a machine (ropes and pulleys are like the intestines which resemble rope), and lets a strange life emerge from the 'dead' body; machinery makes for something uncanny, where the boundaries of life and death are confused. It is Freud's point, in *The Uncanny* (*SE* 18.217–56). The boundaries are muddied when surgeons grab bodies questionably dead, as Linebaugh describes happening in detail. Technology downgrades the human; the dog becomes the recipient of Tom Nero's heart; another primitivism is promoted by the bones cooking in an all-but witches' cauldron on the picture's left, below the studious medic who is dissecting Tom's feet and ankles, reducing him to a skeleton. The rope and pulley system is a variant on the rope used for hanging. Snaking intestines speak of life as a process, resembling the plan of the pictures. Intestines pass to the floor via a bucket containing a head, as if recalling *Macbeth*'s witches' apparitions, and, being pulled by one of the surgeons, become an image for a continuity of narrative. They spill out below (being subservient to) the magistrate's rod which points (as the skeletons point, and the doctors point at them) from the

---

[23] Tom Paulson, 'Fielding, Hogarth, and Evil: Cruelty', in Claude Rawson (ed.), *Henry Fielding (1707-1754): Novelist, Playwright, Journalist, Magistrate – A Double Anniversary Tribute* (Newark: University of Delaware Press 2008), 179 (article 173–200). The treatment of the cadaver should be compared with Géricault's treatment of severed heads and limbs in his art; see 'Public Hanging in London', perhaps of the London Cato Street conspirators (1 May 1820) – Lorenz E. A. Eitner, *Géricault: His Life and Work* (London: Orbis 1983), 223, and 182, 183, 310.

[24] See Elizabeth T. Hurren, *Dissecting the Criminal Corpse: Staging Post-Execution Punishment in Early Modern England* (London: Palgrave Macmillan 2016), 106–12.

back of the picture to the centre. Antal notes the travesty of Rembrandt's *The Anatomy Lesson of Professor Tulp* (1632: The Hague, Mauritshaus).[25] In this masterclass, the atmosphere is febrile, as though once the master withdraws to the professorial or magisterial chair, everyone knows exactly how to act. They have been given their head.

It is hideous – and comic. Baudelaire speaks of the 'absolute comic', which he finds in the grotesque. His principal example comes from the English pantomime, which he had seen in Paris. As with Hogarth, the comic works here more in the visual than depending on language.[1] Baudelaire declares violence to be the distinctive mark of this type of the comic (2.538), which relates to the violence in Hogarth.[1] Pierrot acts with excess throughout (as everything in pantomime, and the comic is marked by hyperbole), and he must be guillotined. The French stage is itself surprised to see a guillotine appearing in relation to the English mode of execution; however, guillotining allows the trick whereby Pierrot is decapitated, but, as the inveterate thief, walks off with his own head, which he has stolen. The whole gives the experience of 'le vertige', which Charvet translates as 'intoxication'.[26] This state has to do with the confrontation with a tumultuous fate: with death, so that the excess in the creation of the grotesque has to do with an excess in the subject who is seeing his own subjectivity questioned in the most radical way, where no moralizing works. The point relates to Hogarth: Baudelaire responds to those who say that Hogarth is the death of the comic by saying that he is the comic in death ('le comique dans l'enterrement').[27] The English pantomime, and Hogarth, make the absolute comic into a strange, non-state, into the perception of a divided state, in its strangest state, a perception of death. Hogarth's grotesque looks beyond death. If it signals that the absolute trauma of capital punishment never stops, it adds that this cannot easily be eliminated because capital punishment, like the pantomime, may be the source of an absolute joy for those engineering or seeing it, as well as absolute violence. Such perversity can never be factored in, but it must be. Shock pervades the comic; and that elision of comedy and violence is perhaps so much inside identity that it works against abolition.[28]

---

[25] Frederick Antal, *Hogarth and his Place in European Art* (London: Routledge & Kegan Paul 1962), 166.
[26] Baudelaire, *Selected Writings on Art and Artists*, trans. P. E. Charvet (London: Penguin 1972), 157.
[27] Baudelaire, *Oeuvres complètes*, ed. Claude Pichois, 2 vols. (Paris: Gallimard), 2.565.
[28] This develops from my *Histories of the Devil: From Marlowe to Mann and the Manichees* (London: Palgrave 2016), 163–93.

Fielding and murder

Hogarth on cruelty is more complex than Fielding's moralism; less bourgeois; perhaps F. R. Leavis's comment that 'by *Amelia*, Fielding had gone soft'[29] finds an echo in his strange justifications for the death penalty. There is the outstanding example of the hanging of the young man Bosavern Penlez on 18 October 1749. He was made a scapegoat in the aftermath of a series of riots carried out on three brothels in the Strand by sailors, disaffected because they had been fleeced in one of them. While Fielding defended himself in *A True State of the Case of Bosavern Penlez* published on 18 November 1749, Peter Linebaugh seems right in saying that Fielding showed himself 'frankly polemical and self-interested', serving political interests, and that Penlez and the fourteen others hanged with him represented a miscarriage of justice.[30] Strange, too, was his softness towards Elizabeth Canning in 1753, a woman eventually transported to America for perjury. She claimed she had been abducted by two roughs and carried away to a brothel in Enfield, till she had escaped a month later, and Fielding defended her story in *A Clear State of the Case of Elizabeth Canning* (20 March 1753).[31] The author who had so mocked Pamela's virtue in *Shamela* and *Joseph Andrews*, and had found hypocrisy there, was more affirmative of the woman's virtue in Elizabeth Canning's case. This was in contrast to the gypsy woman Mary Squires and her accomplice Susannah Wells, who was condemned to be hanged, until the tide turned against Elizabeth Canning.

Whatever happened in the Canning case, it is hard not to feel that Fielding's inconsistency illustrates the unreliability of any system of justice. It does not create confidence. Further, in comparison with the probings into cause and effect, and the ironies which run through *The Four Stages of Cruelty*, Fielding is less interested in motivations than Hogarth, and, speaking of the ruffians who supposedly abducted Elizabeth Cannon, dismisses the need for finding a motive for their actions, so surrendering any firm social or political analysis:

---

[29] F. R. Leavis, *The Great Tradition: George Eliot – Henry James – Joseph Conrad* (London: Penguin 1962), 12.

[30] Peter Linebaugh, 'The Tyburn Riot against the Surgeons', in Douglas Hay et al. (eds.), *Albion's Fatal Tree: Crime and Society in Eighteenth-Century England* (London: Penguin 1977), 90. Lance Bertelsen, *Henry Fielding at Work: Magistrate, Businessman, Writer* (New York: Macmillan 2000), 12–13 takes a more conservative view than Linebaugh.

[31] Both papers are in *An Enquiry into the Causes of the Late Increase of Robbers and Related Writings*, ed. Malvin R. Zirker (Oxford: Clarendon Press 1988), 31–60, and 281–312; see Introductions to both (xxxiii–lii; xciv–cxiv. See the brisk treatment of both cases in Tom Paulson, *The Life of Henry Fielding: A Critical Biography* (Oxford: Blackwell 2000), 269–70, 312–15.

> How many Cruelties indeed do we daily hear of, to which it seems not easy to assign any other Motive than Barbarity itself? In serious and sorrowful Truth, doth not History as well as our own Experience afford us too great Reason to suspect, that there is in some Minds a Sensation directly opposite to that of Benevolence, and which delights and feeds itself with Acts of Cruelty and Inhumanity? And if such a Passion can be allowed any Existence, where can we imagine it more likely to exist than among such People as these?
>
> 289–90

It is not a question of finding fault in Fielding's 'softness'. *Jonathan Wild* illustrates the point. Contemporary with *Amelia* and with the reissue of *Jonathan Wild* appeared Fielding's *Examples of the Interposition of Providence in the Detection and Punishment of Murder* (1752), whose contents are given by the subtitle, *Containing Above Thirty Cases, in which this dreadful Crime has been brought to Light, in the most extraordinary and miraculous Manner; collected from various Authors, antient and modern*.[32] Fielding regards 'the dreadful crime of murder' as increasing, and his task is to explain how the crime discovers itself. In Example XVIII he gives an instance of a murderer who breaks down in the dock though the evidence against him is insufficient: 'At his death he averred that the ghost of the murdered person had appeared before his eyes at his trial' (203), a detail which Dickens might have used for Bill Sikes's death/suicide, pursued by Nancy's 'eyes'. Example XXXIII is Mary Blandy, tried at Oxford and executed (6 April 1752) for poisoning her father, incited to it by her lover, William Cranstoun, whose 'gallantry' Fielding satirizes in the *Covent-Garden Journal*, while being sympathetic to the woman.[33]

Fielding discusses poison in *Tom Jones*, in relation to slander, seeing the two as analogous. Poison is 'a means of revenge so base, and yet so horrible, that it was once wisely distinguished by our laws from all other murders, in the particular severity of the punishment' (*Tom Jones* 500). Apparently in the sixteenth century, the poisoner could be boiled to death (see *Tom Jones* 939). It is interesting to see that the rationalist in Fielding seems to accept that murder is motivated by revenge. He drew on John Reynolds's *The Triumph of God's Revenge Against the crying, and execrable Sinne of Wilful and Premeditated Murder, with their Miraculous Discoveries, and Severe Punishments thereof: In Thirty Tragical*

---

[32] Included in *An Enquiry into the Causes of the Late Increase of Robbers and Related Writings*, ed. Malvin R. Zirker (Oxford: Clarendon Press 1988), 175–217.
[33] Zirker, 214–15, and Goldgar, 134–9 (10 March 1752). See Margaret Anne Doody, '"Those Eyes are Made so Killing": Eighteenth-Century Murderesses and the Law', *Princeton University Library Chronicle* 46 (1984), 49–80. See also Bertelsen, 189.

Histories (Digested in Six Books) Committed in divers Countreys beyond the Seas (1621-2), called an 'excellent book' in *Jonathan Wild* (91, 110). The significance of sixteenth- and seventeenth-century murder, as in *Hamlet* and *Macbeth*, haunts here, as does *Richard the Third*, when Lady Anne is wooed by Richard over the corpse of Henry the Sixth:

> O gentlemen, see, see dead Henry's wounds
> Open their congeal'd mouths and bleed afresh.
>
> 1.2.55-6

The anonymous play *Arden of Faversham* (c. 1591) makes much of the murdered husband's wounds bleeding ('cruentation') in front of the murderous wife.[34] Cruentation implies that the dead body retains a sacral quality, which may recall the point that the older sense of 'victim' is someone – or an animal – offered in sacrifice to a deity. It proclaims the murderer, as it does with Henry, and with the murdered woman in 'Cruelty in Perfection', the third stage of *Four Stages of Cruelty*. As Zirker points out, Reynolds's book may be the one lying beside the dead woman (Zirker, xc).

Reynolds (c. 1588–after 1655) lived, apparently in France, and presented his thirty narratives as translations from the French (see *ODNB*). The fourth story of the First Book is material used for Beatrice-Joanna, De Flores and Alzamero in *The Changeling*, while the wolf that digs up and partially eats the murdered (poisoned) man De Laurier in Book 6 story 2 will recall Cornelia's mad Dirge in *The White Devil* (1612):

> Call for the robin red breast and the wren,
> Since o'er shady groves they hover.
> And with leaves and flowers do cover
> The friendless bodies of unburied men ...
> But keep the wolf far thence, that's foe to men,
> For with his nails he'll dig them up again.
>
> 5.4.91-4, 99-100[35]

It also evokes the dog eating Tom Nero in 'The Reward of Cruelty'. These murders, which bring about God's 'revenges' are presented as 'tragedies', taking place in Italy, or Spain, or Portugal, or France: they are absolutely of the moment of

---

[34] See Malcolm Gaskill, *Crime and Mentalities in Early Modern England* (Cambridge: Cambridge University Press 2000), 203-41 for crimes of blood.
[35] John Webster, *The White Devil and Other Plays*, ed. René Weis (Oxford: Oxford University Press 1996), 89. See also *The Duchess of Malfi* 4.2.301-3 (175).

Jacobean drama, stressing intrigue between people who poison, or stab or shot who stand between them and adultery and its discovery. They are modern, not classical instances: as tragedies, they connect to the place given to murder in Elizabethan and Jacobean revenge tragedy; secret murder, carried out for private gain, not now as part of a blood feud, and the subject of excited narrative which probes and unearths secrecy, as God's revenge is said to do. Murder has become Fielding's theme, having a special place in *Jonathan Wild* (see Book 3 chapter 3), yet as with Bosavern Penlez, Fielding did not think the death penalty should be confined to punishing murder.

Arguing that innocence will be preserved, taken from Providential, largely traditional narratives, comprises one aspect of *Jonathan Wild*, and contradicts the other part which shows that plots are not Providentially ordered, being rather farcical, like Ben Jonson's *The Alchemist*. The Jonsonian plots which involve different rooms and spaces where different people may be gulled appear for instance in the comedy of situations and tricks which Wild practises in Book 2 chapter 5. Fielding's terms of reference are the drama; hence Wild reads Molière (*Les Fourberies de Scapin* – 1.3.11), and Falstaff. The latter's braggadocio in recounting the Gad's Hill robbery in *I Henry IV* 2.4 is echoed by the Count's exaggerations (1.11. 310) – and Falstaff is recalled for his speeches on honour (1.14.48). This comedy of situations, however, at its most farcical with the sexually motivated visits to Laetitia Snap (1.9), where the winner is the person most able to practise on someone else, lacks Providential support. Chance, not a controlling destiny, is at work. Fielding cannot argue simultaneously that Providence ensures that the innocent are never hanged, and that murder will out, and then write a comic plot: the one sentiment belongs to the moralist who cannot afford the possibility that a Heartfree might hang, and the other to the novelist, who derives his material from just such a possibility. The magistrate speaking from the bench cannot claim the novelist's authority, operating with a profounder sense of the strange workings of uncanny chance and complications of plot. The lawgiver can hardly systematize, in the way that Fielding compiles examples of how the guilty have been brought to an unexpected justice. Fielding's views on capital punishment must be taken as inadequate; they risk a sentimentalism inseparable from finding people cruel, even when the criminal is Jonathan Wild, with whom the narrative retains a sympathy, since he is the great engineer of plots, his resources being the drama.

3

Barnaby Rudge, Poe and Caleb Williams

Dickens's pro-abolition letters in 1846 reflect on his authorship of *Barnaby Rudge*, a novel about hanging, and claiming interest for that alone. *Barnaby Rudge* is a wonderful study of crime and prisons, and hanging, and should lead into thinking about each of those topics – especially crime, which this chapter will give it. It gives, in short, a clue to Dickens.

Appearing in weekly form (February–November 1841), in the miscellany *Master Humphrey's Clock* which Dickens edited, *Barnaby Rudge: A Tale of the Riots of 'Eighty* was published in book form on 15 December 1841. It was well prepared for, since Dickens had contracted to write *Gabriel Vardon, the Locksmith of London* in May 1836 for the end of that year, as a Scott-like historical novel.[1] It opens in 1775, remembering a double murder which had taken place on 19 March 1753, and with the sense impending that the murderer will be discovered some time in the future, on a 19 March (chapter 1). It is, then, first of all a detective story. So Edgar Allan Poe read it, tracking down the mysterious stranger of chapter 1, who plagues Mrs Rudge, and is her husband. He murdered Reuben Haredale and also the gardener, with whom he swapped identities after killing him. Rudge's guilt and his need to return to the scene of the crime give him away, and he makes a partial confession in Newgate (chapter 62). The son, Barnaby, has features of the father, and despite his natural 'innocence' as a Wordsworthian idiot boy, partakes of something else within his father, his criminality.

This is one strand in a novel whose chapter 33 jumps to 1780, to the anti-Catholic Gordon Riots, which include everybody in their scope. Those involved show Dickens's absorption with madness and the grotesque which extends through Barnaby Rudge and his raven Grip ('I'm a devil' – 25.209); to Hugh, the

---

[1] On the novel's progression from 1833 onwards, see John Butt and Kathleen Tillotson, *Dickens at Work* (London: Methuen 1957), 76–89, and Kathyrn Chittick, *Dickens and the 1830s* (Cambridge: Cambridge University Press 1990), 152–77. Good discussion comes in Steven Marcus, *Dickens from Pickwick to Dombey* (London: Chatto & Windus 1963).

'centaur', son of Sir John Chester and of a hanged gypsy woman, given a magnificent illustration when shown asleep (11.97); and finally Dennis the hangman, who declares his work to be 'sound, Protestant, constitutional, English work' (37.301). These become leaders of the riots, stirred up by the madness of Lord George Gordon, who, with his steward Gashford, incites anti-Catholic rioting in June 1780. There is a mad obsessiveness, too, in Varden's apprentice, Sam Tappertit, keenly preserving his masculinity, and running an extra-legal 'Prentice Knights' group, which, if transported into the 1930s, would easily qualify as a Fascist organization; he also joins in the riots.

Madness, as melancholia, and deep obsessiveness, affects Geoffrey Haredale, brother of the murdered Reuben, owner of the old house, the Warren, situated outside London. Geoffey is an early version of Mr Jarndyce, as the Warren also suggests Bleak House. Haredale has a dual hatred: of the murderer, Rudge, whom he tracks down and arrests (chapter 56), and of Sir John Chester, a long-time rival, who married the woman he loved, and whom he kills. Further, madness affects the crowd, which is at the heart of the novel. Rudge, who is maddened by guilt, and has the sense of being haunted by the dead Haredale, says: 'I have seen him, on quays, and market-places, with his hand uplifted, towering, the centre of a busy crowd, unconscious of the terrible form that had its silent stand among them' (62.493). The riots, including the burning of Newgate, are written with intense enthusiasm. They form the public part of the novel, and bring out Dickens's own double position in writing, being on the side of law, and on that of the rioters, as when he tells Forster, regarding chapters 63 and 64, 'I have just burnt into Newgate, and am going in the next number to tear the prisoners out by the hair of their heads' (11 September 1841, *Letters* 2.377). It is impossible not to see in that 'I' an identification with the rioters.

A third strand in the book, fascination with the gallows, is illustrated in the letter T which opens chapter 49 (389). It shows especially with Dennis the hangman. A memorandum of Thursday, 31 January 1839 written by Dickens, says: 'Gaspey – Chapter of Executioners' (*Letters* 1.639), about which the editors say that this was probably a note to himself directing him to read this chapter by Thomas Gaspey (1788–1871), a journalist and novelist whom Dickens would have known from his writings for *Bentley's Miscellany* (*Letters* 1.363, 29 January 1838). Gaspey had written about the Gordon Riots in his novel *The Mystery, or Forty Years Ago* (1820), which included Ned Dennis, the executioner from 1771 to 1786; further, he had written an execution scene with a reprieve in *History of George Godfrey* (1828).

The turn in Dickens towards thinking about executioners seems significant. The Preface to the First Edition says that the account in the Tale of the main features of the Riots is 'substantially correct', and that 'Mr Dennis's allusions to the flourishing condition of his trade in those days, have their foundation in Truth, not in the Author's fancy. Any file of old Newspapers, or odd volume of the Annual Register, will prove this with terrible ease' (3). He then references chapter 37, which we have already noted. Gashford and Dennis talk, are agreeing that there are about fifty hanging laws at present in Britain. Dennis describes his work, noting that half of those who should come to him are taken as soldiers, and Dickens becomes journalistic:

> Parliament says 'If any man, woman, or child, does anything again any one of them fifty acts, that man, woman, or child, shall be worked off by Dennis' … sometimes he [George III] throws me in one that I don't expect, as he did three years ago when I got Mary Jones, a young woman of nineteen who come up to Tyburn with a infant at her breast, and was worked off for taking a piece of cloth off the counter of a shop in Ludgate-hill, and putting it down again when the shopman see her, and who had never done any harm before, and only used to do that, in consequence of her husband being pressed three weeks previous, and she being left to beg, with two young children – as was proved upon the trial. Ha ha! – Well! That being the law and the practice of England, is the glory of England …
>
> 37.301

On this hanging, which Dennis carried out on 16 October 1771, the Preface comments:

> Even the case of Mary Jones, dwelt upon with so much pleasure by the same character, is no mere effort of invention. The facts were stated exactly as they are stated here, in the House of Commons. Whether they afforded as much entertainment to the merry gentlemen assembled there, as some other more affecting circumstances of a similar nature mentioned by Sir Samuel Romilly, is not recorded.
>
> 3–4

The 'merry gentlemen' elides these MPs with Fagin, often called that. In the 1849 Preface, Dickens enlarges on the Mary Jones case 'as related by SIR WILLIAM MEREDITH in a speech in Parliament, on Frequent Executions', in 1777:

> 'Under this act', the Shop-lifting Act, 'one Mary Jones was executed, whose case I shall just mention; it was the time when press-warrants were issued, on the alarm about Falkland Islands. The woman's husband was pressed, their goods seized for some debt of his, and she, with two small children, turned unto the

streets a-begging. It is a circumstance not to be forgotten, that she was very young (under nineteen), and most remarkably handsome. She went into a linen-draper's shop, took some coarse linen off the counter, and slipped it under her cloak; the shopman saw her, and she laid it down: for this she was hanged. Her defence was (I have the trial in my pocket), 'that she had lived in credit, and wanted for nothing, until a press-gang came and stole her husband from her' but since then, she had no bed to lie on; nothing to give her children to eat; and they were almost naked; and perhaps she might have done something wrong, for she hardly knew what she did'. The parish-officers testified the truth of this story; but it seems, there had been a good deal of shop-lifting around Ludgate; an example was thought necessary; and this woman was hanged for the comfort and satisfaction of shopkeepers in Ludgate Street. When brought to receive sentence, she behaved in such a frantic manner, as proved her mind to be in a distracted and desponding state; and the child was sucking at her breast when she set out for Tyburn'.

7–8

Several histories combine. One gives material for the history of women, and men pronouncing on women. Another speaks to the history of madness, as the language used indicates: 'she hardly knew what she did' – 'frantic' – 'distracted' – and 'desponding'. This maps onto women, and their conditions of life; and though the cases of madness in *Barnaby Rudge* are all male, it influences the idea of desperation there, as with Mrs Rudge. A third history indicates how capital punishment always claims hard cases, where life is barely sustainable for the one to be hanged; then there is a local history where the proximity of Ludgate to Newgate is to be noted (nor can this be outside Dickens's thinking in charting the progress of the riots around Newgate). Further, there is a history of window displays, consumerism, and shoplifting, which was legislated against first in 1699, and only made a non-capital offence in 1832; the last hanging being in 1822.[2] This hanging shows the preference given of property over lives, which shows when Hugh, about to join the 'division' led by Dennis, turns 'No Popery' into 'No Property' (38.305). How much Hugh is conscious of the slippage may be questioned. The novel is certainly aware.

The politician mentioned in the Preface, the Whig Sir William Meredith (1724–90) had an interest in criminal law:

---

[2] Rachel Shteir, *The Steal: A Cultural History of Shoplifting* (New York: Penguin 2011), 19–34. For Mary Jones, see Peter Linebaugh, *The London Hanged: Crime and Civil Society in the Eighteenth Century* (London: Allen Lane, 1991), 338.

[Horace] Walpole described Meredith as 'remarkably averse to punishments that reached the lives of criminals' (Walpole, *Memoirs*, 3.208) and he moved for an inquiry into the state of the criminal law on 27 November 1770. He raised the issue again on 13 May 1777 with a reasoned plea against capital punishment for minor offences. His speech was published shortly afterwards as *Punishment of Death* (1777), but Meredith was far in advance of prevailing opinion. However, in the changing climate of the early 1830s the third edition of his text ran to 60,000 copies and further reprints followed.

Patrick Woodland in ODNB

A further history deducible from Mary Jones's case is how colonial interests disturb, and create further injustices at home. Criminals were recruited for the American War, itself the subject of chapter 31, where Joe Willett is recruited. In chapter 72 (577) when Joe returns, he has lost an arm in the defence of Savannah, Georgia (1779). Meredith's allusion to British adventurism in the Falklands, islands so named in 1690, and disputed by the French, Spanish and British between 1764 and 1771, shade in another aspect of *Barnaby Rudge*: colonial wars create complacency (John Willett and the Maypole) or nervousness, and shortages at home. Mary Jones provides the inspiration for Hugh's mother, seduced by Mr Chester and hanged. John Willett, the ponderous landlord of the Maypole, and not much better than Dennis, says of Hugh:

> his mother was hung when he was a little boy, along with six others, for passing bad Notes – and it's a blessed thing to think how many people are hung in batches every six weeks for that, and such like offences, as showing how wide awake our government is.
>
> 11.98

Dickens expects his readers to do the multiplication to realize how many people are hanged – and incidentally gives the lie to those who say that he exaggerates; here, at least, he brings out the significance of numbers.

Dennis must explain his profession to Simon Tappertit, who has found him 'odd', and cannot work him out. There is indeed something uncanny in the concept of the hangman. In chapter 39, in a series of euphemisms, Dennis calls himself an 'artist', a 'fancy workman', as if continuing the aestheticizing trend in Fielding associated with public hanging. Yet he says he was not apprenticed to it; he learned his trade by 'natural genius … it come by natur' (316). Dennis's knotted stick, 'the knob of which was carved into a rough likeness of his own vile face' (37.299) was carved by a gypsy, one of his victims, it is revealed (75.604), one who 'died game' (39.317). Dennis took the stick, and his clothes, and declares:

'this very handkercher that you see round my neck, belonged to him that I've been speaking of' (39.317).

This, which recalls pickpocketing for handkerchiefs in *Oliver Twist*, enforces a further connection with Mary Jones and reinforces the injustice: *she* shoplifted for cloth; *he* appropriates the cloth he wants. His boasting takes over and he speaks, too, of his coat, of his shoes, which have 'danced a hornpipe' before and when the man was hanged, and of his hat: 'I've seen this hat go up Holborn on the box of a hackney-coach' (39.318). Here the equivalence of what is thieved – a hat, or coat – with the value of a person's life is underlined: life is taken in order that property may be preserved. In an excellent reading of the character, Myron Magnet notes that with his talk of being 'constitutional' (37.300), Dennis thinks that 'capital punishment [was] the sole function of the state, and a citizen's prime political right his right to be hanged (Magnet, 165, and 162–71). His view of the constitution requires hatred of anything that would include criticism of it. Hence he is glad that Hugh, whose neck he admires, from a professional point of view, can neither read nor write:

> these two arts being (as Mr Dennis swore) the greatest possible curse a civilised community could know, and militating more against the professional emoluments and usefulness of the great constitutional office he had the honour to hold, than any adverse circumstances that could present themselves to his imagination.
>
> 38.306

The combination of 'emoluments' (to himself) and 'usefulness' is neat. The state thrives on maintaining – or creating – ignorance, which if it was alleviated would show Dennis up for what he is. The rioters he would normally be hanging are created by 'bad criminal laws, bad prison regulations, and the worst conceivable police' (49.393). Such ineptitude leaves people with little choice other than to join the revolt. Dennis is part of that ignorance which thinks itself superior, because constitutional; hence his prating over the technology of hanging as opposed to being shot: 'when it's well done, it's so neat, so skilful, so captivating, if that don't seem too strong a word, that you'd hardly believe it could be brought to such perfection' (74.594). He has joined the rioters 'with the great main object of preserving the Old Bailey in all its purity, and the gallows in all its pristine usefulness and moral grandeur' (70.558), taking hanging as particularly Protestant, and deliberately omitting that it pays for his living.

This praise of the constitution gently ribs Fielding's Preface to *An Enquiry into the Late Increase of Robbers*, which he identifies the constitution with the Laws, and with 'the Order and Disposition of the whole', meaning by that the spiritual harmony within the body, the 'Disposition of the several parts in a State' – i.e. the way they function together (66). For Fielding, the older feudal disposition has been altered by 'the introduction of Trade' (69), and because that has increased the 'power of the Commonalty', Fielding wants an equivalent strengthening of the Civil Power; the aim of the *Enquiry* being to 'rouse the CIVIL Power from its present lethargic State', to make the Constitution function again. His design is to oppose

> those wild notions of Liberty that are inconsistent with all Government, and those pernicious Schemes of Government, which are destructive of true Liberty. However contrary indeed those Principles may seem to each other, they have both the same common Interest; or rather, the former are the wretched Tools of the latter: for Anarchy is almost sure to end in some kind of Tyranny.
>
> 73

Zirker's annotation argues that Fielding's characteristic definition of liberty is negative – it is 'the enjoyment of all those Privileges which the Law allows' (73, footnote). There is something circular here; the new conditions of trade threaten a loosening up of morals: indeed, they bring the constitution into question. New laws are needed which will maintain the status quo, which is threatened by what Fielding sees as growing 'anarchy' in the streets. Though pernicious government may restrict liberty, yet liberty is dictated to, as a state, by government and its laws, and Fielding does not let up on this. The guardian of that enforcement is the hangman, as the embodiment of someone from among the people who is willing to identify himself with the interests of the state, indeed, to take pride in them.

Dennis does not reveal his profession to Simon Tappertit, or Hugh, in a pattern of betrayal characterizing this novel. Hugh, whom Sir John Chester intimates will be hanged, thus following his mother, does not know what Dennis does (40.322–5), and Dennis betrays both him and Barnaby (69.553–8). Dennis is overreached and arrested in chapter 74, and must confront Hugh, and the point that he himself hanged Hugh's mother (74.595), who is revealed to have had gypsy blood (75.603). This aligns her with Fielding's Mary Squires, and with Molly in *Great Expectations*, whom Jaggers gets off from the death penalty. In chapter 75, further details emerge: Dennis knows Hugh's identity as the son of the woman he hanged, and knows Sir John Chester to be Hugh's father, since the stick which the other gypsy carved for him bears the word 'Chester' on it. It suits Sir John to let Dennis hang, as well as Hugh, his son, in order to preserve silence.

Rudge the murderer, Dennis, and Hugh are hanged, Dennis with the horror of knowing what is involved in being the hangman: when Hugh says 'how often, before I knew your trade, did I hear you talking of this [being hanged] as if it was a treat?'

> 'I an't inconsistent', screamed the miserable creature; 'I'd talk so again, if I was hangman. Some other man has got my old opinions at this minute. That makes it worse. Somebody's longing to work me off. I know by myself that somebody must be'.
>
> 76.610–11

The statement is one of the best testimonies to the need for abolition, and to Dickens as an abolitionist. It may not be possible to kill without enjoyment, then, or after; without having the pleasure of having someone else wholly in one's power, reducing them to how Dickens describes Dennis, using an Hogarthian mode: as 'a hound with the halter round his neck'.

Dennis remains a minor horrifying Dickensian figure. Dickens's willingness to consider the hangman continues in a *Household Words* essay of 17 May 1850: 'The Finishing Schoolmaster' (*Journalism* 2: 350–6). The 'schoolmaster' is the hangman, and Dickens prints twelve letters submitted as applications to hang a woman, Maria Clarke, at Ipswich Gaol, for the crime of infanticide. Calcraft was unavailable to do the hanging, and a substitute was advertised for in *The Times*. The letters, from as far afield as Cockermouth, Wigan, Manchester and Deal, are masterpieces of what Dickens calls 'Pecksniffian morality'. He notes one where the applicant calls himself a married man which 'shows considerable delicacy', and another where the man has been 'for some time after the birth [*sic* – berth] and am well acquainted with calcraft and I wonder he did not mention my name when you dispatched a messenger to him. I made application at horsemonger lane for the last job there [the hanging of the Mannings] but Calcraft attended himself'. The benefits of competitive tender show when it seems that one man wants £5, another £60. The tone of small-business enterprise (one man will travel by rail), of education being beamed at getting a job, and the sheer willingness to indulge in this sadism since it pays are more versions of Dennis, showing that Dickens never lost his abolitionist tendencies.

The men in Newgate are marked by 'reckless hardihood' (Hugh), and 'abject cowardice' (Dennis). Dickens writes that these are the two commonest states of mind of persons brought to that pass. The observation, which may come from a fascinated knowledge Dickens has acquired, is followed by another paragraph, showing the men held by something which prevents thinking, and action. The writing reaches towards something else it intuits. Sensations Dickens had attempted to consider with 'Fagin's Last Night Alive' appear more abstractly, the drifting anxiety described exceeding an adequate language for it, because there is no objective focus for these *condamnés*:

> The wandering and uncontrollable chain of thought, suggesting sudden recollections of things distant and long forgotten and remote from each other – the vague restless craving for something undefined, which nothing could satisfy – the swift flight of the minutes, fusing themselves into hours, as if by enchantment – the rapid coming of the solemn night – the shadow of death always upon them, and yet so dim and faint, that objects the meanest and most trivial started from the gloom beyond, and forced themselves upon the view – the impossibility of holding the mind, even if they had been so disposed, to penitence and preparation, or of keeping it to any point while that hideous fascination tempted it away – these things were common to them all ...
>
> 76.611

The prisoners are in the state of 'fascination', or, in the terms of the philosopher Emmanuel Levinas, they feel the power of the *il y a*, the 'there is', which, nameless, impossible to isolate or to pin down, speaks of the impossibility for the one who experiences it, in a state of anxiety, or of sleeplessness, of there being nothing. It is Macbeth's sense of 'nothing is but what is not', holding these prisoners by no definable reality, but still real and dispossessing them.[3]

While Barnaby Rudge is reprieved, Dickens notes those who were hanged, as 'for the most part, the weakest, meanest, and most miserable' among the rioters (67.623) . He finishes with a young man hanged in Bishopsgate Street, attended by his father. 'They would have given him the body of his child, but he had no hearse, no coffin, nothing to remove it in, being too poor, and walked meekly away beside the cart that took it back to prison, trying, as he went, to touch its lifeless hand.' We know this victim's name: William Brown, who was to be hanged 'in Bishopsgate St., as near as may be to the house of Charles Daking'.[4] We have an image historical, and starkly allegorical, indeed Blakean.

The sites of capital punishment remain miniatory. On the exterior wall at St Mary's, Ely, a tablet records: 'Here lye Interred in one grave the Bodies of William Beaviss, George Crow, John Dennis, Isaac Harley, and Thomas South, Who were all executed at Ely on the 28th Day of June 1816, having been convicted

---

[3] See Maurice Blanchot, 'Literature and the Right to Death', *The Work of Fire*, trans. Lydia Davis, ed. Charlotte Mandell (Stanford: Stanford University Press 1995), 332.
[4] Quoted, Gatrell, *The Hanging Tree*, 31.

at the Special Assises holden there of divers Robberies during the Riots at Ely and Littleport in the Month of May in that Year. May their awful Fate be a warning to others.' These riots, relating to agricultural fears in the years of reaction leading up to Peterloo, exemplify the church's connivance with the state in harshness; lacking even words hoping for mercy; they remain a permanent attempt to justify capital punishment.

Poe, Godwin and *Caleb Williams*: 'An epoch in the mind'

We must mark the reaction of one of Dickens's best early readers, Edgar Allan Poe (1809–49), to *Barnaby Rudge*. It opens up issues which, while in the hinterland of capital punishment, are essential reading. Its significance is to ask what crime means, what its detection involves, and what complicity police and detectives have with crime; and what the sphere of mystery which all these elements are inside amounts to, and why it is so important. This and the following sections move to Poe to Godwin, and back to Dickens, this time examining *Bleak House*.

Poe had reviewed *Sketches by Boz* in the Richmond-based *Southern Literary Messenger*, calling 'The Black Veil' 'an act of stirring tragedy'.[5] Reviewing the early numbers of *Pickwick Papers* in November 1836, Poe noted the interpolated story, 'A Madman's MS', where 'the writer is supposed to be an hereditary madman, and to have laboured under the disease for many years, but to have been conscious of his condition, and thus, by a strong effort of the will, to have preserved his secret from the eye of even his most intimate friends' (207). In May 1841 he reviewed *Master Humphrey's Clock*; one story from this, 'A Confession Found in a Prison in the Time of Charles the Second' probably influenced 'The Tell-Tale Heart' (1843). And in December 1840, Poe wrote 'The Man of the Crowd', a text impossible without Dickens, and surely recalling *Barnaby Rudge*, whose first three instalments Poe reviewed in May 1841, and the rest in February 1842. When Dickens visited Philadelphia on his American visit, Poe sent Dickens his review, plus *Tales of the Grotesque and Arabesque* (1840).

Dickens let Forster know that Poe had told him that Dickens had '"awakened a new era" in his mind'.[6] Poe's language in the review is stronger, with more sense

---

[5] See Poe, *Essays and Reviews* (New York: Library of America 1984), 206.
[6] To Forster, 15–17 April 1842, *Letters* 194, notes 6–8: it is ambiguous whether Dickens read this in Poe's first review of *Barnaby Rudge*, or whether Poe said it to Dickens; see, for Poe's statement, *Essays and Reviews*, 224.

of himself: Dickens's books 'have formed an era in the reading of every man of genius' (*Essays and Reviews* 224). Dickens seems to have kept up with Poe's writings, this decisive 'era' affecting both.[7] Poe's phrase adopts William Godwin's 1832 Preface to *Fleetwood* (1805), where Godwin recalls that he had wanted to 'write a tale which will form an epoch in the mind of the reader, that no-one, after he has read it, shall ever be exactly the same man that he was before' (*CW* 338). *Caleb Williams* (1794) indirectly references the French Revolution, as in the prison scenes closing volume 2, which mock the Englishman boasting that 'we have no Bastille' (181). In Valmy, in September 1792, Goethe, after a French Revolutionary victory, had announced: 'from this place and from this day forth commences a new era in the history of the world'.[8] The French Revolution had made a difference, which Poe thinks chimes with Godwin's writing ambition. *Caleb Williams*'s revolutionariness exceeds its political impact, affecting Poe and Dickens, forming a context for discussing *Barnaby Rudge*, Dickens and Poe.

Poe saw *Caleb Williams* and *Barnaby Rudge* as about crime. Rudge's raven, Grip, recalls Shakespearian readings: 'the raven himself is hoarse / That croaks the fatal entrance of Duncan / Under my battlements' (*Macbeth* 1.5.38–40); and 'the croaking raven doth bellow for revenge' (*Hamlet* 3.2.247).[9] Poe, while criticizing Dickens, sees Dickens as focused on the double murder, and the discovery of the murderer; the riots being 'almost *forcibly* introduced' (236). Reading *Barnaby Rudge* as a detective piece, he is comparatively disappointed that the identity of the murderer is evident, given away by tell-tale clues; he says that the thesis of the novel 'may be regarded as based on curiosity. Every point is so arranged as to perplex the reader and whet his desire for elucidation' (232).[10]

---

[7] Poe reacted negatively to *American Notes* (*Letters* 3.348). See *Letters* 3.375 and 3.384–5, where Dickens regrets that he has not been able to place Poe's writings with any English firm (but this implies that he had read them), adding that he thinks of Poe with 'a pleasant recollection'. There is another possible allusion to this attempt (letter to Cornelius Mathews, 28 December 1842 (3.406)), and to James McCarroll, 28 February 1862 (*Letters* 10.40), which shows awareness that Poe was published in England in 1852: this implies that Dickens had kept up with Poe.

[8] Quoted, David Andress, *The Terror: Civil War in the French Revolution* (London: Little, Brown 2005), 115.

[9] Poe's poem, 'The Raven', derives from Rudge's Grip; and leads to *David Copperfield*: 'Never more, oh God forgive you, Steerforth! to touch that passive hand in love and friendship. Never, never more!' (*DC* 29.444). See *Letters* 3.107 notes, on Dickens and Poe; including Poe's anger in 1844, that Dickens might have slighted him in an article in *Foreign Quarterly Review* on 'American Poetry' – almost certainly written by Forster.

[10] Coleridge comments on *The Mysteries of Udolpho*: 'Curiosity is raised oftener than it is gratified; or rather, it is raised so high that no adequate gratification can be given it; the interest is completely dissolved when once the adventure is finished, and the reader, when he is got to the end of the work, looks about in vain for the spell which had bound him strongly to it' – quoted, Coral Ann Howells, *Love, Mystery, and Misery: Feeling in Gothic Fiction* (London: Athlone Press 1978), 55–6.

Yet Dickens throws away that interest in mystery, as if unable to keep a secret: Poe knew who murdered Haredale all along. Hence:

> [Dickens] possesses no 'genius' for that metaphysical art in which the souls of all *mysteries* lie. *Caleb Williams* is a far less noble work than *The Old Curiosity Shop*, but Mr Dickens could no more have constructed the one than Mr Godwin could have dreamed of the other.
>
> ER 244

We must dwell on this criticism, contrasting Dickens with Godwin for an understanding of mystery. The implications go deep. We should note Dickens's comment, replying by letter to Poe's critique, and saying he would be pleased to meet him in Philadelphia (they met twice), and his citation of Godwin's statements, from the 1832 Preface to his novel *Fleetwood* (1805):

> apropos of the 'construction' of *Caleb Williams*. Do you know that Godwin wrote it *backwards* – the last Volume first – and that when he had produced the hunting-down of Caleb, and the Catastrophe, he waited for months, casting about for a means of accounting for what he had done?[11]

Dickens might have known this Preface, which we will discuss, through Hazlitt, who had praised *Fleetwood* in *The Spirit of the Age* (1825), or through Bulwer. *Caleb Williams*'s subject, *Things as they Are* – the original title which became the subtitle – was Pitt's tyrannous reactions to the French Revolution; the suspension of liberties such as habeas corpus, and the hunting down of political radicals. Godwin's *Enquiry Concerning Political Justice* preceded it by a year.[12] Its book 7 discusses punishment and will have nothing of coercion – which he calls injustice (*Enquiry* 645) – as a means of improvement. Godwin finds it absurd to punish an individual whose violence is over (643). Violence cannot be used for restraint against some possible future injury which may be committed; that argument justifies tyranny. Coercion cannot produce reformation nor new ways of thinking, nor act an example to others, being cruel itself. Punishment is 'employed against a person not now in the commission of offence, and of whom we can only suspect that he ever will offend. It supersedes argument, reason, and conviction' (648). The last chapter holds that 'delinquency and punishment are,

---

[11] *Letters*, 6 March 1842, 3.107. Poe was so impressed by this that he quoted Dickens's letter to him in his essay, 'The Philosophy of Composition', four years later.

[12] William Godwin, *Enquiry Concerning Political Justice and Its Influence upon Modern Morals and Happiness*, 3rd ed., ed. Isaac Kramnick (London: Penguin 1976). See Gary Kelly, *The English Jacobin Novel* (Oxford: Clarendon Press 1976) and Pamela Clemit, *The Godwinian Novel: The Rational Fictions of Godwin, Brockden Brown, Mary Shelley* (Oxford: Clarendon Press 1993), 35–69.

in all cases, incommensurable' (649). To attempt to measure one crime against another is impossible; motives and actions for murders cannot be compared fairly against each other. Nor can motives for actions be known by another; perhaps scarcely even by their actor. How much is there, he asks, in an action of 'that sudden insanity which hurries the mind into a certain action by a sort of incontinence of nature, almost without any assignable motive and how much of incurable habit?' (653). He finishes that no one can approve a sentence, because of how it reduces actions and motives, adding what Lamb would have agreed with: 'who does not know that there is not a man in England, however blameless a life he may lead, who is secure that he shall not end it at the gallows?' (655–6). He ends with the possibility of innocent people being hanged in error, and on the time which passes between trial and execution; if a master 'do not beat his slave in the moment of resentment, he often feels a repugnance to the beating him at all' (657). That is because reflection teaches the injustice of punishment. Governmental 'rooted habits of injustice' (673) multiply punishments, and crimes.

Chapter 8 of the *Enquiry* considers Law, as 'an institution of the most pernicious tendency' (689), sanctioned by 'the wisdom of our ancestors' – Dickens shares Godwin's contempt here – which wisdom represents as 'lust for power' (690). Godwin recommends abolishing law, replacing it by an appeal to reason within the criminal – 'I must teach him to feel himself, to bow to no authority, to examine the principles he entertains, and render to his mind the reason of his conduct' (692). He want to abolish pardons, too, as producing only patronage and deference. Thomas Holcroft argues similarly in his Jacobin novel, *Hugh Trevor* (1794–7), for Trevor says:

> I doubted whether any man could bring an action against another without being guilty of injustice. I considered crime and error as the same. The structure of law I argued was erroneous, therefore criminal; and I protested against the attempting to redress a wrong, already committed, by the commission of more wrong.[13]

Godwin, in 1795, noted that his 1794 Preface to *Caleb Williams* was perforcedly withdrawn because it criticized Pitt's English government. 'Terror was the order of the day' (*CW* 2) – 'terror' in its reactionary English manifestation. Caleb Williams, the self-educated orphan, writing his memoir, is tracking the chivalrous Mr Falkland, whose servant he is. Falkland's strange, anti-social behaviour has

---

[13] Thomas Holcroft, *The Adventures of Hugh Trevor*, ed. Seamus Deane (Oxford: Oxford University Press 1978), 424.

been apparently, rationally explained by Mr Collins, Falkland's bailiff. For Williams, contradictorily, this explanation apparently conceals a secret:

> the story I had heard was for ever in my thoughts, and I was peculiarly interested to comprehend its full import. I turned it a thousand ways, and examined it in every point of view. In the original communication it appeared sufficiently distinct and satisfactory; but as I brooded over it, it gradually became mysterious.
>
> 107

The secret would make Falkland guilty of plural murder (of the brutish squire Tyrell, and then of the Hawkinses, by having them hanged, to cover up the first murder). Williams, however, tells Falkland, 'innocence and guilt are too much confounded in real life' (117), adding

> I remember an affecting story of a poor man in the reign of Queen Elizabeth, who would have infallibly been hanged for murder upon the strength of circumstantial evidence, if the person really concerned had not been upon the jury, and prevented it.

There echoes how 'murther, though it hath no tongue, will speak / With most miraculous organ' (*Hamlet* 2.2.593–4), and how it speaks when *The Murder of Gonzago* is played before Claudius.[14] Williams's statement arouses Falkland, and resonates with those reassuring Fielding narratives declaring 'murder will out', but the first half of Williams's statement is more questioning than Fielding, for it is not just that the juror, the one sworn in, is guilty and the man in the dock innocent, but rather, guilt and innocence may not be single categories. Murder raises these issues, for Tyrell, whom Falkland murdered, was far worse than Falkland, and as a murderee attracted, virtually created, his murderer.

Further, while Falkland may be guilty, Williams feels guilty, too, and his memoir, though describing Falkland's persecution of him, is at the end a justification of Falkland, told 'that thy story may be fully understood' (326). The aristocratic Falkland murdered the thuggish squire, Tyrell (a name which recalls the hired murderer in *Richard the Third*), who attacked his honour, and these two point to ambiguities marking the English ruling class. Tyrell may reflect Warren Hastings, whom Burke, reactionary in relation to the French Revolution, had impeached in Parliament in 1788 for 'high crimes and misdemeanours' committed as governor-general of the East India Company in India (1772–85). Godwin approved of Burke here; Hastings was, however, acquitted by the House

---

[14] See Robert Kaufman, 'The Sublime as Super-Genre of the Modern, or *Hamlet* in Revolution', *Studies in Romanticism* 36 (1997), 541–74.

of Lords in 1795. Falkland's views on chivalry make him sound like Burke, anachronistic in saying that 'the age of chivalry is gone'.[15] Chivalry had been a subject for parody since *Don Quixote*: it characterizes the eighteenth-century novel. Further, Falkland's sympathies are with the colonizing class, for, in a dialogue with Williams, he approves of Alexander the Great (110–12), though, Williams says, Alexander's 'headlong rage' 'spared neither friend nor foe' (112). For Williams the aristocracy is better considered through Fielding's characterization of Jonathan Wild (110).

The ruling class's guilt indicates Godwin's Jacobinism. In the novel's first ending, it uses the power of the judiciary to silence Williams's denunciations by shutting him in a madhouse or otherwise ruining him. The novel actually has two endings, the first – which has been described – being left in manuscript form; the second, which was published – which Dickens and Poe knew – showing Williams's sympathy for Falkland, though he has gained ascendancy over him. Thus the process of working back from Godwin's original conclusion (the one left in manuscript form) produces the need to write another. Tracing causes from effects produces the opposite result from the one intended. When the causes and actions are written out, the ending must be changed, or rather, the beginning must be changed, since that manuscript ending *was* the beginning of writing the novel. Effects, it seems, do not follow from the causes. Or the cause of writing (i.e. the original ending) does not produce the same effect as Godwin had expected, making him change it. We see how 'innocence and guilt are too much confounded in real life', since telling a memoir cannot establish either innocence or guilt – Falkland's, or Williams's – as discrete entities. Brooding over Mr Collins's narrative gives a paradigm for what happens in reading over a document; it confuses agency. In his aphorisms collected as 'On the Concept of History', Walter Benjamin quotes Karl Kraus, 'Origin is the goal' (*SW* 4.395). This reverses expectations; it means that an ending must be a beginning, and a conclusion, or a state of affairs must find the conditions which would produce it, a point guiding Benjamin's sense of how history must be written. With *Caleb Williams*, Godwin seems to have thought that there was no inevitability which would produce the first conclusion, hence his revision. The purpose of contemplating a goal, or destiny, must be to review whether the steps producing it are inevitable. We may generalize from that to say that capital punishment avoids these questions. It accepts that a life has effectively come to a conclusion at the moment when it

---

[15] Edmund Burke, *Reflections on the Revolution in France*, ed. Conor Cruise O'Brien (London: Penguin 1969), 170.

is punished – indeed that is why it *can* be punished; it accepts that the processes leading to that 'conclusion' were inevitable ones, the essential ones to be factored in in punishing. That allows 'closure' to take place, by which the future is cut out. For 'closure', a misused term, and essential for Derrida, only ever means simplifying, making issues resolvable into a binary choice, innocent or guilty, definite and defining terms.

Williams's 'curiosity', 'the great inquiry which drank up all the currents of my soul' (126), is to discover the contents of Falkland's locked trunk. His obsessionalism resembles Hamlet's wanting to catch the conscience of the King; hence the 'enthusiasm' of Williams's self-dramatizing: 'It is out! It is discovered! Guilty upon my soul!' (129). Yet, he says, 'in the very tempest and hurricane of the passions, I seemed to enjoy the most soul-ravishing calm'. The quotation eroticizes Hamlet's intensity in his advice to the players: 'in the very torrent, tempest, and as I may say, whirlwind of your passion, you must acquire and beget a temperance that may give it smoothness' (*Hamlet* 3.2.6–80). The piling up of synonyms in Hamlet and in Williams needs comment, but Williams's further statement, 'it was possible to love a murderer' (130), goes in a different direction, to Williams's dependency upon Falkland. Discovery of guilt becomes a sexually exciting fulfilment of the 'will to truth', which Nietzsche and Foucault see as inherent in wanting to know something: a will to knowledge has taken over. Williams's excitement at knowing, in the garden where he hides, makes his innocence impossible. He becomes less like Hamlet than Iago, in his insistent curiosity which becomes voyeurism.

Falkland sees himself as Hamlet, and Williams as like Rosencrantz and Guildenstern: 'Do you think I will be an instrument to be played on at your pleasure, till you have extorted all the treasures of my soul? (118 – compare *Hamlet* 3.2.354–61). Both men claim a Hamlet-like authority over the other, as if they shared one identity. When Falkland confesses to Williams, his preparations in doing so prompt Williams to another Shakespearian line: 'what bloody scene of death has Roscius now to act?' (134, compare *3 Henry VI* 5.6.10). It is as if he was Henry VI, the saintly and innocent king, about to be murdered by the future Richard III. That murder of Henry VI was a regicide, a treasonous act, whose parallel, according to the text, is in the French Revolution. Yet Williams, as Henry, is less the assassin than someone watching a momentary surrender of power: the murderer is vulnerable. Williams sees murder as drama, the murderer as acting out, and quoting from *3 Henry VI* confers a new sexual and murderous frisson. Falkland, confessing that he has murdered Mr Tyrell, hounds Williams, saying 'your innocence shall be of no service to you' (154). The amateur detective is destroyed by the criminal, though the question is who feels more guilty, who more inquisitional.

The locked trunk remains unopened, a mystery; Williams is 'persuaded that the secret it incloses is a faithful narrative of [murder] and its concomitant transactions, written by Mr Falkland' (315). His memoir, which is both a confession, and tendentially boastful, acknowledges 'a mistaken thirst of knowledge', and an 'ungoverned curiosity' (4, 133):

> In the high tide of boiling passion I had overlooked all consequences. It now appeared to me like a dream. Is it in man to leap from the high-raised precipice or rush unconcerned into the midst of flames? ... I had acted upon no plan. I had conceived no means of concealing my deed, after it had once been effected. But it was over now. One short minute had effected a reverse in my situation, the suddenness of which the history of man perhaps is unable to surpass.
>
> I have always been at a loss to account for my having plunged thus headlong into an act so monstrous.
>
> 133

All happens in an inexplicable moment, that is, one incapable of fitting into a narrative, as perhaps all events must, since they are specific, not necessarily interpretable, and a narrative must be that which can be generalized from, its events definable beforehand. Pursuing truth is suicidal and criminal. Lacan speaks of a rush towards suicide as the *passage à l'acte*, a term derived from French clinical psychiatry to denote a sudden psychotic move from thought to action. In Lacan, it is a desire in the self to get out of the way which he connects with deep personal embarrassment.[16] Suicide is an apt example, and the phrase serves well here. The 'boiling passion' is Williams's curiosity, the desire to probe the other. Falkland comes before him with threats with the force of Terror in them, but whether this is the radical French terror or repressive English terror is questionable. He claims omnipresent powers (144), and it is clear that Williams cannot sever himself from him, because of the feudal relationship, and because the price of curiosity is to become part of what is witnessed.

Caleb Williams is imprisoned, and escapes, Jack Sheppard-like. In London he becomes a writer, and 'by a fatality, *for which I did not know how to account*, my thoughts frequently led me to the histories of celebrated robbers, and I related from time to time, incidents and anecdotes of Cartouche, Gusman d'Alfarache, and other memorable worthies, whose career was terminated upon the gallows or the scaffold' (159, my emphasis). The 'fatality' is precisely the sense of mystery

---

[16] Jacques Lacan, *Anxiety: Seminar X*, ed. Jacques Alain-Miller, trans. A. R. Price (Cambridge: Polity Press 2014), 114–30. See Dylan Evans, *An Introductory Dictionary of Lacanian Psychoanalysis* (London: Routledge 1996), 136–7.

which is symptomatic of what Godwin possesses, and Dickens does not; it relates to the indecision as to who is criminal and who not. These names combine the fictional, and real criminal. Mafeo Alemán's *Guzmán de Alfarache* (1599–1604) is the autobiography of a *converso*, denied status, for which he is always trying to compensate, making him a *picaro* on the road from Seville to Madrid and Italy, living as a trickster, and ultimately going to the galleys. Translated by James Mabbe as *The Rogue* (1622), its tradition anticipates Jack Sheppard, Hogarth's Idle Apprentice and Oliver Twist. The Sheppard interest parallels Louis Dominique Garthausen, or Cartouche, or Bourguignon (1693–1721), broken on the wheel at the Place de Grève, as a highwayman and a gang-leader.[17] Godwin's interest in the 'great criminal' accompanies curiosity about murder, hence Williams's reading of *God's Revenge Against Murder* (see 340). He notes Richard Weston (201), one of those condemned for the murder of Sir Thomas Overbury, poisoned in the Tower of London (1613). This murder apparently resulted from the instrumentality of Frances Howard and Robert Carr, a royal favourite, created Earl of Somerset. Frances had obtained a divorce from Robert Devereux, the Earl of Essex, whom she had married in 1603, on the questioned grounds of his impotence. Her remarriage to Carr, orchestrated by her uncle, the powerful Henry Howard, Earl of Northampton, was criticized by Overbury. Several accomplices were hanged, but the royal favourites went free. Resembling a Jacobean tragedy, it inspired some.[18] Williams reads, fascinated with crime, as if the criminal and the one who reads about it, become indistinguishable, both guilty. That was something of the 'new epoch' Godwin created.

'The Man of the Crowd' and the criminality of great cities

Through this crowd, self-absorbed as usual – with them, not one of them – Eugene Aram slowly wound his uncompanioned way. What an incalculable field of dread and sombre contemplation is opened to every man who, with his heart disengaged from himself, and his eyes accustomed to the sharp observance of his tribe, walks through the streets of a great city! What a world of dark and troubled secrets in the breast of every one who hurries by you! Goethe has said

---

[17] Colin Jones, *The Great Nation: France from Louis XV to Napoleon* (London: Penguin 2002), 77.
[18] See Alastair Bellany, *The Politics of Court Scandal in Early Modern England: News Culture and the Overbury Affair 1603–1660* (Cambridge: Cambridge University Press 2002). Plays influenced by the scandal include Middleton's *The Second Maiden's Tragedy, The Witch*, and *The Changeling*. A play by Richard Savage, *Sir Thomas Overbury*, was staged at Drury Lane in 1723.

> somewhere that each of us, the best as the worst, hides within him something – some feeling, some remembrance that, if known, would make you hate him. No doubt the saying is exaggerated; but still, what a gloomy and profound sublimity in the idea! What a new insight it gives into the hearts of the common herd! With what a strange interest it may inspire us for the humblest, the tritest passenger that shoulders us in the great thoroughfare of life! One of the greatest pleasures in the world is to walk alone, and at night, while they are yet crowded, through the long lamp-lit streets of this huge metropolis.[19]

The 'new epoch' is marked by something else: the crowd, whose existence, and the need to confront its criminal potential, indicates modernity.[20] Bulwer's 'Newgate novel' *Eugene Aram* (1831), informed by *Caleb Williams*,[21] shows the murderer walking in London on an autumn evening in London in 1758. The second sentence of the quotation is ambiguous: does it include Aram, though his heart is not disengaged from himself? Is the street potentially full of criminals, or does it let the criminal be the *flâneur*? Bulwer's concessive 'no doubt the saying his exaggerated' gives the clue to why he failed as a novelist: he fails to rise to the uniqueness of events, in an impulse to generalize. Nonetheless, the paragraph prompts 'Night is generally my time for walking', opening *The Old Curiosity Shop*, and activates *Barnaby Rudge* chapter 16 where highwaymen are active in the capital, and Dickens criticizes the superficiality of response to the latest outrage:

> rumours of this new act of daring on the road yielded matter for a few hours' conversation through the town, and a Public Progress of some fine gentlemen (half drunk) to Tyburn, dressed in the newest fashion and damning the ordinary with unspeakable gallantry and grace, furnished to the populace at once a pleasant excitement and a wholesome and profound example.
>
> 16.136

---

[19] Bulwer, *Eugene Aram* (London: Collins, n.d.), 316–17. See Walter Benjamin, *The Arcades Project*, 440.
[20] See essays in Jeffrey T. Schnapp and Matthew Tiews (eds.), *Crowds* (Stanford: Stanford University Press 2006), especially Jobst Welge, 'Far from the Crowd: Individuation, Solitude and "Society in the Western Imagination"', 335–58. For eighteenth-century crowds, see George Rudé's 'history from below': *The Crowd in History: A Study of Popular Disturbances in France and England 1730–1848* (New York: John Wiley & Sons 1964); *The Crowd in the French Revolution* (London: Oxford University Press 1972); *Wilkes and Liberty: A Social Study* (London: Lawrence and Wishart, 1983), on the years 1763–74 especially. Rudé attacks the view that called the people who defended Wilkes 'the rabble' or 'the mob', or, in *The Crowd in the French Revolution*, that they were Burke's 'swinish multitude' (8) . Rudé notes Carlyle's fascination with the crowd (4). See Harvey J. Kaye, *The Face of the Crowd: Studies in Revolution, Ideology and Popular Protest: Selected Essays of George Rudé* (London: Harvester Wheatsheaf 1988).
[21] Both are discussed in relation to the Newgate Calendar and the Newgate novel by Jan-Melissa Schramm, *Atonement and Self-Sacrifice in Nineteenth-Century Narrative* (Cambridge: Cambridge University Press 2012), 73–105.

The phrase 'Public Progress' uses Hogarthian language, as if *all* progresses produce a lift to the gallows – as expected in *Oliver Twist: The Parish Boy's Progress*. After these highwaymen 'one man' (i.e. Rudge) is described, 'who prowled and skulked in the metropolis at night'. He disappears into the 'night-cellar' with the 'outcasts', 'a spectre at their licentious feasts; a something in the midst of their revelry and riot that chilled and haunted them' (16.136–7). This in turn prompts Poe's 'The Masque of the Red Death' (1842), where the figures at Prince Prospero's 'masked ball' (208) want to know the identity of the unknown murdering mummer who appears among them. Rudge in chapter 17, is in Southwark, extorting money from his wife. Barnaby, the son, has seen him outside and neither knows he is in the house nor who he is, and imitates him, talking about him going to Tyburn. The father's fate is pronounced by the son. In chapter 18, Rudge is a city-wanderer, and outcast:

> more utterly alone and cast away than in a trackless desert; – this is a kind of suffering on which the rivers of great cities close full many a time, and which the solitude in crowds alone awakens.
>
> 150

Solitude in crowds has become the subject, and should be compared with Poe's 'The Man of the Crowd', whose subject is indecipherability. This opens:

> It was well said of a certain German book that '*es lässt sich nicht lesen*' – it does not permit itself to be read. There are some secrets which do not permit themselves to be told. Men die nightly in their beds, wringing the hands of ghostly confessors, and looking them piteously in the eyes – die with despair of heart and convulsion of throat, on account of the hideousness of mysteries which will not *suffer themselves* to be revealed. Now and then, alas, the conscience of man take up a burthen so heavy in horror that it can be thrown down only into the grave. And thus the essence of all crime is undivulged.
>
> P 131

Secrets – sexual, murderous, criminal – must, yet can hardly be, confessed. Poe's quotation from an unknown German source translates the German; however, translation shows that texts may be unreadable, making the definition of secrets that they *cannot* be revealed. A translatable secret is not a secret. If the essence of all crime is undivulged, the solutions of the detective police may lack relevance. Like Aram, people carry secrets with them, as their own locked room.

The narrating and convalescing 'I', looking at newspapers, in a London coffee house, attempts to 'read' the people in the room, and then those outside, noting the old man, who is like a strange version of Dickens's Master Humphrey, though not so much observing as under observation. Speculating 'how wild a history ... is written within that bosom', and singling out the old man from the urban types, he follows him, as he walks through the London streets. Thomas Mabbott, Poe's editor, notes derivations in Poe's writing from *Sketches by Boz*: 'The Pawnbroker's Shop' for the prostitutes; 'Thoughts about People'; and 'Gin Shops'.[22] Nothing can be said of the man, save for the momentary *punctum* when 'through a rent in his closely-buttoned and evidently second-handed *roquelaire* which enveloped him, I caught a glimpse both of a diamond and of a dagger' (136). The man is in disguise; a dandy, perhaps an assassin; if the diamond is interpreted in terms of clothing, he may be Harlequin-like and carnivalesque, though he is also described as Mephistophelian; at any rate, he has the heterogeneity marking crime. He walks throughout the night, seeking out crowds. Finally the narrator confronts him, 'gazing at him steadfastly in the face', but he ignores him, being, the narrator decides,

> the type and genius of deep crime. He refuses to be alone. *He is the man of the crowd*. It will be in vain to follow; for I shall learn no more of him, nor of his deeds. The worst heart of the world is a grosser book than the 'Hortulus Animae' and perhaps it is but one of the great mercies of God that *es lässt sich nicht lesen*.
> P 139–40

The old man returns to his addictive wish for the crowd, as the collective embodiment of secrets. Ending and beginning, in this story, seem indistinguishable.

Baudelaire calls Poe 'the most powerful pen of his age', and the narrator the man of the crowd, the *flâneur*.[23] He, then, is the detective (so like Pelham). Baudelaire confuses who is the criminal, who the detective, following, in that, the new 'epoch'. Emphasis has shifted from the criminal as exceptional to the crowd as the sphere of crime.[24] Dickens would have agreed with this, from his analysis of crowds at a hanging, and thinking of crowds as viciously hunting people down (*OT* 1.10.77), but Poe gives something less objective and knowable about a

---

[22] Thomas Ollive Mabbott (ed.), *Collected Works of Edgar Allan Poe: Vol. 2: Tales and Sketches 1831–1842*, (Cambridge, MA: Harvard University Press 1978), 505–18.
[23] Baudelaire, 'The Painter of Modern Life': see Charvet, 395–402.
[24] George Rudé (see above) intends to scotch this argument, which was to be taken up in an atavistic reading of the crowd by Le Bon: see *The Face of the Crowd*, 111. Rudé's 'Crime, Criminals and Victims in Early Nineteenth-Century London', 242–65 distinguishes between acquisitive crime ('strictly in pursuit of material gain'), survival crime, and protest crime (261), so de-mystifying criminality and crowds, though at the expense of removing the subject of crime from the record, and separating criminality from the gregariousness of the crowd, though he says that 'to the pickpockets, the greatest boon was the crowd' (250).

crowd, which is not a known entity; indeed not an entity at all. Its anonymity makes it unreadable, and because it is never one thing, since it always replaces itself, it is always in a state of repetition, being never the same: identity and difference together. You cannot step into the same crowd twice. It defies identity; whoever would affirm their individuality using it as a mirror cannot; it offers a series of momentary identities making identification with it impossible. This multiplication negates all forms of uniqueness. The sense of not being able to read something objectively, or keep a sense of objectivity may suspend judgment, inducing paranoia in whoever feels that their difference is threatened by the crowd, which is what Walter Benjamin calls it – 'the veil through which the familiar city beckons to the *flâneur* as phantasmagoria' (*Arcades* 10). It attracts; it inspires fascination or curiosity; it pulls in the spectator to behaviour analogous to its own. It produces uninterpretable behaviour, so making a definition of crime as that which resists interpretation, being 'monstrous' (so Caleb Williams), outside what can be named, or demonstrated, or pulled into a discourse of 'truth'. The 'man of the crowd' wants the crowd, as if it was the scene of the crime, and as being uninterpretable, as comprising mysteries which will not '*suffer themselves*' to be revealed. Poe distinguishes between two character types within the crowd: those with a business-like demeanour, pushing on mechanically; and those who, impeded by the crowd, and disturbed, 'appeared overwhelmed with confusion', which implies their loss of subjectivity. Georg Simmel, theorizing the city in 'The Metropolis and Mental Life' ('Die Grosstädte und das Geistesleben' 1903) notes the blasé attitude which the city induces, and the reserve it creates in people, who are marked by 'a slight aversion, a mutual strangeness' in confronting strangers:

> Our psychic activity still responds to almost every impression of somebody else with a somewhat distinct feeling. The unconscious, fluid and changing character of this impression seems to result in a state of indifference. Actually this indifference would be just as unnatural as the diffusion of indiscriminate mutual suggestion would be unbearable. From both these typical dangers of the metropolis, indifference and indiscriminate suggestibility, antipathy protects us. A latent antipathy and the preparatory stage of practical antagonism effect the distances and aversions without which this mode of life could not at all be led.[25]

Antipathy, tendentially paranoia, protects against these other states which Simmel fears as city-products: (a) indifference, (b) subjection to indiscriminate

---

[25] Kurt H. Wolff (ed.), *The Sociology of Georg Simmel* (New York: The Free Press, 1950), 416.

suggestion, the suggestibility being related to the crowd because this is an infinite series, whose repetitions pluralize the self. 'Suggestion' has a precise sense in the age of hypnotism, and implies not only the self being taken over, but the power of imitation, which the sociologist and criminologist Gabriel Tarde (1843–1903) called a fundamental explanation of social phenomena, with the capacity to spread indefinitely. Tarde, interested in 'the criminality of great cities' (348), and – thinking of the numbers of unidentified bodies from drowning in the Paris Morgue (353) – the imitative character of suicide (355), thought of suggestion as coming about through association; associative ideas spread in crowds.[26] 'Suggestion' was a key for the reactionary Gustave Le Bon in *Psychologie des foules* (1895). Here, the crowd is dangerous in comprising 'criminal' elements. Following Lombroso, Le Bon considers the criminal as definable physiologically, and the crowd being full of atavistic elements, inherently or potentially primitive. So does Georges Sorel in *Réflexions sur la violence* (1908). Le Bon makes suggestibility the condition producing the crowd mind; suggestibility comes from persuasion, and the leader's prestige.[27] As related to hypnosis, and the power of 'autosuggestion' (*OED* first citation 1885), it was vital to F. W. Myers (1843–1901), founder of the Society for Psychical Research, who defined 'auto-suggestion' as 'a suggestion conveyed by the subject himself from one stratum of his personality to another without external intervention'.[28] Myers wrote: 'I define suggestion as a successful appeal to the subliminal self' (129).

If 'suggestion' reaches to the self which does not know itself, that applies equally to the crowd, if this is a body, or a mind, which does not know itself (so Le Bon). Freud's essay, 'Group Psychology and the Analysis of the Ego', notes these terms, and supplies another. He says that the state wherein 'suggestion' takes place is 'the state of "fascination" in which the hypnotized individual finds himself in the hands of the hypnotizer' (*SE* 18.75–6). Fascination – that key concept – motivates, then, directing the man of the crowd, and his follower; indicating how the self is drawn towards confessions holding and withholding their secret, and to that sense of mystery Poe thought lacking in Dickens. Saying that it will be impossible to learn anything of the old man and quoting '*es lässt*

---

[26] Gabriel Tarde, *Penal Philosophy*, trans. Rapelje Howell (London: Heineman 1912), 196. For Tarde, see Terry N. Clark (ed.), *Gabriel Tarde on Communication and Social Influence: Selected papers* (Chicago: University of Chicago Press 1969), 1–69, for Clark's Introduction. See Tarde's essay 'The Public and the Crowd', 277–94.

[27] For an introduction, see Robert A. Nye, *The Origins of Crowd Psychology: Gustave Le Bon and the Crisis of Mass Democracy in the Third Republic* (London: Sage 1975), here, 71.

[28] F. W. Myers, *Human Personality and its Survival of Bodily Death* (London: Longman Green 1903), 156.

sich nicht lesen', the opening is rejoined; we are left asking about the relation of the opening and the rest of the story to each other. Nothing has been learned; we have a mystery, no solution.

In Poe's detective short story, 'The Murders in the Rue Morgue' (1841, revised 1845), uninterpretability looms since everyone claims to have recognized the language which was heard from inside the locked room (P 160–1). Everyone thinks it was a different language, but of course it was no language at all. The detective is summoned, but his work is problematized. The story in its revised version, opens:

> The mental features discoursed of as the analytical are, in themselves, but little susceptible of analysis. We appreciate them only in their effects. We know of them, among other things, that they are always to their possessor, when inordinately possessed, a source of the liveliest enjoyment.
>
> P 141

There is a mystery in analysis, and only its effects are seen. The narrator says that it depends on, as in chess, the analyst 'throwing himself into the spirit of his opponent'; he 'identifies himself therewith' (142). The word 'possessed' makes the art of analysis demonic, and the art of identifying with the opponent devilish. Such identification is the clue to Poe's later detective *conte*, 'The Purloined Letter' (1845), where the schoolboy wins at the game of 'even and odd' (the game of asking how many marbles are in my clenched fist?) by 'an identification of his intellect with that of his opponent' (P 291). And that is a taking over of the self.[29]

'The Murders in the Rue Morgue' shows the strange non-rational nature of analysis. The 'I' describes setting up home with Dupin, furnishing an apartment in 'a style which suited the rather fantastic gloom of our common temper, a time-eaten and grotesque mansion, long deserted through superstitions into which we did not inquire, and tottering to its fall in a retired and desolate portion of the Faubourg St Germain' (P 145). (Much here short-circuits Dickens's writing, even that of *Little Dorrit*.) They live in shuttered darkness during the day, and walk the streets at night, Dupin being 'enamoured of the Night for her own sake' (P 145). Dupin observes people in a manner 'frigid and abstract', as if his observations were divided from himself, so that

---

[29] The implications are worked through in J. T. Irwin's comparative study of Poe and Borges, *The Mystery to a Solution: Poe, Borges, and the Analytical Detective Story* (Baltimore: Johns Hopkins University Press 1994).

> I often dwelt meditatively upon the old philosophy of the Bi-Part Soul, and amused myself with the fancy of a double Dupin – the creative and the resolvent.
>
> P 146

These two parts work separately, independently, as the criminal and detective form a pair. Poe (156) alludes to Vidocq (1775–1857), the criminal turned police informant, who rose to become head of the Sûreté. Vidocq's *Memoires* (1828) make law and crime indeed 'bi-part'. Dupin understands the train of thought that has been going through his companion's mind, and marks out the staging-posts of his semi-conscious thinking. After watching him for a period, he intervenes and gives the sequence of thought in reverse. The 'I' narrating says that 'there are few persons who have not ... amused themselves in retracing the steps by which particular conclusions of their own minds have been attained' (P 147). And that follows the mode of *Caleb Williams*. When Dupin, however, unfolds how he deduced what the 'I' was thinking, his actions – his changes of expression, the words he occasionally mutters – are said to happen each time *after* Dupin has thought about him, hence confirming Dupin's yet silent thoughts (his inductive thinking). It would have made no difference if Poe had written things the other way round. Deduction, working backwards, and induction, working forwards, seem equivalents.[30] Interpretation *precedes* the action it claims to illuminate. In *Eureka* (1848), Poe's 'prose poem':

> In human constructions a particular cause has a particular effect; a particular intention brings to pass a particular object; but this is all; we see no reciprocity. The effect does not re-act upon the cause; the intention does not take relations with the object. In Divine constructions the object is either design or object as we choose to regard it – and we may take at any time a cause for an effect, or the converse – so that we can never absolutely decide which is which.[31]

Effects become causes, as in Godwin. Causes, as opposed to effects, are matters which judicial procedures with criminals are unwilling to consider. If courts looked at them, they might have to consider the complicity of the state, and even the courts themselves, in producing the criminal effect. Godwin prompts Poe in showing that the two endings of his narrative, either of which are acceptable in the light of the causes he has created, cannot be intuited from what has gone before. Events are excessive to explanation. Dupin's logic, creative and resolvent,

---

[30] See Loisa Nygaard, 'Winning the Game: Inductive Reasoning in Poe's "Murders in the Rue Morgue"', *Studies in Romanticism* 33 (1994), 223–54.
[31] Poe, *The Scientific Fiction of Edgar Allan Poe*, ed. Harold Beaver (London: Penguin 1976), 292.

cannot adhere to the logic of cause and effect, whatever he says. As causes must be invented to identify the result which is to be discussed, interpretation becomes more difficult since putting myself into the mind of my opponent means putting myself into his mind as it was then. That ignores a time lag (a *différance*, in Derrida's terms): the opponent has moved on, putting my thinking about him/her in arrears. Representations of events, attempts to say what has happened, or what my opponent is like, are problematic in omitting this *différance*. If Godwin began by describing the hunting down of Caleb Williams by Falkland's agents, that reflects the ambiguity about who is the detective and who the criminal – who is the creator (active, demonic) and who is resolvent (reactive). Williams says his questionings about Falkland were 'a fatal impulse that seemed destined to hurry me to my destruction' (*CW* 121). Many criminals would say the same; and motivation remains opaque.

Unsurprisingly, in 'The Purloined Letter', pretensions to cause and effect have gone. The police raiding the Minister's apartment, knowing that the letter he purloined from the Queen must be there, cannot find it. They resemble the convalescent 'I' in 'The Man of the Crowd'. Dupin intuits that they could not see it because the letter was in full view, and he re-purloins it, leaving behind a facsimile to revenge himself on the Minister who will not therefore realize that he has lost it, nor know that he has lost his advantage over the Queen (presumably as a blackmailer possessing an incriminating letter). In this respect, the Minister resembles Mr Tulkinghorn, calling his knowledge of Lady Dedlock's secret 'my secret' (*Bleak House* 48.745). Like Dupin, the Minister is a poet – which the policeman thinks makes him 'only one remove from a fool' (P 285). Ignorance of poetry, which requires knowing how to arrange letters, and following another order than that of cause and effect, explains why the police cannot solve the mystery. Further, depending on the meaning given to the *Macbeth*-like line said by the Police, that the Minister (called D-) 'dares all things, those unbecoming as well as those becoming a man' (P 283); the apparent sexual inversion is a familiar marker of the criminal's transgressiveness, and associating with his poetry, makes him an aesthete.

Dupin's last speeches in the narrative make two reversals implicit. The Minister will have a precipitate 'downfall' (P 299), while Dupin has become now the plotter, lacking sympathy or pity for the one who descends. 'He is that *monstrum horrendum*, an unprincipled man of genius.' This references the Cyclops Polyphemus, (*Aeneid* 3.658), as one-eyed as the police. Dupin shows fascination with the monstrous, and distances himself from it, in a manner like the police, yet in practising this 'revenge', because the Minister had done him 'an evil turn' in Vienna, he becomes heterogeneous himself, revealing a certain spite underlying detective work. The demonic identification with the other already mentioned is fratricidal as indicated in the concluding words left for the Minister to read: 'un dessein si funeste / s'il n'est digne d'Atrée, est digne de Thyeste' (P 265). Translating 'funeste' as 'cruel', the design (the plot, the revenge), if it is not worthy of Atreus, the avenger, is worthy for Thyestes, who seduced Atreus' wife Aërope, for which Atreus killed Plisthenes, the fruit of that union, and served him to Thyestes at a banquet. Fraternal hatred is displaced onto the killing of sons; in Crebillon's *Atrée et Thyeste*, the banquet is replaced by a loving cup which contains the son's blood. It makes Dupin another *monstrum horrendum*, locating blood-lust as the other side of rational detection.

In giving solutions, these Dupin stories point in the other direction from 'The Man of the Crowd' where crime exceeded knowledge. Yet Derrida indicates how these texts may be alike. Opposing a reading of 'The Purloined Letter' given by Lacan, he sees the triangular structure which Lacan sees pervading the narrative, as omitting the uncanny, and the doubling, in a belief that the tale reveals itself to analysis.[32] Derrida wants to criticize this view from a distaste from psychoanalysis as being like detective work, both activities believing they are capable of delivering a definite 'truth' about the person they examine. Finding a structure of four, not three, entails the detective and the criminal both having a bi-part mind. Two (detective/criminal) are four because both are internally split, neither knowing the self or the other. That insight was palpable, too, in Caleb Williams and Falkland.

If the essence of all crime remains unrevealed, that makes the closure of capital punishment singularly otiose. It comments on the inadequacy of considering causes as producing criminal effects. That absence of explanation relates to the 'new epoch' which fascinates Poe. Giving up on these means that we are left with the unpredictable crowd, or else with acts whose motivations go too deep to be confessed; they remain unconscious, or, unpredictable, like the *passage à l'acte*.

---

[32] Lacan's Seminar on 'The Purloined Letter' (1957) argues that the letter holds its sway over the subject who comes under its power: *Ecrits*, 6–48. Dupin's ratiocination, which enables him to read the Minister and to act, will only start another mystery, as the minister attempts revenge. Curiously, that is repeated, or mirrored, as Irwin says, in the Lacan and Derrida dispute over 'The Purloined Letter', Lacan seeing in it a structure of three people (so odd) within repeating situations, Derrida a structure of four (so even) and using that to attempt to knock out Lacan's argument. See Jacques Derrida, 'Le facteur de la verité' (first published 1975) in *The Postcard: From Socrates to Freud and Beyond*, trans. Alan Bass (Chicago: University of Chicago Press 1987), 411–96. See Irwin, 5, cp. 448–9, and Barbara Johnson, 'The Frame of Reference: Poe, Lacan, Derrida', in *The Critical Difference* (Baltimore: Johns Hopkins University Press 1980).

Dickens, Poe and secrecy

Nothing absorbs Poe, and Dickens, more than crime. Poe saw that in Dickens, who seems to have responded to Poe. *Martin Chuzzlewit* (1843–4), written after Dickens's American journey, develops *Eugene Aram*'s sense of secrecy within city life, with the detective Mr Nadgett, who is spying on Jonas Chuzzlewit to the point of being the policeman (*MC* 51.736). He 'belonged to a class; a race peculiar to the city; who are secrets as profound to one another, as they are to the rest of mankind' (27.425–6). Dickens gets back with interest a Bulwer-derived interest in cities which he passed on to Poe. Like 'The Murders in the Rue Morgue', *Martin Chuzzlewit* experiments with a locked room. Jonas Chuzzlewit is supposed to be in it, though he creeps out through another door to commit murder (chapters 46 and 47).[33] Dickens combines the locked room, the murderer outside, with Jonas's sense of being doubled, fantasizing that Tigg whom he murdered might be in the room on his return (47.682). In this fantasy questioning identity, Jonas becomes murderer and murdered man (he will soon murder himself). Every move one part of the self makes betrays the other. Dickens writes of Jonas: he 'was at once the haunting spirit and the haunted man' (47.681).

Everything about Nadgett is a secret, though it is 'as if he really didn't know the secret himself'. He seems 'bi-part' in Poe's sense, since the letters he writes 'never appeared to go to anybody, for he would put them into a secret place in his coat, and deliver them to himself, weeks afterwards'. Nadgett, a 'man of mystery' (38.554), says 'nothing has an interest to me that's not a secret' (38. 558). As Poe's madmen write manuscripts opening themselves up to the world, however much they leave their mysteries intact, Nadgett writes secret letters to himself and burns them. Nadgett may respond to Dupin, anticipating Inspector Bucket in *Bleak House* (1852–3), even perhaps in name, though Dickens might have remembered for the latter writing of those 'who live solitarily in great cities as in the bucket of a human well' (*OCS* 15.123).

Yet Dupin and Bucket contrast; one is aristocratic, the other bourgeois, and serving the aristocracy. Bucket, unlike Dupin is married and practises less ratiocination than his French counterpart. Dupin is superior to the police but Bucket *is* the police: one of the Metropolitan Police who were created in 1829,

---

[33] See my *Lost in the American City: Dickens, James, Kafka* (New York: Palgrave 2001), 49–76. See Nancy Aycock Metz, *The Companion to Martin Chuzzlewit* (London: Helm Information 2001), 361–2. She notes, for Jonas Chuzzlewit, Dickens's use of Thomas Hood's poem, 'The Dream of Eugene Aram, the Murderer' (465, 481, 484).

and who were supplemented by a plainclothes Detective Department in 1842 after criticism of police inefficiency (the Criminal Investigation Department – the C.I.D. – followed in 1878). Bucket is based on Charles Field (1805–74), an ex-Bow Street Runner, and Chief of the Detective Department in 1846.[34] He has been mentioned already in the Introduction, in connection with William Palmer's trial. In literary terms Bucket/Field has been seen as a continuation of Gines, the agent of the law with power to hunt down the individual in *Caleb Williams*.[35] And Gines, the thief turned detective, has been compared with Jonathan Wild.[36] Bucket, however, is a moralizing force. Dupin needs another narrator, while Bucket, seeking out the murderer of Tulkinghorn, has a 'bi-part soul', being the voice of the law, and even educative for Esther or Mrs Snagsby, yet subverting law in tricking Mr George, or Gridley, both in chapter 24, or in bribing Skimpole (*BH* 57.885), for which he blames Skimpole, though Skimpole justly blames him for it (61.935). Dickens supplements the bipartite character by scattering these Bucket qualities inside two narratives, the present-tense impersonal one, and another in the past-tense narrative of Esther, pursuing Poe's idea of how the time lag makes the other unknowable, through two time sequences in the narratives. Thus Bucket controls Snagsby by addressing him as though he was the other whom he but no one else could know:

> you're a man it's of no use pumping; that's what you are. When you know you have done a right thing, you put it away [secrecy again, as though Snagsby was Nadgett] and it's done with and gone, and there's an end of it.
>
> 22.365

He then goes outside the room with Jo (22.364), making their conversation unheard. It needs Esther's past-tense narrative to discover that Bucket warned Jo out of London at that moment (31.489–91, 57.872–3).

Bucket 'mounts a high tower in his mind' to speculate on Lady Dedlock's whereabouts (56.864), as if, Poe-like, trying to put himself into her mind. He

---

[34] See 'On Duty with Inspector Field', *Household Words* (*HW*) 14 June 1851 (*Journalism* 3: 356–9). See *Letters* 6.689 note, and pp. 130, 172, 380, and Slater's notes to the two essays 'A Detective Police Party', 27 July 1850, and 10 August 1850 (Slater, *Journalism* 265–82). The articles reappeared as one in *Reprinted Pieces*. They succeeded W. H. Wills's article, 'The Modern Science of Thief-Taking', *HW* 13 July 1850; see also 'Three Detective Anecdotes' (*HW* 14 September 1850) (see *Reprinted Pieces*), 'Down with the Tide' (*HW* 3 February 1853), and 'The Metropolitan Protectives' (*HW* 26 April 1851 – written with Wills).

[35] Kenneth W. Graham, *The Politics of Narrative: Ideology and Social Change in William Godwin's Caleb Williams* (New York: AMS Press 1990), 27.

[36] Erin Mackie, *Rakes, Highwayman, and Pirates: The Making of the Modern Gentleman in the Eighteenth Century* (Baltimore: Johns Hopkins University Press 2009), 187 (179–91 for her account of *Caleb Williams*).

then follows her, thinking that she is Jenny, who is the 'other' to Lady Dedlock. Only when he realizes that he is following the wrong 'other' does he get on 'the track' from 'the lost trace' and go into reverse (57.886–7), telling Esther 'they [Lady Dedlock and Jenny] changed clothes at the cottage . . . and one returned, and one went on' (59.615). He has not known the woman's mind, nor seen that she has doubled her identity. Nor did the now dead Tulkinghorn, that 'sacked depository of noble secrets' (53.805) 'get' women. All Tulkinghorn could say of them was 'these women were created to give trouble' (42.664). Hortense, his killer (and we will remember the discussion of Mrs Manning) was seen earlier walking barefoot through wet grass, angry at her dismissal by Lady Dedlock, showing 'that cool relish for a walk that might have ended in her death-bed' (so Mr Jarndyce comments: 44.688). 'Cool relish': the ambiguities in that phrase convey a desire for death. The wet grass is akin to blood (18.299–300), and Esther thinks Hortense 'brings visibly before me some woman from the streets of Paris in the reign of terror' (23.368).

The literature of the Terror, discussed in the Second Part, is that which knows that every citizen has 'a right to death'; individual life is pronounced unimportant. In the Terror, thinking is 'cold, implacable; it has the freedom of a decapitated head'.[37] Hortense, a masochist, as is apparent in her defiant walking, stands outside normal British self-interestedness, ready to serve Esther for nothing. Her hatred towards Tulkinghorn, after being used by him, makes him threaten prison and the treadmill (chapter 42). Arrested by Bucket, she remains beyond self-interest and rational norms in relation to being hanged: 'It is but the death, it is all the same' (54.837). The citizen affirms that all she has, all that anyone has, is the 'right to death', taking this away from the sovereign's right over people, as happened in the French Revolution. For the literary theorist Maurice Blanchot (1907–2003), friend of Levinas, Foucault and Derrida, the 'right to death' marks literature, taking away the 'right' of the writer who believes in his or her sovereignty over the text, undoing intention and the writer's attempts at a self-centring affirmation. In that way literature acts like death:

> it is the being which protests against revelation, it is the defiance of what does not want to take place outside [i.e. in the open]. In this way, it sympathises with darkness, with aimless passion, with lawless violence, with everything in the world that seems to perpetuate the refusal to come into the world.
> 330

---

[37] Maurice Blanchot, 'Literature and the Right to Death', 320.

On the one hand, absolute purity, which Terror reinforces; on the other, the secrecy of the man of the crowd, and the point that death is the unknowable which is inside literature. Literature – and Dickens – sides with the criminal, and with what remains in the shadows. Unlike philosophy, literature knows that its language undoes its commitments to meaning; Dickens knows that literary language is 'the life that endures death and maintains itself in it'.[38]

'Springing a Mine', the title of the chapter of Hortense's arrest, opens saying that Bucket is preparing for a 'field-day' (54.816), so bringing in Inspector Field. It indicates Dickens's ambiguity; for while he is critical of Bucket, did he, and his *Household Words* editorial policy, have to so flatter the police as they did – a point which several Dickens critics have noted? Not just flattering their philistinism – which the police shared with those applicants to become hangmen – the flattery affects the moral certainties or complacencies which *Household Words* indulged in, sometimes damagingly. And what of the voyeur's pleasure at going 'on duty with Inspector Field'? Though, to be fair, even that essay shows fascination with the poor and destitute, even if seeing them from the 'official' point of view which objectifies everything. Those complacencies are found in such essays as 'Pet Prisoners' (*HW* 27 April 1850) and 'A Walk in a Workhouse' (*HW* 25 May 1850). Some of the enthusiasm for the police reads as near-infantility, as if Field was wanted as a father figure, stabilizing, as the voice of the law, an otherwise anarchic city space; the other side of that is Dickens writing to Bulwer that Field 'is quite devoted to me' (*Letters* 6.380), and in his belief that he can command Field's services. That itself reads strangely; over-reverentially, complacently, as though Dickens wants to have the law working for him, just as if he responded to the police as to a superego. The police seem to have challenged Dickens's sense of self and of the other; he could never have invented Dupin's irony then. Perhaps they challenged in him the sense that literature's 'right to death' means that it cannot endorse a polarization of life/death, nor have unqualified sympathy with police morals: Dickens's defence of abolition showed, at some level of being, identification with the criminal.

As the option of transportation for criminals ceased in the 1850s, and Dickens, among other members of the middle class, suspected the new forms of imprisonment, *Household Words* encouraged emigration, to relieve

---

[38] Blanchot, 336, quoting Hegel, *The Phenomenology of Spirit*, trans. A. V. Miller (Oxford: Oxford University Press 1977), 19.

overpopulation, especially in towns.[39] It reveals a strange Utilitarian flatness, and leads to a last point for this First Part: that something in Dickens craved police normativity, and acted as though he and they had the key to unlocking social problems. That normativity affected even his sense of plotting, in terms of cause and effect, up to *Bleak House*. That was something which Poe spotted, in finding that Dickens never possessed the genius for mystery, i.e. for criminal unknowability and secrecy, however much genius he had for the uncanny. While the doubling of criminal and police held him as an idea, and as an insight which was burned into him, he remained 'on duty', an agent for uncovering mystery. That tension between different positions relates to Dickens as a split subject. The zeal for order hardly accounts for those other appeals in his writing, to what precedes literature as meaning and affirmation. Things are more complex for him, and unresolved.

Dickens will be returned to in Part Two via *A Tale of Two Cities*, reviewing in that work his sense that literature may claim the right to death. Another sense of mystery connects with what we will discuss of Derrida on identity ('ipseity') and which I will therefore leave hanging, but it should be remembered there: it is Esther Summerson narrating:

> I had for a moment an indefinable impression of myself as being something different from what I then was.
>
> *BH* 31.489

---

[39] Ken Lewandoski, 'A New Transportation for the Penitentiary Era: Some Households Words on Free Emigration', *Victorian Periodicals Review* 26 (1993), 8–18. Referring to the 21 million of the 1851 census, he quotes from George Sala, writing 'The Key to the Street' in *HW* 6 September 1851 on the '196,000 in barracks, prisons, workhouses, lunatic asylums, hospitals, and charitable institutions' and the '18,249 homeless, - gypsies, beggars, strollers, vagrant, tramps, outcasts, and criminals, and others unrecorded', and on crime as resulting from 'bad training and ignorance, drunkenness and other kinds of profligacy, poverty, habits of violating laws engendered by the creation of artificial offences, other kinds of unjust legislation, temptations to crime caused by uncertainty or insufficiency of punishment' (Dickens, Henry Morley and W. H. Wills, 'In and Out of Jail', *HW* 14 May 1853). The way that laws are blamed is noteworthy, as is a stress which Lewandoski notes, on crime as disease, and disease as inseparable from crime, metaphorically and literally. To many of these problems, emigration to Australia seemed a solution. On transportation, see Helen Johnston, *Crime in England 1815-1880: Experiencing the Criminal Justice System* (London: Routledge 2015), 73–87.

Part Two

Derrida – The French Revolution Onwards

4

Deconstruction and Justice

Derrida's Seminars on capital punishment are parts of his meditations on justice, as a care for the 'other'. Jacques Derrida became prominent in the 1960s, but in the 1990s, his work, which had put into circulation the main terms of 'deconstruction', such as 'supplementarity', *differance*, the trace, the *pharmakon*, 'life-death', the aporia, undecidability and 'hauntology', was marked by renewed discussion of responsibility to 'the other', where he was engaging with the philosopher Emmanuel Levinas (1906–95). In the 1940s and 1950s, Levinas was associated with Maurice Blanchot and Georges Bataille. Influences from these fan out to Pierre Klossowski's readings of Nietzsche, Gilles Deleuze and Foucault, Many of these inform everything discussed here. Derrida, student of the Hegel scholar Jean Hippolite, worked in the shadow of these, commenting on them, not always in agreement.

By the 1990s, Derrida's preoccupations were such ethical issues as hospitality, forgiveness and the meaning of being 'cosmopolitan', i.e. not refusing the stranger, but rather welcoming the stranger as other, because accepting that one is already also a stranger, and can, ultimately, claim no rights. Opening up to the other, which involves risk, depends on seeing no state as absolute, and time as not something that I can possess: time as the other.[1] A central term to be contested was 'sovereignty', i.e. belief in personal autonomy, as much as political sovereignty. Sovereignty may be defined, technically, as 'the power held by every ipseity ... to be able to be itself, to say "I can", to define itself, and to posit itself sovereignly as a self, as the same, as the self-same'.[2] This term 'ipseity', which has already been used as a contrast to what Esther Summerson feels about itself, means 'personal identity and individuality, selfhood' (*OED*).

---

[1] See Martin Hägglund, 'The Autoimmunity of Religion', in Edward Baring and Peter E. Gordon (eds.), *The Trace of God: Derrida and Religion* (New York: Fordham University Press 2015), 178–98.
[2] Laura Odello, '"The Greatest Possible Mastery, the Greatest Possible Self-Presence of Life": Derrida and the Deconstruction of Sovereignty', trans. D. J. S. Cross, *CR: The New Centennial Review* 17 (2017), 141–62, quotation 144. Latin *ipse* translates Greek *autos*: and author, authority, autonomy, autobiography may be heard here.

In *The Beast and the Sovereign*, Derrida's last seminars (2001–3), another term enters: 'biopolitics', and its cognate, 'biopower'. Derrida quotes Giorgio Agamben on this: Agamben in turn quotes Foucault's Conclusion to *The History of Sexuality* (1976): 'Right of Death and Power over Life', which launched the term. Foucault writes:

> For millennia man remained what he was for Aristotle: a living animal with the additional capacity for political existence; modern man is an animal whose politics calls his existence as a living being into question.
>
> BS 1.328[3]

Foucault contrasts the political Sovereign who, until the European nineteenth century possessed the absolute right to put to death (with widespread use of the death penalty) with the present order. This – risking irresponsible generalization on my part – emerges with the French Revolution, where 'life and its mechanisms' have come 'into the realm of explicit calculations'.[4] A new power enters, dethroning an older sovereignty, and being less that of the law, but rather of the state, which establishes norms, claiming a right to determine the conditions within which people are allowed to live, using 'continuous regulative and corrective mechanisms' (*Biopolitics* 48), demonstrating that power now controls life (*bios*), especially through the discourses of sexuality, which could be seen as a keen weapon to calculate and control interior life, and according people 'rights', i.e. medical, social, even pronouncing, and defining, and redefining, when individual life starts, as with abortion, and defining death.

Derrida's argument that no philosopher has criticized the death penalty is only formally right as regards Foucault, who is content to show that the death penalty *is* an anachronism in his argument about the 'biopower' which has displaced it. From its being out of place and out of time comes the chance that the death penalty may not survive. Yet it implicitly illustrates the power of anachronism that certain nation states, while using advanced weapons of technology (informational, military), nonetheless have also returned to the old sovereign power of capital punishment (and some have never left off). Derrida's project involves him being symptomatically critical of Foucault, continuing a strain which had motivated his disagreement over the latter's *Histoire de la Folie* in the

---

[3] Derrida criticizes Agamben's *Homo Sacer* (as also at pp. 92–6); he criticizes Agamben's reading of Foucault, but faults Foucault for neglecting to credit Heidegger – presumably for such essays as 'The Question Concerning Technology', and 'The Age of the World Picture'. But Foucault's intense reading of Heidegger is a matter of record.

[4] Foucault, 'Right of Death and Power over Life', in Timothy Campbell and Adam Sitze (eds.), *Biopolitics: A Reader* (Durham, NC: Duke University Press 2013), 47.

1960s – here, underplaying the radical stimulus within Foucault's Conclusion though all the while working with it. The politics of the ongoing dispute, while challenging both, makes Derrida slighter, however speculative – but there is so much to say here that the problem must remain flagged up only.

Derrida's concentration on justice had been anticipated in Heidegger's 1946 reading of the 'Anaximander Fragment' (1946), deriving from the Presocratic philosopher Anaximander (c. 610–546 BCE). Nietzsche had lectured on Anaximander, with other 'Presocratics', aligning their philosophy with poetry rather than with the rationality which Plato's version of Socrates thought comprised philosophy.[5] Heidegger remains the philosopher about whom Derrida wrote most; we should note, incidentally, that Derrida finds his silence on the subject of the death penalty 'strange' (*DP* 1.237). And Heidegger rightly divides critical attention because of his Nazi sympathies, which endured until 1945. What was the relation of his fascism to his project, which is to think outside humanism, since this elevates the sovereign subject, whose *Dasein* ('being there') questions such humanism, above everything else within what Heidegger terms 'being'? Heidegger's reading and translation of the fragment is controversial, using a punning etymology complexly, and unorthodoxly, and the essay is difficult. An attempt to paraphrase his take on the fragment might, however, yield the following reading: seeking after justice must accept that there is no originary error-free condition. Further, the self cannot assume self-identity, because existence is temporal, and time disallows any stable unchanging being. No one can insist on their own permanence. Demanding justice occludes that, in claiming an absolute right of and for the person wanting it, to which no one has entitlement. For Heidegger, Derrida and Blanchot, there is no self-identity, no ipseity: the self is never fully present to itself, and lacks a knowable stable essence. To argue the opposite, that there are enduring stable entities which are speakable

---

[5] See Nietzsche, *Philosophy in the Tragic Age of the Greeks*, trans. Marianne Cowan (Washington, DC: Regnerey 1962), 45–60, and Parkes's note to *Thus Spoke Zarathustra*, 306, translating the fragment as: 'according to necessity, for they pay penalty and retribution to each other for their injustice according to the assessment of time'. See John Barnes, *Early Greek Philosophy* (London: Penguin 1987), 75, and Martin Heidegger, *Early Greek Thinking: The Dawn of Western Philosophy*, trans. David Farrell Krell and Frank A. Capuzzi (New York: Harper & Row 1984), 13–58, and Derrida's critique in his book on Marx and justice, *Spectres of Marx; The State of the Debt, the Work of Mourning and the New International*, trans. Peggy Kamuf (London: Routledge 1994), 21–7. See Karin de Boer, 'Giving Due: Heidegger's Interpretation of the Anaximander Fragment', *Research in Phenomenology* 27 (1997), 150–66. Other relevant sources for Derrida: 'Totem and Taboo', Kafka's 'Before the Law', and Blanchot's 'The Madness of the' Derrida, 'Before the Law', in *Acts of Literature*, ed. Derek Attridge (London: Routledge 1991), 181–220. For Derrida and Marxism, see Michael Sprinker (ed.), *Ghostly Demarcations: A Symposium on Derrida's 'Spectres of Marx'*, (London: Verso 1999).

of in the present, and in history – such isolatable concepts as 'nature'/'human nature', 'evil', 'identity', 'time', and indeed, 'history' – is 'metaphysics'.

Derrida's readings undo the elisions and repressions in language which conceal differences in such concepts, moments of *differance* which make them not unitary. The 'metaphysics of presence' critiques the assumption that the human's essence can come into presence – the clarity of knowability – within the present moment.[6] There can be no single concept, nor single identities, which must take account of a *differance* within them, preceding known and definable differences between entities. The relationship of speaker or writer to language prevents meaning being self-evident: language dispossesses, divides author from text, making authorial 'intention', for example, a rationalization after the event (in a major division from traditional 'humanist' criticism). 'Presence' assumes a 'now', that there can be a positive relationship with the punctuality of the present. But any 'now' is a repetition of previous 'now's', disappearing as the word is spoken, and each repetition is different, constituted by *differance* (a pun implying difference and deferring). *Differance* means the delay of presence, full meaning, in any sentence (unless the last sentence of the law), focusing on gaps (aporias) and hesitations, signs of the 'other' which disallow single meaning, and make this something forced. History is not a narrative of progress within time's continuity, the past being calculable and knowable, the future a subject for calculation. Derrida's hostility towards capital punishment relates to its calculatedly treating life in terms of a knowability established by a constant sense of time and progress. Calculability versus the incalculable are essential terms for Derrida.[7]

'Force of Law'

Derrida's essay, 'Force of Law: The Mystical Foundation of Authority' (1990 – revised 1994), took issue with Benjamin's 'Critique of Violence', which we have already noted when discussing the 'great criminal'.[8] Benjamin argues that the

---

[6] For 'the metaphysics of presence' in, e.g. *Of Grammatology*, trans. Gayatri Chakravorty Spivak (London: Routledge 1976), 49, where wishing for it is for full meaning; and *Writing and Difference*, trans. Alan Bass (London: Routledge 1978), where it relates to belief in personal experience – i.e. self-presence.

[7] See Kas Saghafi, 'Calculus', in Kelly Oliver and Stephanie M. Straub (eds.), *Deconstructing the Death Penalty: Derrida's Seminars and the New Abolitionism* (New York: Fordham University Press 2018), 139–55.

[8] On 'Force of Law', see Jacques de Ville, 'Desire and Language in Derrida's *Force of Law*', *Archives for Philosophy of Law and Social Philosophy* 95 (2009), 449–73; and for Benjamin's essay, see Alison Ross, 'The Distinction between Mythic and Divine Violence: Walter Benjamin's *Critique of Violence* from the Perspective of Goethe's *Elective Affinities*', *New German Critique* 121 (2014), 93–120.

state claims the monopoly when it comes to violence. Wanting that monopoly, it forbids it in others. Benjamin and Derrida note how maintenance of order has passed from the absolute state to the police, whose unaccountability in using violence makes them simultaneously law-preservers and lawmakers. For Benjamin, the death penalty is a test case. Defenders of it believe that

> attack on capital punishment assails not legal measure, not laws, but law itself in its origin. For if violence, violence crowned by fate, is the origin of law, it may be readily supposed that where the highest violence, that over life or death, occurs in the legal system, the origins of law jut manifestly and fearsomely into existence... For in the exercise of violence over life and death, more than in any other legal act, law reaffirms itself. But in this very violence something rotten in the law is revealed.
>
> CV 242

The law's arbitrariness, as well as its majesty, shows itself in the death penalty with its power of life and death. The death penalty shows up the 'rottenness' in law, recalling *Hamlet*'s 'something is rotten in the state of Denmark' (1.4.90). Benjamin calls police power a 'nowhere-tangible, all-pervasive, ghostly presence in the life of civilised states' (*CV* 243). Derrida adds to that 'ghostliness' the idea that 'spirit is the capacity to exercise dictatorship'.[9] 'Spirit' conjures up the amorphous invisibility of police power, its 'ghostly presence'. Since 'law and laws may be unwritten, ignorance of the law is never protection against punishment' (*CV* 249). We should, then, distrust the 'spirit' of the law, which the New Testament deems superior to, replacing, the literal Ten Commandments (2 Corinthians 3.6). Invoking the 'spirit' of anything may sound liberatory (e.g. when we do things in the 'spirit' of the law, not its 'letter'), but it is actually coercive, because 'the spirit' of anything is not easily challenged, because no one can quite say what it is. Not following the general 'spirit' is liable to be thought of as blameworthy, marginalizing, potentially ostracizing.

Benjamin calls justice – as opposed to law – 'the principle of divine end-making' (*CV* 248). He contrasts the concealment inherent in the 'mythic' (i.e. ideological) character within which law enwraps itself, and with which it imposes guilt, with 'divine violence', or 'sovereign' (*waltenden*) violence. Law-making violence threatens people, being 'bloody power over mere life for its own sake'. Divine violence, which destroys laws and boundaries, is 'pure power over all life

---

[9] Derrida, 280, quoting Walter Benjamin, *The Origin of the German Trauerspiel*, trans. Howard Eiland (Cambridge, MA: Harvard University Press 2019), 89.

for the sake of the living' (*CV* 250). 'Divine violence' has 'incomparable effects' (*CV* 252), being separate from the law-bound cycle of guilt and retribution. Divine violence might happen in revolution; hence Benjamin's last page endorses the possiblity of 'revolutionary violence, the highest manifestation of unalloyed violence by man' (*CV* 252).

Derrida agrees with this thesis of violence's primacy in forming law, and peaceable conditions, so that 'every philosophy of non-violence can only choose the lesser violence within an economy of violence'.[10] His *Glas* (1974), an extraordinarily creatively inventive comparison between Hegel and Genet (philosopher and writer), noted Rousseau, Kant and Hegel accepting the death penalty as a kind of 'strict' freedom, making the subject's actions independent. He also noted Hegel arguing that 'death's infinite and thus non-constraining constriction, produces the strict: what is called spirit, freedom, the ethical and so on. The people must risk its life, must not hesitate to let itself be destroyed as an empiric people in order to become a free people' (*Glas* 99, 101). The case of Antigone, in Sophocles' play, undergoing death from the state for the individual freedom to bury her brother, occupies Hegel's thinking, which *Glas* discusses. Law installs and falls back on violence. No solutions to human problems are possible, says Benjamin, 'if violence is totally excluded in principle' (*CV* 247).

'Force of Law' is less certain than Benjamin that law proceeds from violence, arguing a performative act brings law into force, the act being neither just nor unjust. Law can only be brought in as lacking a foundation other than itself: it institutes an order which rests upon itself, upon its own existence. Whereas laws can be 'deconstructed', because they have been constructed, 'justice' cannot; rather, 'deconstruction is justice' (243), 'incalculable', unlike law (245), addressed to the singular case, though necessarily claiming universality (248). The singular case requires the reinventing of law each time (251). Justice points to what is in excess of law, as deconstruction does. Making a legal decision requires suspending the 'undecidable', and is performative, i.e. a legal decision initiates a new state of affairs, including for the one who judges. Here Derrida cites Kierkegaard saying that the moment of decision is madness (255). Hence the moment of founding that new state is terrifying, because the accompanying violence – suspending law to establish law to come – is uninterpretable, indecipherable, 'mystical', justified by the future, not by the present (269).

---

[10] Derrida, 'Violence and Metaphysics', 313 n. 21, quoted in Hent de Vries, *Religion and Violence: Philosophical Perspectives from Kant to Derrida* (Baltimore: Johns Hopkins University Press 2002), 135.

A critical decision suspending the other point of view, or argument, shows the violence inhering in deciding on *one* reading, *one* decision – as must happen in law courts. Justice must be in the interest of an 'other', elsewhere it is called 'the affirmative experience of the coming of the other as other'.[11] 'Force of Law' evokes Levinas (254), who stresses that violence is done to a face, the face of the 'other', which always makes a silent appeal for justice. No wonder those about to be executed are hooded or blindfolded.

Derrida is puzzled by Benjamin on 'divine violence', which closes the essay, and on the idea that it could be recognized *après coup*, after it had happened – that it could actually happen – and that it would be a 'sovereign' act:

> Divine violence may manifest itself in a true war exactly as it does in the crowd's divine judgment on a criminal. But all mythic law-making violence which we may call 'executive' is pernicious. Pernicious, too, is the law-reserving, 'administrative' violence that serves it. Divine violence, which is the sign and seal, but never the means of sacred dispatch, may be called 'sovereign' violence.
>
> *CV* 252

Derrida thinks Benjamin cannot maintain the difference between the two forms of violence which he would distinguish. What would a 'true war' be? With the 'great criminal', does divine judgment mean his release, or his instantaneous destruction by a crowd? How would that differ from lynching? Is Benjamin ambiguous about putting someone to death? We will return to crowd judgments, and to 'divine violence' via *A Tale of Two Cities*. Derrida thinks 'divine violence' may sanction the worst forms of violence, and finds Benjamin's essay fascinated by violence, and also that it implies something too definitive, too certain, too present, one implying an absolute judgment of God (298), like Billy Budd suddenly killing the accusing and vindictive Claggart in Melville's novella *Billy Budd*. As Captain Vere exclaims after the impulsive blow that unexpectedly kills Budd's false accuser Claggart: 'Struck dead, by an angel of God! Yet the angel must hang.'[12] Where, then, does Derrida stand on the possibility, or desirability, of revolution? Or Dickens? Asking that of Dickens means noticing how full of contradictions he necessarily is, patent and concealed, which help explain why deconstruction is essential for reading him.

---

[11] Derrida, *Negotiations: Interventions and Interviews 1971–2001*, ed. Elizabeth Rottenberg (Stanford: Stanford University Press 2002), 104.
[12] Herman Melville, *Billy Budd, Sailor, and Other Tales*, ed. Robert Milder and Stephanie J. Gannon (Oxford: Oxford University Press 1997), 333.

There is something strangely unresolved, about Derrida turning away from Benjamin's endorsement of divine violence, repeating a problem in Benjamin's essay itself. Perhaps the problem lies in thinking there can be no law without violence. An argument adopted from the writings of Friedrich Hölderlin (1770–1843) suggests that law begins as the difference between me and another, which it measures – because knowledge takes place on the basis of there being a sense of the other, and it emerges as the difference between two entities.[13] This difference sets a limit, or measure, between the self and other, and implies my finitude. 'Finitude', Derrida's and Blanchot's term, derives from Heidegger, being glanced at in discussing the 'Anaximander fragment', which affirms it. Finitude implies that death is inherent to life (and gives it purpose). As I do not know the hour of my death, so my knowledge and language are marked by an absence, cutting off knowledge even of what I am, say or write. All speaking contains an underside of meaning from which I am occluded. Finitude includes my dying (my non-absoluteness), as well as the impossibility of my dying, for, as Blanchot, who writes extensively on Hölderlin, argues, actual dying – even in suicide – is actually not in my control. That is, suicide cannot give the subject a place or status. It cannot affirm his/her will, willpower or centred identity, for I can neither die, assuredly, of my own volition, and yet nor can I not die. Death is what I cannot know, and I cannot know what I do not know – death eludes my grasp; I can only wait for it, and waiting will continue in death.

Derrida sees this law which is inherent in knowledge of the other, as the basis of my responsibility, or obligation to, the other. But when such a measure is commanded into law, it becomes questionable, because with that, desire to infringe the taboo comes in. The issue is as live in Derrida as it is in Dickens. The death penalty tries to destroy finitude by making an absolute life/death distinction; it thus misreads both. That is at the heart of Derrida's contending against it.

The Beast and the Sovereign

'Force of Law' was one of those activating the Seminars on the death penalty, and *The Beast and the Sovereign* (2001–3). Derrida argues that two types are outside the law, one, the sovereign, the other, the 'beast'. The moral overtones of 'beast',

---

[13] See Leslie Hill, '"Not in our Name": Blanchot, Politics, the Neuter', *Paragraph* 30 (2007), 141–59.

when applied to humans, demean animal life, which is never beastly. Derrida derives the 'sovereign' as a concept from the Nazi jurist Carl Schmitt (1888–1985), for whom sovereignty connotes the ruler's power, particularly the power of 'exceptionalism', i.e. his power to establish law and a political state and to make exceptions in the execution thereof. It colours a point implicit in Derrida, that arguments about the right to life are always theologically based – that is, underpinned by appealing to a centre which is regarded as having holding power (God), and by concepts – e.g. what is good, or evil – held, therefore, to be absolutes, beyond debate.

A third type outside the law is the criminal (*BS* 1.17), another instance of sovereignty, but customarily considered as bestial, i.e. as showing *bêtise* (folly, or stupidity). These three, says Derrida, have a troubling, uncanny and mutually haunting relationship with each other; hence Derrida plays with the term 'rogue'. When Cordelia thinks of her father 'fain . . . / to hovel thee with swine and rogues forlorn / In short and musty straw' (*King Lear* 4.7.39–40), the identification of rogue with the animal becomes clear. Cordelia combines things that do not go together; she draws out the singularity of the 'rogue', who does not associate with others of his kind, though Lear, the sovereign, must 'hovel' with him. The rogue does not even respect the law of the animal community, or the pack, or the horde – and so may include the designation of a country as a 'rogue state' (1.19), including the United States as only one of those which breaks international law.

The state can be figured as the animal, as in Hobbes's *Leviathan*, which, Derrida says, after an excursus on terror, is the mainspring for controlling people. It works by fear, being an 'animal-machine designed to cause fear' (1.39). A definition of sovereignty, which Derrida discusses next, is that it feels no compulsion to respond to 'the other' (1.57) That state is common to bestiality, divinity and death. Crime is not possible without a sovereign power: a point from Hobbes; that power works by fear, which is a property of the human, 'the origin of both law and crime' (1.41). For Derrida quotes from Hobbes that 'a crime may be committed through fear'.[14]

What is the human as distinct from the beast and the sovereign? After discussing the werewolf, who may be aligned with the outlaw, Derrida affirms that the human is uniquely capable of *bêtise* and bestiality (1.98). Here *The Beast and the Sovereign* discusses Lacan's essay, 'A Theoretical Introduction to the Functions of Psychoanalysis in Criminology' (1950: *Écrits* 102–22). Derrida is

---

[14] Hobbes, *Leviathan*, ed. C. B. McPherson (London: Penguin 1968), 343.

consistently critical, not always fairly, of Lacan, even when agreeing with him, accusing him of a limiting humanist logic, which is Cartesian in how it views the animal, the non-human (1.110). Nonetheless he agrees with Lacan's Hobbesian statement that 'with Law and Crime begins man' (Lacan 106). The concept of 'man' as separable from animals, and responsible, and knowable and describable in a term which occludes women, may be what emerges in the eighteenth century. The 'Black Act' (see Chapter 1) may be its concomitant in Britain or, even, following Lacan's logic, its starting point. Lacan's meaning is more abstract, however, than reference to the eighteenth century implies. He means 'man', as accountable, and able to be defined, for example, as capable of responsibility. He begins from the issues of Freud's *Totem and Taboo*, which argues that the two twin peaks of criminal behaviour, incest and parricide, found the law (Lacan 106). The law is the expression of the superego, the punishing agency within the human, the internalization of the power of the father. But the dependency of Crime upon Law means, as it does for Freud on the superego, that 'the Law can be criminal, the superego can be criminal' (1.103).

Further, this associates with the idea of crime as self-punishment:

> to the extent that, according to the formula in which the icy humour of the legislator is expressed, given that no-one is supposed to be ignorant of the law, everyone can foresee its incidence and therefore be held to be seeking out its blows. This ironic remark ought, by obliging us to define what psychoanalysis recognises as *crimes or felonies issuing from the superego*, to permit us to formulate a critique of the scope of this notion in anthropology.
>
> BS 1.103, quoting Lacan 107, my emphasis

Criminology was first the preserve of anthropologists, and retains that objectifying characteristic. Lacan notes the morbid nature of crimes which show their symbolic character, for as he quotes the anthropologist Marcel Mauss, 'the structures of society are symbolic'. It follows, therefore, that the forms that crime takes in those who are neurotic subjects of the superego within the family structure are also symbolic. Such symbolic features within crime are, of course, what literature notices, psychoanalysis explores, and politicians deny when intoning about 'senseless violence'. Neurosis expresses 'the family unit's structural anomalies' (Lacan 109). Psychoanalysis, noting the non-Utilitarian character of the crimes which mark the neurotic (Lacan must have Freud's 'Criminals from a sense of guilt' in mind) would gain access to 'the imaginary world of the criminal which can open the door to reality for him' (Lacan 110). The neurotic dwells in the 'imaginary' stage, which is outside the 'symbolic order' established within the family headed by the patriarchal superego, who, heading up the family, and as the superego, institutionalizes neurosis within it. The 'Imaginary' stage, as the mirror stage – solipsistic, narcissistic – seems to legitimize neurotic behaviour, and here crime shows itself.

The criminal's superego differs from that associated with the Kantian sense of duty ('the categorical imperative'), which is also peremptory and dominating, in having a more fantasized form. Society is built on the premise of 'responsibility – that is, 'punishment' (Lacan 112), which implies that punishment may be what the criminal seeks. Utilitarianism could never understand this. Lacan illustrates – from an array of early psychoanalytic writers – what psychoanalysis has noted in criminal behaviours, and argues for the non-existence of 'criminal instincts'. The criminal, however delinquent, cannot be considered as the 'beast'.

Derrida, of course, agrees with this, noting that for Lacan, crime offends against 'the order of eternal brotherhood' (Lacan 122), a view which, while Derrida honours it, he declares inadequate, since much violence is directed against what is not recognized as brotherhood, and which is 'unrecognizable'. An ethics, and politics, must be founded on that. Derrida is thinking of cruelty to animals, subject, of course, of Hogarth's *Four Stages of Cruelty*, and he argues that crime is not necessarily directed against man. An ethics must include, begin with, the 'unrecognizable'. Hogarth knows that, and starts with cruelty towards things not recognized as belonging to the world of man. For him, as for Blake, in 'Auguries of Innocence', as for Derrida, the line between human and animal has been drawn unwarrantably.

Year two of the Seminar uses contrasted texts, *Robinson Crusoe* and Heidegger's *The Fundamental Concepts of Metaphysics* (1929), in a deconstruction of the particularly eighteenth-century distinction between nature and culture. He meditates on a Heideggerian word, *Walten*, which for Derrida complicates a nature–culture distinction in that it implies that there is an originary violence. Or it means 'to rule violently' (*BS* 2.30). *Walten*, which shares a theme with the 'force' of the title 'Force of Law', operates in *physis* and logos (i.e. nature, and the laws of culture) together (2.46, 2.72).[15] *Walten* includes, for Derrida, what Freud calls *Trieb*, which the Standard Edition of Freud translates as 'instinct', though 'drive' would render it better. *Trieb* is a primary pushing power which is neither

---

[15] See Michael Naas, *The End of the World and Other Teachable Moments: Jacques Derrida's Final Seminar* (New York: Fordham University Press 2015), and David Farrell Krell, *Derrida and our Animal Others: Derrida's Final Seminar, The Beast and the Sovereign* (Bloomington: Indiana University Press 2013).

of nature nor culture but precedes both, as *differance* (2. 126), and makes either of them unsatisfactory rationalizations. As the power of death, *Walten* defies the ability to speak of it. As sovereignty, it precedes designating any power as 'sovereign'. It is a sovereignty, and violence within nature, indeed creating it.

Writing at the time of the American and British invasion of Iraq (19 March 2003), punitive state terrorism which was part of the 'war on terror' taking occasion from the 11 September 2001 destruction of New York's World Trade Center towers, Derrida muses on the human as 'exposed to the violence of *Walten*', and 'in a position to exercise this violence himself, to do violence' (2.287). Such ability for violence, and such claiming authority over death, produces Derrida's horror about the power of the death penalty: awarding death to someone, believing in a sovereignty which could authorize this. *Walten* names a driving power inside everything, a violence which awards death, and so witnessed in televised accounts of bombings in time of war, from Syria to Ukraine, Yemen and Ethiopia. Derrida concludes the seminar by saying that the question is 'that of knowing who can die':

> To whom is this power given or denied? Who is capable of death, and through death, of imposing failure on the super- or hyper-sovereignty of *Walten*?
>
> 2.290

State power, federal power, imperial power may impose death. Its sovereignty is seen in such destructiveness, but, remembering Blanchot, no one is capable of death, in the sense of having mastery over their own death, for that means yielding to one's own passivity. Death counters power: the *Walten* that arrogates death to someone, in war, terrorism, or as in capital punishment, forgets its own subjection to *Walten*; its pretentions to power cover over that impotence.

After this overlong, and necessarily oversimplifying introduction to Derrida, we may turn to the Seminars on the death penalty, since we have arrived at its arguments.

5

The Death Penalty Seminars

The first year of the Seminar makes the point that the death penalty is the property of the state.[1] Without it, the state could not wage war: it could neither ask/demand people to die for it, nor put to death those who are defined as enemies. That problem was something Hegel – writing *The Phenomenology of Spirit* which dwells on Antigone, in the shadow of the French Revolution, while Napoleon's armies conquered Jena in 1806 – accepts, even welcomes.[2] A final reckoning with capital punishment would necessitate confronting the state, states and nationalism. Derrida notes that, for Carl Schmitt, politics begins with the distinction between friends and enemies, and that to distinguish these is a sovereign decision (*DP* 1.87). That is where the state starts and a demand for total abolition must, therefore, question the existence of the sovereign state. In that sense, Derrida agrees that his discourse is abolitionist, adding that abolitionist discourse is contestable: while it may question what the state has the right to do, no state, as state, will rescind the right to kill on its statute-book (1.5) – unless, that is, we could lose the idea of separate nation states.

---

[1] On the first seminar, see E. S. Burt, 'The Autobiographical Subject and the Death Penalty', *Oxford Literary Review* 35 (2013), 165–87, Miriam Jerade, 'Mors certa, hora incerta: Derrida on Finitude and the Death Penalty', *The New Centennial Review* 17 (2017), 103–21, Gwynne Fulton, '"Phantasmatics": Sovereignty and the Image of Death in Derrida's First *Death Penalty* Seminar', *Mosaic* 48 (2015), 75–94, Peggy Kamuf, 'At the Heart of the Death Penalty', *Oxford Literary Review* 35 (2013), 241–51. On both, see Marguerite La Caze, *Derrida Today* 2 (2009), 186–99, Elizabeth Rottenberg, 'The "Question" of the Death Penalty', *Oxford Literary Review* 35 (2013), 189–204, Michael Nass, *Derrida from Now On* (New York: Fordham University Press 2008), 66–7, 244. More work appears regularly in *Derrida Today*. On Derrida's relationship to Foucault, and for sexual difference (discussed via Hugo), see Michael Naas, 'Violence and Hyperbole: From Cogito and the History of Madness to the Death Penalty', and Penelope Deutscher, '"This Death which is not one: Reproductive Biopolitics and the Woman as Exception in *The Death Penalty, Volume 1*', in Olivia Custer, Penelope Deutscher and Samir Haddad (eds.), *Foucault / Derrida Fifty Years Later: The Futures of Genealogy, Deconstruction, and Politics* (New York: Columbia University Press 2016), 38–60, 166–84. Nass reproduces Derrida calling Foucault's book on madness as 'totalitarian' , so highlighting – without criticism – a problematic *parti pris* in some of Derrida's work, affecting his judgments: of Foucault, of Lacan, of Marx, and Nietzsche.

[2] See Blanchot's account of this, Maurice Blanchot, *The Instance of My Death*, and Jacques Derrida, *Demeure: Fiction and Testimony*, trans. Elizabeth Rottenberg (Stanford: Stanford University Press 1998), 7.

Given that crux, Derrida aims at the 'deconstruction' of the arguments which uphold the death penalty. Why, for instance, did Robespierre defend abolition, yet recommend the execution of Louis XVI? (1.18). Permitting this kind of inconsistency results from a point of view which accepts the sovereignty of the state. Justifications of the state and the death penalty become 'theologico-political' (1.23), even if they are maintained separately from the Bible, or other religious systems, as well as from, in the West, the authority of Greek philosophy. Derrida argues not that a 'theologico-political' system – claiming power, as being a central force and an ultimate sanction – creates the death penalty. Rather, the death penalty created a theologico-political force which exists where the death penalty does.

Derrida can argue that this is because the death penalty, uniquely among punishments in its absoluteness, is currently practised as an instance of exceptionalism. This returns to Carl Schmitt's words opening his *Political Theology* (1922 – 1.83): 'Sovereign is he who decides on the exception.' This demand for sovereignty, which is godlike, suspends the law (1.86) in a form of 'decisionism'. In the sovereign state claiming rights over each body may be seen as that which Beccaria had questioned, i.e. that the state should have any rights other than those which are practically useful. Beccaria's questioning of those extra rights earned his doctrine – even in his own day – the name of 'socialism'.[3] The suspension of law accords with the arguments in Dostoevsky's *Crime and Punishment*, where Raskolnikov defends a paper which he has written and which declares, apparently, that what defines the ruler is his right to override law.[4]

Derrida uses Foucault, whose *Discipline and Punish* begins, in a chapter on 'Torture', with the torture-and-execution of a would-be regicide Damiens (1757). This, incidentally and significantly, intersects with *A Tale of Two Cities*, which refers to the Damiens case. Derrida notes how Foucault comments on the death penalty inside the *ancien régime* as being 'spectacle' (1.42) and follows the argument that punishment was moved from the public to a private space in the nineteenth century, into the prison, whose ideal form was the Panopticon. Taking punishment out of the public sphere , though, does not diminish its visibility. Derrida speaks of Foucault's theme as

> the historical transformation of the spectacle, with the organized visibility of punishment, with what I will call, even though this is not Foucault's expression,

---

[3] See Richard Bellamy's Introduction to *Beccaria: On Crimes and Punishments and Other Writings* (Cambridge: Cambridge University Press 1995), xxiv (citing the critique of Beccaria by Ferdinando Facchinei).

[4] Dostoevsky, *Crime and Punishment*, trans. Jessie Coulson, ed. George Gibian (New York: W.W. Norton & Co. 1989), 219–27.

the '*seeing-punish*' [*voir-punir*] essential to punishment, to the right to punish as right to see-punish(ed), or even as duty-to-see-punish(ed) [*devoir de voir punir*].

1.43

Derrida plays with Foucault's French title. While *surveiller* loses its force in the English translation 'discipline', surveying and surveillance emphasize (super)vision, where the supervisor is a voyeur. So Iago taunts Othello about Desdemona and Cassio being together, asking how he might be 'satisfied': 'would you, the supervisor, grossly gape on? Behold her topp'd?' (*Othello* 3.3.394–6). Displaying, making visible, as how the sovereign state expresses itself, is essential to punishment, and the second session aligns it with *cruelty* (1.48), a major topos here, for, as in *The Beast and the Sovereign* (1.104), he affirms that the animal cannot be cruel, since it cannot do evil for evil.

On fascination

Derrida reads differently from the usual way of taking Foucault's work on the Panopticon, which sees it as erasing public spectacle – even the guillotine diminishes spectacle, according to Foucault – and as 'hardly touching the body' by way of torture (1.43). Derrida's stress on visibility argues that the Panopticon does not hide prisoners from torture. Rather, putting them on the inside of the prison, it acts as a system of secrecy. France's last public execution was that of Eugene Weidmann (b. 1908), on 17 June 1939; this is discussed by Derrida in relation to Genet's *Our Lady of Flowers* (1.28). The death penalty was ended in 1981, in Mitterand's presidency, largely thanks to the work of Robert Badinter (b. 1928), whose father was murdered at Sobibor. Derrida discusses Badinter in the Second Section (15 December 1999), and his book *L'exécution* (1973), on the trials of Claude Buffet and Roger Bontems. Badinter notes the public joy and hatred – the sadism – displayed in the courtroom when Bontems, an accomplice, not the murderer, was sentenced to be guillotined alongside Buffet, the actual murderer (1.57). The process of guillotining in the years between 1939 and 1981, when the guillotine was inside prison walls, did not make capital punishment less part of a 'theatre of cruelty' (1.58). Rather, it was

> put under the sign of fascination, of *fascinatio*, of what is going to tie voyeurism, the scopic drive, the desire for drama to the charm, the enchantment that chains the spectator to the spectacle.

1.58

What, then, is fascination? A first gloss of *fascinatio* comes in relation to a *fasciola*, a wrapping or bandage. We may remember Jeremiah Flintwinch's bandages in *Little Dorrit*, which are uncannily reminiscent of him being hanged, as the Ghost of Jacob Marley has a bandage round his head, of the sort put on corpses to keep the lower jaw from dropping (*CB* 1.60). Dickens had noted the desire for drama in the spectacle of hanging, but 'fascination' not only implies tying things together, but suggests the evil eye, and so enchantment. To be fascinated was a synonym for being bewitched, hence the word implies an action done towards a person, or animal, and means that whoever is held in a state of fascination puts himself or herself in that position. It suspends a clear subject–object antithesis. *OED* notes, in a 1651 translation of Cornelius Agrippa, that 'fascination is a binding' – attaching someone to the power of the 'witch', or the 'serpent'. Fascination also implies the phallic for behind it stands the Latin *fascinum*, which bears that sense (see *Oxford Latin Dictionary*), as that meant, too, a phallic-shaped amulet worn round the neck to ward off witchcraft – for instance, in the Roman triumph. There was even a Roman deity, Fascinus, who was one of those tended in the Temple of Vesta. To be under the power of fascination is to be held by what disempowers, castrates. Capital punishment must in some sort be public, visible: what watches it has the power of the evil eye. Yet what is fascinating resists castration, as being phallic itself. Blindfolding at an execution may be a form of clemency, though the psychoanalyst Edward Glover thought it was a way for the executioners to avoid the prisoner's evil eye.[5]

Blanchot calls fascination 'passion for the image'.[6] The phrase, not self-explanatory, may imply that there can be no more powerful image than that the hanged person conjures up, as Flintwinch's look, and Mr Jaggers's trophies in his office testify. Yet the hanged person is a double image, resisting state phallic destruction and destructiveness, in being a figure beyond shame. For Blanchot, 'what fascinates us robs us of our power to give sense'; it fits neither in 'the temporal present' and 'presence in space'. It erases the present time, and destroys the spectator's distance. Hence the fascination, which comes from, and is defined as

> vision which is no longer the possibility of seeing, but the impossibility of not seeing, the impossibility which becomes visible and perseveres – always and

---

[5] Edward Glover, *The Roots of Crime* (London: Imago 1960), 354.
[6] Maurice Blanchot, *The Space of Literature*, trans. Ann Smock (Lincoln, NE: University of Nebraska Press 1982), 32.

always – in a vision that never comes to an end: a dead gaze, a gaze become the ghost of an eternal vision.

32

In that 'dead gaze', spectators find their own death, their own impotence. The image, in fascination, is not one thing. It is anamorphic, robbing us, as Blanchot says, of our power to give sense to what we see; and, as simulacral, pointing to the phantasms which engender its power.[7] Blanchot's essay, 'Two Versions of the Imaginary', dwells on the image as not representing something recognizable, rather keeping us 'outside', and making 'of this outside a presence where "I" does not recognise "itself"'.[8] The image within the spectacle of the gallows has the unique capacity to throw viewers outside themselves, to disorganize all possibilities of being in control. That is its fascination.

The spectator is held suspended through witnessing the phallic, hence the significance of Derrida's word 'voyeur', derived from Freud, whose 'Instincts and their Vicissitudes' (1915) speaks of 'scopophilia' (*SE* 14.129), marking its connection with sadism, since such voyeurism implies the reduction of the other, the one looked at. There is hardly any spectatorship of violent death without a sexual undercurrent within it; the fascination Derrida speaks of includes scopophilia. Derrida notes the relationship of an erection, and of orgasm, to decapitation (1.58). Doubtless Dickens knew this, as with the metonymy of the hanged Bill Sikes and his 'stiffening hand' (*OT* 428), in a scene replete with a crowd whose motivations exceed the quest for justice. The image of capital punishment induces a scopophilia, more intense the more it is put out of sight.

Derrida, calling fascination a 'virtual involvement with perversity or perversion' (1.59) and thinking of what it means in relation to the sight of an execution, conjoins the following: the theatre of cruelty, fascination, spectacle, and the medieval Christian mystery play, which gave the Passion of Christ, in carnival conditions, and so identifies with the torturers, however grotesque (as in Bosch's 'Christ Crowned with Thorns' (National Gallery, London)).[9] The ambiguity of this fascination, that it is essential, cannot be discarded; Artaud's 'theatre of cruelty', silently referenced, argues that the theatre must, however 'cruel', however uncomfortable, challenge traditional, bourgeois representation,. The 'involvement' becomes *more* voyeur-like when 'virtual' – that is, when it is

---

[7] Allen S. Weiss, 'An Eye for an I: On the Art of Fascination', *SubStance* 15 (1986), 87–95.
[8] Blanchot, *The Space of Literature*, 263.
[9] I argue this in my *Histories of the Devil*, 69–70.

concealed by the respectability of having issued from a judge imposing the death sentence, or of being one of those officials who must witness, or carry out, the execution. The hidden object becomes, in every sense, 'obscene'. 'Involvement' produces fascination with the human form as distorted, ruined, as with the crucified Christ in Grünewald's Isenheim Altarpiece (Unterlinden Museum, Colmar), just as the guillotine is a rudimentary human form (1.62–3). Similarly anthropomorphizing, Fagin called the gallows 'an ugly finger-post, which points out a very short and sharp turning that has stopped many a bold fellow's career on the broad highway' (*OT* 3.2.361). 'Turning' evokes 'turn off' (*OED* 1.4., 'to hang'). It appeared in Swift's poem about Tom Clinch. A 'turn-off' repels, or disgusts, bearing a negative sexual sense; but what of Dennis the hangman's expression 'work me off'?

The Seminar evokes the theatre of cruelty when discussing Nietzsche, for whom Kant's 'categorical imperative' – i.e. the maxim 'so act that the maxim of your will could always hold at the same time as a principle of a universal legislation' – smells of cruelty (*Genealogy of Morals* 1.148, 158).[10] The categorical imperative permits no contingency, being a formal rule which dictates, regardless of circumstances. It is compulsive – i.e. both compulsory, and a repetitive force, with the force of the superego – hence Freud calls it 'the direct heir of the Oedipus complex' ('The Economic Problem of Masochism, *SE* 19.167), the work of the superego playing on guilt. Nietzsche argues in a related way, since for him disciplining the human animal to remember involves something like branding – causing suffering to fix something indelibly in the memory (1.149). That coldness marks Kant,

> who attempts to raise the categorical imperative of the death penalty above the calculation of interest but in the name of another rationally and morally pure calculation, the principle of equivalence, the *jus talionis* [i.e. the law of retribution] between the crime and the punishment, between the injury and the price to be paid.
>
> 1.151

This disciplinary system is impersonal: a strange memory is served in making injury and penalty equivalents, in endorsing the idea of a 'common measure between a wrong or an injury ... and the suffering inflicted by punishment' (1.152).

---

[10] Immanuel Kant, *Critique of Practical Reason*, trans. Werner S. Pluhar (Indianapolis: Hackett 2002), 45.

This is indeed a problem. Why must crime and punishment be thought of in terms of equivalents? That idea of equivalence supports belief in universal exchangeability, based on commercial relationships that consider only loans and debts. Every injury has its equivalent, and can be 'compensated in a *calculable fashion*' (1.151, my emphasis), following the principle of the *lex talionis*. Derrida quotes Nietzsche's question, with reference to revenge, 'how can making suffer constitute a compensation?' (1.163). The question's validity becomes more apparent if we drop the assumption that a particular crime represents the clear intention of the person committing it towards the other person. It *may*, of course, but it could be a symptom of something else which has gone wrong with the person, not something specifically or uniquely directed to another. To consider what should be done about a crime is different from thinking about how a criminal should be treated. For example, is the crime representative of the person?

Nietzsche sees the categorical imperative as the voluptuous pleasure of 'faire le mal pour le plaisir de le faire'. Derrida calls that a definition of cruelty: doing harm for the pleasure of it (1.155); assuming a 'right to cruelty' (1.156). So Derrida discuss Lacan's essay, 'Kant with Sade' (1963: *Écrits* 645–68) via consideration of masochism, which the Introduction called a sadism turned back against the self. Kant accepts, it seems, that the existence of the death penalty is the foundation of morality, and what Christianity relies on, which gives obedience and morality a certain cruelty, reducing both to prudentialism. Sade opposed the death penalty, as much as Christianity. For Kant, at the end of the scale from Beccaria and Utilitarianism, punishment is not for any good of society, being necessary because the criminal has made himself guilty of a crime, and the law of punishment is a categorical imperative. Anything less infringes on the honour of man. Nor would Kant ever accept the argument of killing in self-defence (2.39–43).

Simone de Beauvoir and Hannah Arendt

At this point, reaching the sixth seminar, a pause, to consider the *lex talionis*.

Simone de Beauvoir, in an essay 'Oeil pour l'oeil' ('An Eye for an Eye'), published in *Les temps modernes* in 1946, supports, in her title and content, the *lex talionis* to explain why she did not sign a petition to reprieve Robert Brasillach, shot by firing squad on 6 February 1945, as the Second World War was ending. Camus, but not Sartre, signed. Brasillach, aged 35, was a Parisian anti-Semitic writer, fascist and film critic, and one effect of his execution was to make him a martyr.[11] As editor of *Je suis partout*, Brasillach had 'denounced people, specified victims, and urged the Vichy government to enforce the wearing of the yellow star in the Free Zone'. Simone de Beauvoir names some of those who had gone to their deaths, and explains the solidarity she felt for these victims: '[I]f I lifted a finger to help Brasillach, then it would have been their right to spit in my face.'[12] She concedes that Brasillach, sentenced for treason, did not directly kill anyone.[13] Hatred is justified towards Brasillach since he has used people as 'things'; she believes that the thirst for revenge is an essential within life, and finds a 'whiff of magic' in the phrase 'an eye for an eye'; for the phrase corresponds to a 'profound human need' (247-8). For 'vengeance is a concrete relation among individuals in the same way that struggle, love, torture, murder, or friendship are' (251).

The complement to this is de Beauvoir's belief in an absolute evil, and the sense that a person is ambiguous in being both 'a freedom and a thing ... isolated by his subjectivity and nevertheless coexisting at the heart of the world with other men' (258). Punishment, if always partially a failure, is an essential response to a person's thingness, i.e. to how that person behaves in the world. To punish, therefore, means 'to recognise man as free in evil as well as in good' (259). Yet the 'eye for an eye' argument hardly allows any value to exceed another in worth; it remains curiously trivial in relation to thinking of what Brasillach was undoubtedly guilty, and how those issues might be addressed as common to a society and not confined to one person.

Simone de Beauvoir on Brasillach and evil compares with Hannah Arendt on Adolf Eichmann (1906-1 June 1962). Eichmann, captured in Argentina in 1960, was tried by three judges in Jerusalem on 11 April 1961 for crimes against the Jewish people, crimes against humanity against Jews, war crimes, and for crimes against humanity against non-Jews.[14] Shoshana Felman finds the Eichmann trial was new in giving voice to survivors: '[T]he mute bearers of a traumatizing destiny become the speaking subjects of [a] history ... It is this revolutionary transformation of the victim that makes the victim's story happen for the first

---

[11] Alice Kaplan, *The Collaborator: The Trial and Execution of Robert Brassilach* (Chicago: University of Chicago Press 2000), 230-4; see 89-201 for the petition.

[12] Simone de Beauvoir, *Force of Circumstance*, trans. Richard Howard (London: Penguin 1968), 28-9. Cp. Deirdre Blair, *Simone de Beauvoir: An Autobiography* (London: Jonathan Cape 1990), 252; 637-8 for Brasillach and Jews.

[13] Simone de Beauvoir, 'An Eye for an Eye', trans. Kristana Arp, in *Philosophical Writings*, ed. Margaret A. Simons (Urbana: University of Illinois Press 2004), 252.

[14] Lori J. Marso, 'Simone de Beauvoir and Hannah Arendt: Judgments in Dark Times', *Political Theory* 40 (2012), 165-93.

time.'¹⁵ Here, uniquely, appears the concept of the victim with a story to tell – that is, one who has been silenced, by shame, or fear, or from the inability of people to recognize that someone has been victimized. Less positively than the spirit of that argument, Hannah Arendt covered the trial for the *New Yorker*, noting much she considered questionable in it. Yet she endorsed Eichmann's execution: something Derrida notes, and though saying he will return to it, curiously not doing so (1.252–3). We must discuss Arendt's agreement, not whether she was fully attentive to Eichmann's anti-Semitism, nor her criticisms of the Jewish Councils during the war, which produced strong reactions against her reporting.¹⁶

Arendt finds that Eichmann partook of the 'banality of evil'. The 'banal' lacks originality, which associates with Eichmann's defence that he was only following orders.¹⁷ This new type of evil, she argues, was the product of totalitarianism, a rule working by terror and the police, and accepting the view that humans were 'superfluous', and committed to eradicating spontaneity.¹⁸ Arendt had begun thinking in terms of Nazi atrocities as monstrous, telling Karl Jaspers that 'for these crimes, no punishment is severe enough ... This guilt, in contrast to all criminal guilt, oversteps and shatters any and all legal systems. That is why the Nazis at Nuremberg are so smug ... we are simply not equipped to deal on a human, political level with a guilt that is beyond crime.'¹⁹ Her Postscript distinguishes Eichmann from Shakespeare's great criminals, Iago, Macbeth or Richard III, noting his 'lack of imagination' and 'sheer thoughtlessness – not identical with stupidity – that predisposed him to become one of the greatest criminals of that period'.

This argument revised a sense of 'radical evil', Kant's phrase which Arendt accepted in her earlier book, *The Origins of Totalitarianism* (1951). There, humans become superfluous, since totalitarianism, as this emerges, shows its 'radical evil' in accepting superfluity, in the perpetrator of the system and in the victim (*Origins* 459). Superfluity meant, in Auschwitz, eliminating the very traces of the victims. The point distinguishes these perpetrators from a murderer –

---

¹⁵ Shoshana Felman, 'Theaters of Justice: Arendt in Jerusalem, the Eichmann Trial, and the Redefinition of Legal Meaning in the Wake of the Holocaust', *Critical Inquiry* 27 (2001), 201–38.

¹⁶ Hannah Arendt, *Eichmann in Jerusalem: A Report on the Banality of Evil* (1963; revised 1965; London: Penguin 1977). See Judith Butler, 'Hannah Arendt's Death Sentences', *Comparative Literature Studies* 48 (2011), 280–95, and Julia Kristeva, *Hannah Arendt*, trans. Ross Guberman (New York: Columbia University Press 2011), 143–51.

¹⁷ See Alice Kaplan, *Reproductions of Banality: Fascism Literature, and French Intellectual Life* (Minneapolis: University of Minnesota Press 1986), 47–52 on banality in French fascism.

¹⁸ Arendt, *The Origins of Totalitarianism* (New York: Harcourt Brace and Co. 1951), 437–75. On spontaneity, see Kristeva, 140–1.

¹⁹ Quoted, Valerie Hartouni, *Visualising Atrocity: Arendt, Evil, and the Optic of Thoughtlessness* (New York: New York University Press 2012), 39.

who, normally, 'destroys a life but he does not destroy the fact of existence itself' (*Origins* 462). In *Eichmann in Jerusalem*, Arendt apparently learned that 'remoteness from reality and such thoughtlessness can wreak more havoc than all the evil instincts taken together which, perhaps, are inherent in man' (288). Eichmann's inability to speak other than in clichés came from an inability *to think* – that is, to think from the standpoint of somebody else' (49).[20] Hence the phrase 'the banality of evil'. Arendt noted Eichmann's empty rhetoric at the gallows – equivalent to that of Brasillach – finding it corroborating the 'banality of evil' . For the trial made little impression on Eichmann; he remained the dull middle-ranking bureaucrat, lacking inwardness, cliché-ridden. Derrida memorably comments on the arrogance of claiming speech and the logos to be markers of the human, who is considered to have the right (as well as the *Walten*) to destroy the non-human world. He narrates a nightmare of having to defend, with the power of the logos, and in a Surrealist Nuremberg trial, Bush and Blair (and other 'world-leaders') being on trial for their Iraq-invading destructiveness (*BS* 2.260–1). Though, in qualification of Eichmann as bureaucrat, we should note the Jewish survivor Mummelstein, who had responsibility in Theresienstadt, telling Claude Lanzmann, in the film *The Last of the Unjust*, that Arendt was wrong about Eichmann, since with a gun in his hand, he was as frenzied and violent as could be, and personally killed his victims, *not* working at his desk.

There seems little doubt that Eichmann was a convinced anti-Semite on race lines: he accepted Nazi ideology, regarding Jews as a race to be eliminated.[21] Hence the trial hardly affected him, as also seemed to be the case at the Nuremberg trials, when footage of the death camps was shown to various Nazis. Neither Brasillach nor Eichmann went to their deaths with self-realization, remaining theatrical, attitudinizing, down to their last words. That implies a futility in the death sentences, to which the vengefulness of de Beauvoir and the rationalism of Arendt were irrelevant. Even on the argument that punishment must teach something, which it can hardly do with the death penalty, it seemed that nothing was learned, and that the sentence could not start Eichmann, or Brasillach, out of an habitual state of mind wherein the death penalty featured prominently already.

---

[20] See Seyla Benhabib, 'Identity, Perspective, and Narrative in Hannah Arendt's *Eichmann in Jerusalem*', *History and Memory* 8 (1996), 35–59. For the radical evil vs banal evil distinction, see Devin O. Pendas, '*Eichmann in Jerusalem*: Arendt in Frankfurt: The Eichmann Trial, The Auschwitz Trial and the Banality of Justice', *New German Critique* 100 (2007), 77–109.

[21] See Bettina Stangneth, *Eichmann Before Jerusalem: The Unexamined Life of a Mass Murderer* (New York: Random House 2014).

For Arendt, the trial proceeded on older lines which did not respond to 'the horror of Auschwitz, which is of a different nature from all the atrocities of the past' (267). It permitted a new thinking of the criminal as carrying out, imitatively, administrative massacre under the power of the totalitarian state whose logic of extermination exceeded 'merely' exterminating Jews; it normalized genocide. Writing to Mary McCarthy, Hannah Arendt concluded from Eichmann that 'extermination would not have come to an end when no Jew was left to be killed. In other words, extermination *per se* is more important than anti-Semitism or racism' (quoted, Hartoumi, 119). Crimes may, then, be against humanity, a concept created at the 1945 Nuremberg trials and reinforced by the Rome Statute in 1998, which created the International Criminal Court (ICC) in 1998, though the concept of 'crimes against humanity' dates from 1915, and to the Turkish genocide of Armenians. The ICC was to deal with crimes of genocide, crimes against humanity, war crimes, and the crime of aggression.[22]

Arendt refuses the demands for vengeance-as-justice as barbaric, quoting Yosal Rogat's *The Eichmann Trial and the Rule of Law* (1961) in that repudiation of revenge and retribution, but continues:

> And yet I think it undeniable that it was precisely on the grounds of these long-forgotten propositions that Eichmann was brought to justice to begin with and that they were in fact the supreme justification for his death penalty. Because he had been implicated and had played a central role in an enterprise whose open purpose was to eliminate for ever certain 'races' from the surface of the earth, he had to be eliminated. And if it is true that 'justice must not only be done but must be seen to be done', then the justice of what was done in Jerusalem would have emerged to be seen by all if the judges had dared to address the defendant in the following terms:

Arendt gives an imagined speech of condemnation wherein the judges note the defence that all Germans were equally guilty, hence no one was guilty, but say:

> if you don't understand our objection, we would recommend to your attention the story of Sodom and Gomorrah, two neighbouring cities in the Bible which were destroyed by fire from heaven because all the people in them had become equally guilty ...
>
> ... you have carried out, and therefore actively supported, a policy of mass murder. For politics is not like the nursery; in politics obedience and support are the same. And just as you supported and carried out a policy of not wanting to

---

[22] See Matthew Talbert and Jessica Wolfendale, *War Crimes: Causes, Excuses, and Blame* (Oxford: Oxford University Press 2019), discussing specifically the tortures at Abu Ghraib prison, Iraq, in 2004.

share the earth with the Jewish people and the people of a number of other nations – as though you and your superiors had any right to determine who should and who should not inhabit the world – we find that no-one, that is, no member of the human race, can be expected to want to share the earth with you. This is the reason, and the only reason, you must hang.

277–9

The Sodom and Gomorrah reference (Genesis 19) may echo Benjamin on 'divine violence' in 'Critique of Violence'; yet if so, it taints it. Genocide is defined as refusal of diversity, or plurality, while 'sharing the earth' brings in questions of justice and sustainability – we live in the world, we do not possess it, and must leave it better than we find it – but there is a non sequitur in saying that no one can be expected to share the earth with the now stateless Eichmann. 'You must hang' almost creates an intolerant tit for tat which makes it necessary that Eichmann must be excluded. If Arendt is right that the new conditions of totalitarianism have unleashed a new biopolitics indifferent to genocide, no single solution to that by hanging individuals measures up to it. The death penalty has no Utilitarian value, being reactive, confirming a history which makes the banality of evil personal to Eichmann. If anti-Semitism persisted in Eichmann throughout, a *ressentiment* in killing him comes from an inability – which would depress anyone – to bring this out or to deal with it. Eichmann should have stayed in captivity; a belief in 'evil', shared with de Beauvoir, makes Arendt identify with executing him.[23]

The language of 'evil' is theological, and as in Kant assumes a prior disposition to do the wrong thing, defining this in relation to practising the good. Eichmann was 'predisposed' towards evil. That is different from concluding that the effect of an action was evil, retrospectively deciding that something has happened which 'absolutely should not have occurred', which is how Peter Dews (8) wants to consider the concept of evil. Assuming the existence of a prior evil makes capital punishment easier to uphold. It contrasts with Adorno speaking of 'the evil of banality', which presumes only people's inert adapting to the world as it is (quoted, Dews, 194). Derrida hardly speaks of evil, because that would be an example of metaphysical thinking, assuming the priority of evil as an entity.[24] As

---

[23] Robin May Schott, 'Beauvoir on the Ambiguity of Evil', in Claudia Card (ed.), *The Cambridge Companion to Simone de Beauvoir* (Cambridge: Cambridge University Press 2003), 228–47.

[24] See Eddis M. Miller, *Kantian Transpositions: Derrida and the Philosophy of Religion* (Evanston, IL: Northwestern University Press 2014), 79–81, and Michael Naas, *Miracle and Machine: Jacques Derrida and the Two Sources of Religion, Science, and the Media* (New York: Fordham University Press 2012), 287–91.

for Dickens, the novelist is much more interested in forms of heterogeneity which may be murderous, yet not containable within the contraries of what goodness means.

On the guillotine: Hugo and Turgenev

The seventh session of *The Death Penalty*, on abolitionist debates in the French nineteenth century, gives space – as in the fourth and eighth sessions – to Victor Hugo (1802–85).[25] It notes the reactionary – indeed proto-fascist – Savoyard Joseph de Maistre (1753–1821), for whom the death penalty was a divine weapon from the sovereign God to the sovereign monarch, fulfilling a providential law (1.181). De Maistre believed the guillotine was necessary to defend hereditary monarchy. De Maistre's thought is theological, and inherently, therefore, anti-the French Revolution, as in his influential *Considerations on France* (1796), which fed the reactionary beliefs of the aristocratic *émigrés* from the Revolution. Living in St Petersburg from 1802 to 1817 as an ambassador, he produced the *Saint Petersburg Dialogues*, which call blood 'sacral', and theorize the executioner and the soldier as two essential praiseworthy figures.[26] The First of these *Dialogues* wonders at the executioner as a truly heterogeneous figure, as

> the horror and the bond of human association. Remove this incomprehensible agent from the world, and at that very moment order gives way to chaos, thrones topple, and society disappears. God, who is the author of sovereignty, is the author also of chastisement.
>
> 192

Further 'the sword of justice has no scabbard; it must always threaten or strike' (193). Le Maistre does not believe in miscarriages of justice; indeed, 'human justice is not entirely without a certain supernatural assistance in seeking out the guilty' (193). The Seventh Dialogue, with war as its subject, and the soldier, repeatedly declares war to be divine (254), indeed part of a divine order; divine in the mysterious glory which it has, and in its results. The dialogue is full of the strange contrast between the executioner and the soldier, both called necessary,

---

[25] Derrida quotes Hugo from the anthology: Victor Hugo (ed. Hubert Nyssen), *Écrits sur la peine de mort* (Avignon: Actes Sud 1979).
[26] Jack Lively (ed.), *The Works of Joseph de Maistre* (London: Allen & Unwin 1965).

despite the soldier being a popular figure, deservedly so for de Maistre, and the executioner an excluded figure, though an equally essential one.[27]

By contrast, Hugo had originally opposed the Revolution, changing his mind with the 1830 July Revolution – which removed the revived Bourbon monarchy (1815–30) – when he became a Republican. His opposition to the death penalty – regarding life as sacred, thus exceeding any demand the Revolution could make for execution – shows in his novella, *The Last Day of a Condemned Man* (*Le dernier jour d'un condamné*, 1829), whose Preface of 1832 Derrida quotes.[28] A first-person account by a condemned criminal, which Dickens could have read – as Dostoevsky, whose *The Idiot* it influenced, did – it hints in chapter 12 that this *condamné* may be a parricide. The absence of male figures in his life may reinforce this reading. (And parricide aligns with regicide in *A Tale of Two Cities*'s account of the *ancien régime*.) In Hugo's chapter 12, a spider tries escaping after its web has been torn down. The web is a prisonous image; the spider suggests the castration fear which compounds dread of the prison and of its engulfing power with the ultimate Oedipal dread (*The Last Day* 48). Refusal of the death penalty reappears in Hugo's short story, *Claude Gueux* (1834), an argument against prison conditions, saying that poverty produced crime ('gueux' means a beggar).[29] Hugo calls the scaffold 'the only edifice that revolutions do not demolish' (1.214). The necessity to abolish the death penalty exceeds the importance of the Revolution, which Hugo identifies with the Terror; for him, revolutions create desire for blood.

Hence Derrida's eighth session discusses the guillotine, as a complex image for the Revolution. Here, some historical context may help. Louis XVI's government convened the Estates General to meet in 1789, the first time since 1614. On 17 June 1789, the Third Estate made itself into the National Assembly. This preceded the storming of the Bastille (14 July 1789), which gives a Carlylean climax to the first volume of his *The French Revolution* (1837), called 'The Bastille'. In Carlyle, the Duke de Liancourt tells Louis XVI: 'it is not a revolt, – it is a Revolution' (1.5.7.154). Revolution means returning to a time before tyranny, as Blake would understand it, or it would be, as for Burke, an upheaval from below

---

[27] For de Maistre and Tolstoy, see Isaiah Berlin, *Russian Thinkers*, ed. Henry Hardy and Aileen Kelly (London: Penguin 1979), 22–81.

[28] On Hugo, see Victor Brombert, *Victor Hugo and the Visionary Novel* (Cambridge, MA: Harvard University Press 1984), 25–48. See *The Last Day of a Condemned Man and Other Prison Writings*, trans. Geoff Woollen (Oxford: Oxford University Press 1992): this includes *Claude Geux*.

[29] See Sandy Petrey, 'Victor Hugo and Revolutionary Violence: The Example of *Claude Gueux*', *Studies in Romanticism* 28 (1989), 623–41, and Allan H. Pasco, 'Reforming Society and Genre in Hugo's *Claude Gueux*', *MLR* 111 (2016), 85–103.

which restructures society.³⁰ In Carlyle, Revolution replaces the 'strumpetocracy' of Louis XV (*FR* 1.6.1.163) with the truly heterogeneous – when 'the Earth yawns asunder and amid Tartarean smoke, and glare of fierce brightness, [there] rises SANSCULOTTISM, many-headed, fire-breathing, and asks, What think ye of *me*?' (1.1.1.164). That emergence of such monstrosity associates with Carlyle's other subject: that 'every man holds confined within him a *mad*-man' (1.1.3.31), and this breaking out constitutes revolution.

The National Assembly deprived the king of a veto, and by its title implied the end to separate groupings as opposed to what it went on to establish: the 'General Will', deriving from Rousseau's *Social Contract*. The General Will contended with individual freedom, marked by the Declaration of the Rights of Man (27 August 1789), which Mary Wollstonecraft followed up on, with *Vindication of the Rights of Woman* (1792). Events in 10 August 1792 (discussed below) consolidated the rule of Danton, Marat and Robespierre, before Louis XVI's trial (10 December) and execution (21 January 1793).³¹ This regicide differs from killing kings in Shakespeare, where the king can be replaced, after usurpation and murder. It was intended to end the rule of kings, as with Charles I, when Cromwell apparently made the proposal to Algernon Sidney (see Chapter 6 for him), 'we will cut off his head with the crown on'.³²

In late 1789, Joseph-Ignace Guillotin (1738–1814) proposed to the Constituent Assembly a form of capital punishment progressive, individualist, egalitarian – and mechanistic because punishment must be meted out equally (1.195). 'The mechanism falls like a bolt of lightning, the head flies off, blood spurts out, the man is no more' (Guillotin, quoted 1.190).³³ Adopted as a proposition in June 1791, first used on 25 April 1792, and often given feminine names, the guillotine prompts thinking of a 'history of blood' (1.191; indeed Derrida asks: 'what is blood?' (1.192), a topic which needs a section to itself. Crime, capital punishment and the power of terror unite, and this returns us to the guillotine. Derrida quotes Daniel Arasse asking why the guillotine is such an object of fear, while

---

³⁰ Ronald Paulson, *Representations of Revolution (1789–1820)* (New Haven: Yale University Press 1983), 47–56.
³¹ On the afterlife of Louis XVI's guillotining, see Susan Dunn, *The Deaths of Louis XVI: Regicide and the French Political Imagination* (Princeton: Princeton University Press 1994).
³² Quoted, Michael Walzer, *Regicide and Revolution: Speeches at the Trial of Louis XVI*, trans. Marian Rothstein (Cambridge: Cambridge University Press 1974), 4.
³³ 'La mécanique tombe comme la foudre, la tête vole, le sang jaillit, l'homme n'est plus' – quoted Michele Vallentini, 'Violence in history and the rise of the historical novel: the case of the Marquis de Sade', in Thomas Wynn, *Representing Violence in France 1760–1820*, (Oxford: Voltaire Foundation 2013), 93–102, 94.

noting the fascination, to the extent of fetishization, which the king's blood had for the people.[34] The guillotine, Arasse (13) notes, is said to promote 'Humanity, Equality, Rationality'. The first of these is illustrated in the language of a Dominican, Labat, in 1730, describing the *Mannaia*, a prototype of the guillotine used in the colonies: 'the device is entirely reliable, and, where an unskilful executioner sometimes requires two or three strokes to detach the head from the trunk, with the *mannaia* the condemned man is not kept waiting' (Arasse 14, compare Derrida, 1.196). The Enlightenment cleric (Arasse notes how interested clerics were in the guillotine's possibilities) disavows the punishment's cruelty with the pretence of gentleness. 'Humanity' applies to the trappings of the punishment, not to the punishment itself. Politeness and manners cover a deeper injustice. Guillotin is appalled to think of hangmen who 'dishonour mankind to such an extent as coldbloodedly to soak their hands in the blood of their fellow men merely in response to orders' (Arasse 14, Derrida 1.200). The hangman and torturer (*bourreau*) becomes an executioner (*exécuteur*). Arasse cites Foucault, in recounting the move to the gentle way of punishment, and on how the casual hangman becomes a professional. The guillotine and the Panopticon seem images of each other, both being what Foucault calls the latter: 'the diagram of a mechanism of power reduced to its ideal form; its functioning, abstracted from any obstacle, resistance, or friction, must be represented as a pure architectural and optical system; it is in fact a figure of political technology that may and must be detached from any specific use' (*DandP* 205).

The guillotine intends at the level of (re)presentation to allay fear, yet its humanization of the inhuman terrifies Arasse. Professionalization of death covers over not only a deeper because a colder cruelty, it makes cruelty not part of what is implied, in putting questions of blood out of court. Modern Western societies would do without blood, desiring an invisibility which its presence denies. This extends to the death penalty as executed in the United States. Derrida notes in contrast the fighting spirit which draws attention to blood, when saying it is the colour of the victims of those who died in revolutionary fighting (1.199). There follows a history of the significance of redness in the nineteenth century (1.199, see also 1.230). Hugo calls the guillotine a 'hideous', an 'infamous' machine (1.204), playing with the point that it was moved in 1832 from its public place, the Place de Grève, in the now renamed Place de l'Hôtel de Ville. It was as if it was moving away from Paris, from civilization, and use, and making blood less

---

[34] Daniel Arasse, *The Guillotine and the Terror*, trans. Christopher Miller (London: Allen Lane 1989), 63.

visible. Hugo announces, in 1848, in the Constituent Assembly: 'I vote for the pure, simple, and definitive abolition of the death penalty' (1.97) – which happened, temporarily, in the Commune.

Hugo claims indebtedness to Beccaria, and, behind Beccaria, to Beccaria's French source – Montesquieu's *L'Esprit des lois* (1.213). But Derrida finds Hugo's abolitionist arguments insufficient, depending on accepting that 'order will not disappear with the executioner' (1.208); instead, that 'the gentle law of Christ will finally permeate the legal code and radiate out from there. Crime will be regarded as an illness' (1.208). Hugo, who had thought that the July Revolution would have ended the reign of the guillotine, believes that it is possible to have a Christian humanism which is compatible with abolition. This accepts 'a sedimented history, a European history, a history of Europe, of Christian Europe, that is getting itself ready or constructing itself by means of the Enlightenment, revolutions, declarations of the rights of man, and so forth' (1.211–12). Hugo ties abolitionism to belief in a purified Christianity; and a Europe accepting this. The Christianity justifies the abolition, or rather, abolition makes sense in the context of accepting a Christian Europe. Later, Derrida notes how belief in God and a hereafter sanctions both capital punishment, and, as in Hugo, the abolitionism (1.262): if these opposites grow together, abolition cannot be based on religious arguments.

Of course the guillotine did not end as Hugo wished. We will take the essay of the Russian novelist Turgenev (1818–83), an admirer of Dickens, whom he had met by 1862, and author of *Fathers and Sons* (1861) which confronted nihilism and terrorism.[35] He describes in June 1870, in a Russian periodical, *The European Herald*, being in Paris that January and invited by Maxime du Camp (1822–94), friend of Flaubert, and 'expert on the statistics of Paris', to witness the execution of Jean-Baptiste Troppmann.[36] Troppmann, not fully 20, had murdered an entire family in Pantin, and had been arrested trying to flee France by M. Claude, the Inspector Bucket-like *chef de la police de sûreté* who also attended the execution. Turgenev describes him novelistically, as he does the executioner, an Alsatian, M. Heidenreich. The party of eight assembles at La Roquette prison at midnight, for a 7 a.m. execution, and the setting up of the guillotine:

> its two beams, separated by about two feet, with the slanting line of the connecting blade, stood out dimly and strangely rather than terribly against the dark sky …

---

[35] Patrick Waddington, *Turgenev and England* (London: Macmillan 1980), 75–80, 137–40.
[36] Ivan Turgenev, *Turgenev's literary Reminiscences and Autobiographical Fragments*, trans. David Magarshack (London: Faber & Faber 1959), 210–31.

> I imagined that those beams ought to be more distant from each other; their proximity lent the whole machine a sort of sinister shapeliness, the shapeliness of a long, carefully stretched-out swan's neck.
>
> 217

It is, of course, Troppmann's neck which has to be separated into two; Turgenev's image strangely replicates that process, and fascination shows when the bird and the machine are described in terms of each other.

There was already a crowd gathering. The party sees Troppmann, who had apparently slept well, at 6.30 a.m., Claude telling him that the 'hour of retribution' had come, and wanting details of accomplices whose existence Troppmann had asserted, this being his defence. Troppmann, as ever, refused sturdily to name anyone else. Turgenev notes 'that when people sentenced to death have their sentences read out to them, they either lapse into complete insensibility and, as it were, die and decompose beforehand, or show off and brazen it out; or else give themselves up to despair, weep, tremble, and beg for mercy' (223). Troppmann, with his absence of emotion, fitted none of these categories, surprising M. Claude, and Turgenev, who cannot understand what sustained him. It was only a minority opinion that Troppmann 'was not in his right mind' in committing the aimless and absurd annihilation of the Kink family.

Turgenev's narrative shows his fascination with what was going on in the young man's mind. He describes in detail Troppmann's being given a new shirt, and made to wear the straitjacket, his being shaved, walking with him to the room where the assistant hangman, from Beauvais, hobbles his legs while another man cuts his hair and the collar, so revealing the neck and shoulder-blades. Troppmann's reaction on finally seeing the guillotine changes. On the scaffold he 'threw his head sideways, convulsively, so that it did not fit into the semi-circular hole. The executioners were forced to drag it there by the hair, and while they were doing it, Troppmann bit the finger of one of them – the chief one' (229).

The last words and actions Turgenev notes for himself are Troppmann at the top of the steps saying 'Dites à Monsieur Claude' and 'two men pouncing on him ... like spiders on a fly. I saw him falling forward suddenly, and his heels kicking' (228). Justice never hears the last words. While the image recalls Hamlet's desire to 'trip' Claudius 'that his heels may kick at heaven' (3.3.93), Turgenev sees no more because he turns away, yet he records horrified reactions, and the sound of the blade descending and stopping which he says was 'as though a huge animal had retched' (229). An animal would recoil. The machine has no such scruples.

Turgenev notes the men who, crawling under the guillotine, 'began wetting their handkerchiefs in the blood that had dripped through the chinks of the planks' (230). These details compromise the neatness and modernity of Dr Guillotin's method, and make mockery of its speedy efficiency (twenty seconds from beginning to mount the ten steps and the body being flung into the basket which was then driven away to the cemetery by a horse and cart in attendance). The speed is actually inseparable from an atavistic violence asserting itself in the crisis moment. At the last it is a triumph of brute force.

In discussion with Maxime Du Camp, Turgenev ponders the execution and thinks of Troppmann's 'contempt for death' – for so he reads it – and wonders if the law-giver can desire that, as well as pondering the spectacle of so many people wanting to see Troppmann killed. He nonetheless pulls back, saying that he knows that 'the question of capital punishment is one of the most urgent questions that humanity has to solve at this moment' (231). As he had wanted the liberation of the serfs, and as he partly identified with nihilists in *Fathers and Sons*, Turgenev is in favour of abolition, and hopes at the least that his essay will lead to the ending of public executions. This inconsistency, or compromise, accompanying the point that he himself could not bear to watch, incensed Dostoesvky, who had been lined up for execution himself. He was one of five who had been made to stand, hooded, awaiting death by firing squad, until the imperial pardon arrived minutes before execution in Semenovsky Square (St Petersburg) on 22 December 1849. This was imperial 'power on display', the reprieve a theatrical trick performed to control the men, one of whom, Nikolay Grigoyev, was so traumatized that he spent the rest of his life insane.[37] Dostoevsky's *Demons* (1871-2) satirizes Turgenev as Karmazinov, a vain 'great writer' who watches a steamer sinking off the English coast, and writes only about himself in relation to this disaster.[38] Dostoevsky must have felt that Turgenev was inadequate in his self-concentration, and inability to identify with Troppmann's death, turning away, rather. In contrast, Georges Bataille was to sign himself as Troppmann, identifying with the heterogeneity of the great criminal, as opposed to the bourgeois morality which condemned him.[39] That morality was not to be identified with, being righteous, but only more subtly violent.

---

[37] Joseph Frank, *Dostoevsky: The Years of Ordeal 1850-1859* (Princeton: Princeton University Press 1990), 51-64.
[38] Fyodor Dostoevsky, *Demons*, trans. Richard Pevear and Larissa Volokhonsky (London: Vintage 1994), 85.
[39] Georges Bataille, *The Story of the Eye*, trans. Joachim Neugroschel (London: Penguin 1982), 70.

'The instant of my death'

Derrida's ninth session returns to Guillotin's selling point for his apparatus: its instantaneity (1.221). Yet it cannot give 'the instant of my death', because I cannot speak about that, as I have no power over my death. *L'Instant de ma mort* is the name of a *récit* by Blanchot which Derrida's *Demeure* discussed: a brief account of someone from a château (a 'demeure' – a residence – Kafka's *Der Schloss* is implicitly recalled) who was lined up against a wall to be shot in 1944, but reprieved at the last moment. It was almost certainly Blanchot himself, though there must be an uncertainty here since the text has a fictional mode. The *récit* concludes:

> Qu'importe. Seul demeure le sentiment de légèreté qui est la mort même ou, pour le dire plus précisément, l'instant de ma mort désormais toujours en instance.
>
> What does it matter. All that remains is the feeling of lightness that is death itself, or, to put it more precisely, the instant of my death henceforth always in abeyance.
> *The Instant of My Death* 10–11

If death is always *en instance*, it is hanging fire, suspended, inside life. The question of what 'remains' after the work of deconstruction haunts Derrida, as does 'what remains' after nihilism has done its work in the absolute act of shooting someone. Derrida's *Demeure* puns on *je meurs* (I die), *demeure* (residence, staying) and *demourance* (which combines dying and staying, so questioning the contrastive relationship between death and remaining, which the word 'arrest' also poses).[40] The *instance*, implying a trial (as with 'the Court of Final Instance'), keeps the person always under trial, as in Kafka's *Der Prozess* (*The Trial*). There is the sense of something *insisting* ('insisting' and 'instance' relate etymologically) within the subject with the force of an unspecifiable and de-centring agency.[41] Death is inside the subject, and the 'instant' is part of a trial, where, as in Kafka, the proceedings gradually merge into the judgment, since

---

[40] See Peter Banki's review-essay, 'Translate – Blanchot', *Oxford Literary Review* 22 (2000), 176–84, and Christopher Langlois, 'Temporal Exile in the Time of Fiction: Reading Derrida Reading Blanchot's *The Instant of My Death*', *Mosac* 48 (2015), 17–32. See Hent de Vries, '"Lapsus Absolu": Notes on Maurice Blanchot's *The Instant of My Death*', *Yale French Studies* 93 (1998), 30–59, and Thomas Davis, 'Neutral War: *l'Instance de ma mort*', in Kevin Hart (ed.), *Clandestine Encounters: Philosophy in the Narratives of Maurice Blanchot* (Notre Dame: Notre Dame University Press 2010), 304–26.

[41] Compare Lacan's title, 'The Instance of the Letter in the Unconscious' (*Écrits* 412 and note 807), which Alan Sheridan's older translation rendered 'The Agency of the Letter'.

guilt is always to be presumed.[42] As with the proceedings in *Bleak House* (chapter 65) – the resolution of Jarndyce v. Jarndyce is Richard Carstone's death sentence.[43] For 'the law kills. Death is always the horizon of the law. If you do this, you will die'.[44] Yet what remains for the one who faced the firing squad is a strange lightness, because Life is now 'dying', in a loss of ego (which gives a new sense of injustice suffered by the other), and acceptance of passivity, not being 'under the threat of which you believe you are called upon to live; you await it henceforth in the future, constructing a future to make it possible at last – possible as something that will take place and will belong to the realm of experience':

> To write is no longer to situate death in the future – the death which is always already past; to write is to accept that one has to die without making oneself present to it. To write is to know that death has taken place even though it has not been experienced. and to recognise it in the forgetfulness that it leaves – in the traces which, effacing themselves, call upon one to *exclude oneself from the cosmic order* and to abide where the disaster makes the real impossible and desire undesirable.[45]

Commenting on Blanchot, Philippe Lacoue-Labarthe argues that literature starts with autobiography, as the record of death, 'autothanatography'.[46] The 'I' of autobiography is an other from the one who writes, and Blanchot's text moves freely from 'I' to 'he'. Writing, in the quotation from *The Writing of the Disaster*, knows that its sphere is the unknown, starting from the death sentence, from language whose origins and meanings are unknown to the speaker and writer, where differences between life/death are suspended. There is an absolute difference from the sovereign imposition of the death penalty which makes an absolute life/death distinction, where encompassing the death of the other instances what Derrida calls *calculation* (1.238), the word being a leitmotif for the rest of the first volume of Seminars, reappearing in the second volume's sixth session. Calculation is an aspect of sovereignty, desiring to master the instant of death, 'and this mastery can only be that of a subject presumed capable of giving death' (1.239). Derrida, like Kafka, like Blanchot, resists the thought of the

---

[42] Kafka, *The Trial*, trans. Breon Mitchell (New York: Schocken Books 1998), 213.
[43] See Mark Spilka, *Dickens and Kafka: A Mutual Interpretation* (Bloomington: Indiana University Press 1963).
[44] Maurice Blanchot, *The Step Not Beyond*, trans. Lycett Nelson (Albany: SUNY Press 1992), 25.
[45] Maurice Blanchot, *The Writing of the Disaster*, trans. Ann Smock (Lincoln, NE: University of Nebraska Press 1986), 65–6; quoted, *The Instant of my Death* and *Demeure*, 51.
[46] Philippe Lacoue-Labarthe, *Ending and Unending Agony: On Maurice Blanchot*, trans. Hannes Opelz (New York: Fordham University Press 2015), 52.

moment of death being knowable, pronounceable within a death sentence. Writing starting from death sees life elliptically, with breaks of non-knowing in narrative, which therefore makes narrative no longer relatable to a known reality. Its gaps are one way wherein the practices of literature illustrate nihilism in the rationalist logic of the death penalty.

The affinities with madness which criminality may have indicate how life and death may be inseparable. A word for that is 'vertigo', which appears in the tenth section, to contrast with the law's sovereignty. Derrida quotes Camus's 'Reflections on the Guillotine' on a murderer's contrary aims. There are here unconscious, unintended echoes of Dickens's letters:

> Man wants to live but it is useless to hope that this desire will dictate all his actions. He also desires to be nothing, he wants the irreparable and death for its own sake. So it happens that the criminal wants not only the crime, but the suffering that goes with it, even and especially if this suffering is beyond measure. When this strange desire grows and takes command, the prospect of being put to death not only fails to stop the criminal, but probably further increases the vertigo in which he loses himself. In a certain way, then, he kills in order to die.

Further, 'the murderer, most of the time, feels innocent when he kills. Every criminal acquits himself before the verdict' (quoted, 1.248).[47]

There seems to be a dual action of wanting to take my life, and keeping it, says Derrida. He thinks of what instantiates itself in the subject as an 'instinct' (an aural pun, and more than that), for which Camus draws in Freud on the death drive ('death instinct', in Camus). This permits questioning the distinction between wanting to murder and wanting one's own death (1.249): this might make murder an act of despair, far from calculation itself, 'killing someone in oneself'. Crime may be calculable, premeditated, but death is not, neither its moment nor its time. It is a criticism of those who believe in the death penalty that they should be so reductive about life that they think someone can be 'turned off' at an instant. A desire to calculate, exhibited in the machine, takes over, though the death penalty itself is an immeasurable, excessive act, destroying neat calculation (1.248) – as with the killing of Troppmann. Derrida interpolates a comment, calling it madness, 'to put an end to finitude' (1.257), when noting:

> the seduction that [the death penalty] can exercise over fascinated subjects, on the side of the condemning power but also sometimes on the side of the

---

[47] Derrida quotes Albert Camus, *Resistance, Rebellion and Death: Essays*, trans. Justin O'Brien (New York: Vintage 1995), 192.

condemned. Fascinated by the power and by the calculation, fascinated by the end of finitude ... by the end of this anxiety before the future that the calculating machine procures. The calculating decision, by putting an end to life, seems ... to put an end to finitude; it affirms its power over time; it masters the future; it protects against the irruption of the other ... [T]his calculation, this mastery, this decidability, remain phantasms.

1.257–8

This comes near to Dickens's letters. 'Fascination' implies the condemning power has control over life and death, that being the dream of phallic power, i.e. of absolute presence and power over someone, which law lives by. For the one being executed, this fascination may activate murder itself. Dickens, Camus and Derrida are in agreement here.

Shakespeare and blood

What, then, to pose Derrida's question, is blood? Writing on capital punishment in Germany in the nineteenth century, the historian Richard J. Evans shows how people watching – especially epileptics – craved to drink cups of blood from people who had been executed. Blood appears as the *pharmakon*, the marker of a condemned life, which is yet life-giving. Evans quotes from a case in 1824 of a rural labourer, Johann Georg Sörgel, murdering in order to drink blood: 'I've killed him so that I can get a poor man's blood to drink; the man has horns on.'[48] Presumably, the murdered man was fantasized as diabolical, or sexually potent – or his horns might have implied he was a cuckold. Evans argues that Protestant blood-drinking at executions corresponded to the Catholic Eucharist, whose power Protestantism disavowed. As the 'sinner' had been shriven, his blood would be in a state of grace. Evans quotes contemporary views which held that the epileptic had temporarily gone out of life, so that the blood of another would replace his death state. Evans, his book useful while anti-Foucault, is incurious about differences of attitude towards blood in various historical moments.

One point comes from the Jewish Bible: 'the life of the flesh is in the blood, and I have given it to you upon the altar to make an atonement for your souls: for it is the blood that maketh an atonement for the soul' (Leviticus 17.11). Sacrifice assumes that 'the gods do nothing without remuneration, and that they

---

[48] Richard J. Evans, *Rituals of Dissolution: Capital Punishment in Germany 1600–1987* (Oxford: Oxford University Press 1996), 92 (see 90–8).

sell their goods to the humans'.[49] Perhaps the gods need to be kept going by sacrifice, this being a necessary concomitant to deal with the guilt felt in hunting; however, sacrifice involves blood, essentially, for blood possesses something of the quality of a divine gift which expresses the value of the sacrifice. It atones for guilt, for 'without shedding of blood is no remission' (Hebrews 9.22). Since the blood must be on the altar, it requires expert handling, what theorists of sacrifice call 'blood manipulation', empowering the priest.[50] But nothing is more susceptible to mythicizing, sacralizing, than thinking that life must be laid down for the nation. The rhetoric of 'sacrifice', reinforced by bloodshed, worked equally well for French Catholicism, the French Revolution, which borrowed Catholicism's language, and for the cynicism of the Dreyfus case. Nor is France exceptional here.[51]

Gil Anidjar approaches Derrida's question by associating blood with the history of Christianity, which maintained differences of blood between Christians and non-Christians. The papacy of Gregory VII (1073–85) and Urban II (1088–98) made shedding the blood of another not forbidden, as before; it was permissible when fighting Saracens in the Crusades.[52] Medieval Christianity makes the blood of others expendable, even purifying; this thinking continues with Spain's insistence on purity of blood, so proclaimed in Toledo in 1449, licensing a racial discourse, by privileging the difference between Christian and Jewish or Islamic, and, a little later, native American blood (Andijar, 65). This discourse of blood purity only intensified through the nineteenth century.

Privileging Christian blood intensifies Benjamin's musing, in 'Critique of Violence': 'It might be well worthwhile to track down the origin of the dogma of the sacredness of life' (for which reason Christianity disallows suicide). Hence

---

[49] Quoted from Walter Burkert, *Homo Necans: The Anthropology of Ancient Greek Sacrificial Ritual and Myth* (Berkeley: University of California Press 1983) in Fritz Graf, 'A Satirist's Sacrifices: Lucian's *On Sacrifices* and the Contestation of Religious Traditions', in Jennifer Wright Knust and Zsuzsanna Varhelyi (eds.), *Ancient Mediterranean Sacrifice* (Oxford: Oxford University Press 2011), 204 (and see Introduction (3–31)). See also William Gilders, *Blood Ritual in the Hebrew Bible: Meaning and Power* (Baltimore: Johns Hopkins University Press 2004). I omit discussion of menstrual blood, blood proclaiming virginity lost, and blood rituals in hunting (*OED*: 'blood' – verb 4). Relevant texts here include Leviticus 12, *Othello*, *Chronicle of a Death Foretold*, Lynda E. Boose, 'Othello's Handkerchief: "The Recognizance and Pledge of Love"', *English Literary Renaissance* 5 (1975), 360–74, and Edward Berry, *Shakespeare and the Hunt* (Cambridge: Cambridge University Press 2001), 39–48). These relate to blood in murder and execution, but go wider.

[50] See Mira Balberg, *Blood for Thought: The Reinvention of Sacrifice in Early Rabbinic Literature* (Berkeley: University of California Press 2017), 65–107.

[51] See Ivan Strenski, *Contesting Sacrifice: Religion, Nationalism, and Social Thought in France* (Chicago: University of Chicago Press 2002).

[52] Gil Anidjar, *Blood: A Critique of Christianity* (New York: Columbia University Press 2014), 132–5, citing Tomaž Mastnak, *Crusading Peace: Christendom, the Muslim World, and Western Political Order* (Berkeley: University of California Press 2002).

the language of Genesis 9.6: 'whoso shedeth man's blood, by man shall his blood be shed', a text which insists on capital punishment, and on life and blood as equal, sacred. Benjamin reflects:

> this idea of man's sacredness gives grounds for reflection that what is here pronounced sacred was, according to ancient mythic thought, the marked bearer of guilt: life itself.
>
> CV 1. 251

Life while sacred, is guilty. That catch subjects everyone, implicitly, to a suspended death sentence. Life's sacredness is marked by blood, despite the race connotations. However, as seen earlier, Benjamin believes that non-democratic, mythic power asserts bloody power over mere life. State power undoes the sacredness of life, while apparently supporting it. 'Critique of Violence' contemplates mythic and divine violence. If the former is bloody, the latter is lethal without spilling blood, working without bloodshed:

> for blood is the symbol of mere life ... Mythic violence is bloody power over mere life for its own sake; divine violence is pure power over all life for the sake of the living. The first demands sacrifice; the latter accepts it.
>
> CV 249–50

The distinction between drawing, and not drawing, blood is neither an absolute nor even a discernible reality; yet calling blood the symbol of mere life indicates that shedding it may be a pointless display of power, a will to empty life out for no purpose save for display; a will to cruelty.[53] The cruelty of 'bloodsports', a term *OED* first cites from 1893, should be weighed. Blood shows sovereignty over mere life, but the symbolics of blood make life sacred, too.

Blood is life in visual form, as when Chaucer, apparently fascinated by murder throughout, describes visual images seen in the Temple of Mars – 'myghty Mars the rede':

> The sleere of hymself yet saugh I ther
> His herte-blood hath bathed al his heer'.
>
> *The Knight's Tale* 2005–6

Perhaps this suicide has cut his throat, hence the blood on his hair. The half-rhyme of heart and hair affirms how blood sticks everywhere. We can compare

---

[53] See Gil Anidjar, 'Blutgewalt', *Oxford Literary Review* 31 (2009), 153–74 for discussion of possible meanings of the relation of blood to mythical violence. See also his 'The Meaning of Life', *Critical Inquiry* 37 (2011), 697–723.

'life blood', for which *OED* cites Spenser, or the idea of blood being on someone's head (*OED* cites Joshua 2.19). *Macbeth* asks Derrida's question, 'what is blood?', in a play essential to Dickens. If 'murder will out', part of its definition is that murder is done in secrecy, a point *OED* tends to confirm. Homicide, contrastedly, however felonious, may be open, part of blood revenge, or a blood feud. Secret murder marks *Hamlet* (1600–1), and *Macbeth* (1606), where murder begins in the secrecy of a soliloquy when the witches have made Macbeth 'rapt', and the first thing to be murdered is rational thought:

> My thought, whose murder yet is but fantastical
> Shakes so my single state of man that function
> Is smothered in surmise,
> And nothing is but what is not.
>
> 1.3.138–41

In this syntax, murder entangles thought, creating a black hole, implying nihilism, while the thought which would allow murder is still only Macbeth's unreal fantasy. The thought *shakes*, a word reawakening an earlier phrase in the speech: 'this supernatural soliciting'.[54] The witches' words produce physical disturbances to heart and hair. Having cut to pieces 'the merciless Macdonwald' (1.1.9–23), Macbeth feels himself a body shaken to pieces by mental terrorizing.[55] Another soliciting appears with the fascination produced when looking at the dagger he 'sees', which then acquires 'gouts of blood' (2.1.46), attracting him, blood tempting him, or perhaps pointing towards suicide. The hallucinatory state continues when he hears, after the offstage murder, 'Macbeth doth murder sleep'. He has killed Duncan sleeping, and has murdered thought and its sustainer, sleep, the power of the unconscious, which gives space for dreams.

The play identifies with Macbeth, the wartime killer; it is as if, like Nietzsche's 'pale criminal', he has all along wanted blood. He says after the Ghost of Banquo appears:

> Blood hath been shed ere now, i' the olden time,
> Ere humane statute purged the gentle weal,
> Aye, and since too, murders have been performed
> Too terrible for the ear. The time has been

---

[54] 'The French *solliciter*, as the English *solicit*, 'derives from an Old Latin expression meaning to shake the whole, to make something tremble in its entirety' – Alan Bass, note to Derrida, *Margins of Philosophy* (Brighton: Harvester Press 1982), 16, and see Derrida, 21.

[55] Andrew J. Mitchell, 'Heidegger and Terrorism', *Research in Phenomenology* 35 (2005), 181–218, p. 198, an essay both interesting and reactionary.

That when the brains were out, the man would die,
And there an end, but now they rise again
With twenty mortal murders on their crowns
And push us from our stools ...

3.4.74–81

Humane statute makes the 'weal' civilized by purging it, sacralizing life, repairing an earlier violence in the 'olden time'. Now murder must surface: 'It will have blood they say, blood will have blood' (half-referencing Genesis 9.6. – 'whoso sheddeth man's blood, by man shall his blood be shed'). 'Augurs' – omens, even speaking birds – have 'brought forth / The secretest man of blood': detecting the most hidden murderer. *OED* traces 'man of blood' to the Vulgate's *vir sanguinus* (1 Samuel 16.7 – the King James line, 'come out thou bloody man, thou man of Belial', has as a marginal reading 'man of blood'). *Macbeth* opens with 'what bloody man is that?' (1.2.1), as if being covered with blood was an equivocal state, making woundedness and a disposition to murder primary states, reappearing in the ambiguous image of the bloody child seen in the witches' cauldron (4.1.75). Similarly, Bill Sikes, on the run from murdering Nancy, may have a bloodstain on his hat, but he does not wait to find out (*OT* 3.10.400–1). In the context of helping put out a fire, even while running away, Sikes 'bore a charmed life' (3.10.404), aligning him with Macbeth. As later with Bradley Headstone (*Our Mutual Friend*), Dickens keeps no distance from Sikes's torment: 'Let no man talk of murderers escaping justice, and hint that Providence must sleep. There were twenty score of violent deaths in one long minute of that agony of fear' (3.10.402). His death by hanging, tracked by his familiar, his dog and by the phantasm of Nancy's eyes, show the criminal the finitude of the charmed life, as Macbeth learns that, too, when he says it (5.8.12). The charmed and the sacred conflict, and sacred life makes detecting murder and murderer inevitable, here, through Banquo's Ghost appearing, as the unspecifiable 'it' which, not necessarily through 'humane statute', 'will have blood'.

Macbeth makes punishment and crime mutual, exchangeable. Macbeth fixes the head of the rebel, Macdonwald, on the battlements in a battle scene which is compared to Golgotha (1.2.23, 30). Cawdor, the traitor, goes to execution in self-fashioning mode:

very frankly he confessed his treasons,
Implored your highness' pardon, and set forth
A deep repentance. Nothing in his life
Became him like the leaving it. He died

> As one that had been studied in his death
> To throw away the dearest thing he owed
> As a mere trifle.
>
> 1.4.5–11

Similarly, Sir Walter Raleigh in 1618 made a half-hour speech before being beheaded. Does Cawdor's speech indicate subservience to the state, or is it equivocation, as Raleigh's speech was 'studied' and theatrical?[56] At the end, Macbeth's head is brought in. *Macbeth*'s reminders of execution include the witches using 'grease that's sweaten / From the murderer's gibbet' – the dead body and the liquids exuding from it having a sacral or destructive value. And Macbeth identifies, unconsciously, with the executioner when emerging from Duncan's chamber with his 'hangman's hands', as if having just dealt out to Duncan the fate of treasonous Cawdor.

That 'fate' was defined by Edward III's Treason Act of 1352, against those who would compass the king's death:

> [to be] laid on a hurdle and so drawn to the place of execution, and there to be hanged, cut down alive, your members to be cut off and cast in the fire, your bowels burnt before you, your head smitten off, and your body quartered and divided at the King's will, and God have mercy on your soul.[57]

What has been quoted here was the last sentence of the law against Edward Stafford, Duke of Buckingham (1478–1521), convicted of high treason in Henry VIII's reign, though having prospered under Henry VII, during whose time the practice of last speeches from the scaffold seems to have begun. Execution erased name, title and body. The Tudor state seems to have increased its terrorizing power. Sir Thomas Wyatt finishes his Senecan translation, 'Stond whoso list', on the dangers of court life, for the one 'much known of other' people in court, with an image resonant of what public execution means, death – like the executioner – gripping the hair:

---

[56] For Raleigh's 'self-fashioning' at his execution, as Stephen Greenblatt discusses it, see Andrew Fleck, '"At the Time of his Death": Manuscript Instability and Walter Raleigh's Performance on the Scaffold', *Journal of British Studies* 48 (2009), 4–28, and Stephen Greenblatt, *Sir Walter Ralegh: The Renaissance Man and his Roles* (New Haven: Yale University Press 1973), 1–20. See J. A. Sharpe, '"Last Dying Speeches": Religion, Ideology, and Public Execution in Seventeenth-Century England', *Past and Present* 107 (1985), 144–67.

[57] Quoted, Lacey Baldwin Smith, 'English Treason Trials and Confessions in the Sixteenth Century', *Journal of the History of Ideas* 15 (1954), 471–88 (p. 484).

For hym death greep' the right hard by the croppe,
That is miche knowen of other; and of him self alas,
Doth dye unknowen, dazed with dreadfull face.[58]

Macbeth was probably written after the execution of the conspirators in the Gunpowder Plot (5 November 1605), including Father Henry Garnet (3 May 1606), whose head ended on a pole on London Bridge.[59] Garnet's only substantial crime seems to have been knowing of the plotting of two of the conspirators, Robert Catesby (1572–1605) and Francis Tresham (1567–1605), through Oswald Tesimond (1563–1636) who revealed it in confession (the secrets of the confessional would not allow this to be revealed).[60] The Porter in *Macbeth*, mock-admitting the equivocator into hell, follows the popular view of Garnet's damnation; he has already admitted a suicide: a farmer who 'hanged himself on the expectation of plenty' (2.3.1–21).

Malcolm calls Macbeth a 'butcher' (5.11.35) but not just because he 'carved out his passage' (1.2.20) en route to disembowelling Macdonwald, when his 'brandished steel' 'smoked with bloody execution' (1.2.18). Butcher and hangman, he and Lady Macbeth create the scene of the crime which he describes:

> Here lay Duncan
> His silver skin laced with his golden blood,
> And his gash'd stabs look'd like a breach in nature
> For ruin's wasteful entrance; there the murderers,
> Steeped in the colours of their trade, their daggers
> Unmannerly breech'd with gore.
>
> 2.3.108–13

'Gashed stabs' comprises a pleonasm; murder – as a professional 'trade' – is emblemized as being completely red. The daggers are unsheathed – hence naked ('unmannerly'), which produces the image of nakedness covered not by breeches but by 'gore', meaning filth, dung and dried blood. The absence of trousers, reflecting on the grooms who are in drunken sleep, is a 'breach' which recalls the gashes as 'breaches' – wide entrances – letting the body be ruined both on the outside, and the inside. How was Duncan's body laid waste? What *did* Macbeth

---

[58] *Collected Poems of Sir Thomas Wyatt*, ed. Kenneth Muir (London: Routledge & Kegan Paul 1949), 164.
[59] Philip Caraman, *Henry Garnet 1555–1606 and the Gunpowder Plot* (London: Longman 1964), 430–40.
[60] See Caraman, 378–82. On equivocation, see Frank L. Huntley, '*Macbeth* and the Background of Jesuitical Equivocation', *PMLA* 79 (1964), 390–44, with reply by A. E. Malloch, *PMLA* 81 (1966), 145–6. Garnet was apparently author of a manuscript, *A Treatise of Equivocation*, based on a Spanish original.

perform upon the unguarded Duncan? Disembowelling? Pyrrhus was seen by Hecuba 'mincing with his sword her husband's limbs' (*Hamlet* 2.2.510). The phrase 'ruin's wasteful entrance' personifies Macbeth as 'ruin' and indicates what blood means: it shows the inside outside, ruin having gone in and ruined what is within. In letting blood spread so indiscriminately, Macbeth has defiled the notion of sacrifice with its blood manipulation, in a will to sacrilege.

Murdering and executing seem equivalents. That Shakespeare might have qualified as an abolitionist is supported by the dialogue defining a traitor as one that swears and lies:

Son And must they all be hanged that swear and lie?

Wife Every one.

Son Who must hang them?

Wife Why, the honest men.

Son Then the liars and swearers are fools, for there are liars and swearers enow to beat the honest men and hang up them.

4.2.51–8

So much for equivocating: everyone does it, though it catches you out, as with Father Garnet, and others who find their words can be turned against them, words being *already* ambiguous *before* anyone tries equivocation. Punishment, however real, only works with commanding authority in the realm of illusion; honest men can hardly prove their difference from liars and swearers. Yet such logic avails little; soon after the boy is dead, having called the murderer a liar when he called his father a traitor. Murder in *Macbeth* seems to come with a supernatural sanction offering 'success', which is the cause of terror to the murderer. In *Coriolanus*, a play following hard on *Macbeth*, blood's attractiveness has no demonic prompting. Coriolanus is a machinic 'thing of blood' (2.2.109), which seems more obviously modern. The unresolved question is how that machinic quality associates with what seems to be its opposite: the sight of blood, where the attraction of that seems to create the desire to open up the blood of the other.

The Death Penalty 2: Confession

We can now approach the second year of Derrida's Seminars.

Derrida begins by saying, that no legislative measure, to date, has prohibited the *desire* to kill – whether in murder, the death penalty or the desire to be killed

(2.6–7). The question of desire opens the way for discussion of the unconscious. The Seminar asks what punishment means, and whether the death penalty can be considered punishment. Derrida cites Benveniste, who finds a single etymological root for the meanings *honour* and *punish*. Does punishment – taking vengeance – pay honour to the prisoner? (2.27–8). Killing a prisoner means, inherently, that he or she cannot pay the penalty, cannot make recompense. The opposite is the case: Derrida envisages a condemned man saying,

> You are exonerating me by making me bear a burden whose weight is infinite, hyperonerous, *incommensurate with my capacities* ... You are cancelling out the punishment; you are imposing on me a harm that no longer even deserves the name of punishment ... that becomes heterogeneous to the very concept of punishment, indeed of expiation, heterogeneous or transcendent to punishment, thus to the right to punish.
>
> 2.33, my emphasis

The essence of punishment must be that the person can take it; if not, it becomes persecution, or, ironically, a way of conferring dignity, or honour, on the prisoner. Punishment must be finite, for an infinite penalty has no value as punishment; it becomes revenge (2.34), which ends up honouring the person undergoing it, so making the link which Benveniste had noticed. The prisoner killed is beyond punishment, and has attained the status of someone who must be honoured for undergoing what is beyond their capacity. At that point Derrida invokes Benjamin's 'Critique of Violence', and finds in his comments on the 'great criminal' an indication that society *does* honour the criminal, for such a one has taken on a challenge to wrest from justice its guarded monopoly on violence, and has claimed sovereignty (2.45, 48), a strange sovereignty which necessarily awards to the criminal the right to death. Derrida's second session finishes by noting a strange connection between honour and dignity, and payment, penalty and punishment, which he thinks Benveniste has noticed, but has lacked the necessary intellectual aggressiveness to develop, beyond finding the connection between words a matter of chance. The connection gives the criminal the suggestion of greatness.

The third session reverts to Freud, and to how death is unrepresentable to the self, and yet Derrida adds from Freud that fear of death, as a debt to be paid, has to do with a sense of guilt (*SE* 14.297 – see 2.77). This is death as debt, death taken as retribution (2.75). This *lex talionis* theme persists into the fourth section, on Kant and the *Critique of Practical Reason*, but it begins with punishment, where 'what needs to be repaired is honour' (2.97). Here 'justice rises above the interest of life' as with the example of the 'honourable' criminal. This one, says Kant, has internalized the need for punishment – and thereby chooses death – whereas the scoundrel-criminal would choose forced labour in the mines (2.101). That this justice which Kant seeks is actually the *lex talionis* appears towards the end of this, and in Derrida's following session.

Its implications are highlighted by the psychoanalyst Theodor Reik (1888–1969), in *The Compulsion to Confess* (1924), the title of which silently acknowledges that guilt impels crime and increases guilt afterwards. It implies that the compulsion is not separate from desire. Reik takes the un-Kantian view that, as Derrida says, 'the death penalty is disavowed murder'. Reik begins, traditionally enough, that 'crime was originally the violation of a taboo', and continues:

> As Freud remarks, punishment not infrequently offers, to those who execute it and represent the community, the opportunity to commit, on their part, the same crime or evil deed under the justification of exacting penance.
>
> quoted, 2.107

This is, of course, an unconscious desire, but it raises the question, what is happening if the unconscious has such a desire, which makes it produce the calculation of the *lex talionis*? We have seen how much Derrida's animadversion is the attempt to make a calculation out of life. Reik uses *Totem and Taboo*, where the brothers kill the father to possess the women he claims, and afterwards erect the totem which represents his authority and which creates the taboos which characterize law (Freud, *SE* 13.1–162). Infringement of the tabooed object brings punishment; further crimes repeat the act of killing the father, who is thus not dead, and never is, nor was, but whose return, in plural forms, disorganizes the sense of time as succession, or a narrative of progress. The dead father reactivates further crimes, while having the force of the totemic. Crime brings about the need for forgiveness, but remorse further activates crime (Derrida cites Freud's 'Criminals from a sense of guilt'). Derrida adds Reik's point that this remorse includes those who support and apply the death penalty (2.122). Guilt, producing crime, and punishment – these are equivalences arising from an unconscious desire for calculability and for the *lex talionis*. This last is not easy to execute with sexual crimes such as rape, where it is impossible. Even so, talionic law involves 'sexual exchange and substitution', since the eye of an 'eye for an eye' and the tooth in a 'tooth for a tooth' (Exodus 21.24) are 'phallic substitutes' (2.168–9). Hence 'the essence of crime' is sexual, or rather it is made so since its punishment may be so interpreted, so retrospectively investing the crime with sexuality.

Nietzsche's pale criminal's conflictual desires, showing themselves in lust for blood, illustrate how sexuality pervades crime.

This sexuality may, however, be unconscious. Derrida adds to a quotation from Reik that 'the unconscious knows no caution' (2.129) another: 'to the unconscious, gratefulness is as foreign as is forgiveness' (2.170). The unconscious remembers, and revenges:

> Forgiveness comes to disavow in consciousness the talion ... which continues to operate in the unconscious ... [T]alionic law never stops governing the unconscious. Forgiveness would be an illusion, a simulacrum, at most a reaction formation of consciousness that would merely confirm the violence of the unconscious talion. Not only, says Reik, does this 'reaction formation' character not exclude the original drives (those that dictate revenge and the talion), but it confirms, on the contrary, their effectiveness and their indestructible permanence.
> 2.173

Hence 'Christian teaching teaches meekness as a reaction to a particularly strong fury and thirst for revenge' (Reik).

We are in a strange world where what is said, or maintained, is what cannot be acknowledged. As Derrida later explains, for Reik, 'forgiveness' is a 'reaction formation, as the reaction to a ... thirst for vengeance' (2.204). In a 'reaction formation', the superego reacts against a desire it deems impermissible and attempts to install its opposite, an example being law itself; but this reaction formation perpetuates a division of the subject (see Freud *SE* 19.34).[61] In Reik, the unconscious insists, in a compulsion to repeat, which is without regulation. Derrida engages here with the unanswered question of how psychoanalysis could engage with those outpourings from the unconscious, which demand revenge. As Christina Howells indicates, the *lex talionis* was included within Jewish law to limit the extent to which retribution and revenge could go.[62]

Following this argument, an abolitionist position would have to declare itself as another reaction formation, working against an impulse to revenge, but which is incapable about doing anything about the unconscious roots of revenge. Following *The Genealogy of Morals*, turning the other cheek (Matthew 5.39) may be a subtle revenge – calculated, not spontaneous – though it is worsened when tabloid and social media virtually encourage victims to insist on their day in court, and, with the connivance of populist politicians, to ratchet up the prison

---

[61] See Anthony Sampson, 'Freud on the State, Violence, and War', *Diacritics* 35 (2005), 78–91.
[62] Christina Howell, 'The Death Penalty and its Exceptions', in Kelly Oliver and Stephanie M. Straub (eds.), *Deconstructing the Death Penalty: Derrida's Seminars and the New Abolitionism* (New York: Fordham University Press 2018), 89.

sentence, encouraging *ressentiment*. Reik argues that in a primitive trial by ordeal (*Urteil*), it was not God who pronounced whether a person was innocent or guilty, but the dead. Since such ordeals took an oral form, requiring the prisoner to consume something, whatever was eaten ('introjected') bore some unconscious relation to the crime, indicating that crimes have, in essence, a cannibalistic base. 'For primitive man, killing and eating was the same thing' (Reik, quoted 2.177). Of course the ambivalence involved in devouring, consuming the other (love and identification plus hatred) is inherent to a consideration of murder. Chapter VI, below, follows up on this insight.

Reik connects this material with the 'unconscious self-punishment of neurotics'. Self-tormenting repeats the ingestion of the victim through a self-imposed ordeal and adheres to the principle of the *lex talionis* as a Kantian categorical imperative. As Reik adds, 'he who kills, kills himself' (2.178). The *lex talionis* enacts a principle already operant in the unconscious. Reik's statement makes it unnecessary to fix a chronology here – hence we have the following possibilities:

> I kill because I want to die;
>
> or
>
> I kill, therefore I doom myself;
>
> or
>
> I kill and I want that death to kill me.

Similarly, 'Criminals from a sense of guilt' disturbs customary chronology, in placing guilt before crime, crime exposing how the person already feels guilt, the crime being a symptom of it (see 2.240). That guilt, as Derrida adds, is Oedipal – and that returns us to the sexual motivation within crime (2.181). Reik's point is that any system of justice must recognize the primacy of guilt, and, if it thought that way, it would break with the *lex talionis* which only perpetuates it. Justice should work at removing guilt, not proceeding with an abstract sense of pure justice needing to be performed as the *lex talionis*, as the principle of reason, i.e. the principle of calculating, which is cruel. The argument continues in the eighth session, where Kant (in *The Metaphysics of Morals* – 1797) is put alongside the unnamed Robespierre, who becomes a subject for Reik.[63]

---

[63] For Kant on the French Revolution, see Ferenc Fehér, 'Practical Reason in the Revolution: Kant's Dialogue with the French Revolution', *Social Research* 56 (1989), 161–85. For Kant on punishment, see 2.36–44, 86–102, and 164–9 where he compares him with Hegel on the death penalty, 183–5, and then the eighth session. For a starting essay on Derrida and Kant, see Marguerite La Caze, 'At the Intersection: Kant, Derrida, and the Relation between Ethics and Politics', *Political Theory* 35 (2007), 781–805, and Hent de Vries, *Religion and Violence: Philosophical Perspectives from Kant to Derrida* (Baltimore: Johns Hopkins University Press 2002).

Robespierre

Robespierre, a Beccaria-like abolitionist, spoke on 2 December 1793 for Louis XVI's execution, insisting that the Revolution was dealing with a system; therefore the judges of Louis are only representing the nation in condemning him. The Jacobins had not wanted to put Louis on trial – itself a problematic act, for how can a king be tried by laws intended for subjects? For example, Charles I had never accepted the legality of his trial. A trial could suggest that Louis might not be guilty – that, in fact, he had never been, effectively, king! As Saint-Just had said, 'no man can reign innocently' (quoted, Walzer, 64). Tyranny, that clue word in Godwin's *Political Justice* and *Caleb Williams*, voids the social contract, and Robespierre said it must be met by returning to the state of nature:

> peoples do not judge in the same way as courts of law; they do not hand down sentences; they throw thunderbolts. They do not condemn kings; they drop them back into the void, and this justice is worth just as much as that of the courts.[64]

And there may be injustice in trying a king under laws which postdate the laws he ruled under, for a revolution, definitionally, alters the laws (see Walzer, 76–7). Yet the Jacobin will to suspend a trial for Louis incites an absolutism instigating the reign of terror. Robespierre identified the Revolution with returning to nature, hence he speaks of 'thunderbolts', but these turn out to mean the guillotine whose machinic force facilitates violence, just as Hannah Arendt notes how implements, machines, are essential for violence.[65]

Robespierre regarded Terror as an argument for the death penalty, as impersonally necessary, but his thunderbolt image implies a religious, even orgiastic, fervour which has been seen as characteristic of revolutionary fervour, and regressive from Enlightenment values, though implicit within what these repress.[66] Hegel notes its resultant 'fury of destruction' (359):

> wholly *unmediated* pure negation, a negation, moreover, of the individual as being *existing* in the universal. The sole work and deed and universal freedom is

---

[64] Stout, 42; see Jean Ducange (ed.), *Robespierre: Virtue and Terror*, speeches of Maximilien Robespierre introduced by Slavoj Žižek, trans. John Howe (London: Verso 2017), 59.
[65] Hannah Arendt, *On Violence* (New York: Harcourt and Brace 1969), 3–4.
[66] See Derrida, *The Gift of Death*, trans. David Wills (Chicago: University of Chicago Press 1992), 21–2, discussing the theologian Jan Patočka; for this, see Rodolphe Gasché, 'European Memories: Jan Patočka and Jacques Derrida on Responsibility', *Critical Inquiry* 33 (207), 291–311.

therefore *death*, a death too which has no inner significance or filling, for what is negated is the empty point of the absolutely free self. It is thus the coldest and meanest of all deaths, with no more significance than cutting off a head of cabbage or swallowing a mouthful of water.[67]

For the fated individual, held to be separate from the general will:

> *being suspected* ... takes the place, or has the significance and effect of, *being guilty*; and the external reaction against this reaction that lies in the simple inwardness of intention, consists in the cold, matter-of-fact annihilation of this existent self, from which nothing can be taken away but its mere being.
>
> 360

The negativity of the abstract will is expressed in 'the *terror* of death' (361). Following Hegel, terror must be exerted against the individual, whose existence as such shows, ironically, that the system of virtue and danger lacks something, in excluding that individual. Denying the subject an outside place constitutes totalitarianism and terror, both saying they have no place for that which is other to them. Robespierre proclaimed on 5 February 1794:

> If the mainspring of popular government in peacetime is virtue, the mainspring of popular government in revolution is virtue and terror both: virtue without which terror is disastrous: terror without which virtue is powerless. Terror is nothing but prompt, severe, inflexible justice: it is therefore an emanation of virtue; it is not so much a specific principle as a consequence of the general principle of democracy applied to the homeland's most pressing needs.
>
> quoted, Ducange, 115

Robespierre's monologism makes him the executioner, combining virtue and terror as alike fearful terms. The lack of awareness of the unconscious in saying 'anyone who trembles at this moment is guilty, for innocence never fears public scrutiny'[68] indicates what is problematic in his statement:

> to punish the oppressors of humanity is clemency: to pardon them is barbarity. The rigour of tyrants has only rigour for a principle; the rigour of the republican government comes from charity.
>
> Ducange, 117; Žižek, 159

---

[67] G. F. W. Hegel, *The Phenomenology of Spirit*, trans. A. V. Miller (Oxford: Oxford University Press 1977), 360.

[68] Speech of 11 Germinal, quoted, Claude Lefort, *Democracy and Political Theory*, trans. David Macey (Cambridge: Polity Press 1988), 64. For Robespierre's life, see Ruth Scurr, *Fatal Purity: Robespierre and the French Revolution* (London: Chatto & Windus 2006).

There is no room for affect here – though interestingly Ruth Scurr's biography of him brings out how warmly Robespierre was supported by women, by his sister, and by those with whom he lodged.

Kant judges Robespierre for the execution of Louis XVI, considering it an unabsolvable crime, in destroying the very basis of law-giving (2.192), being the equivalent to the state committing suicide, in an act of 'auto-immunisation', as Derrida puts it (2.191) – auto-immunisation being a process, analogous to the death drive, wherein the body attacks its own immunity system, destroying itself.[69] But quoting and annotating Kant (omitting these annotations here), the act of condemning the king originates from

> fear of the state's vengeance upon the people if it revives at some future time, and that these formalities are undertaken only to give the deed the appearance of punishment, and so of a *rightful procedure*. But this disguising of the deed miscarries; such a presumption on the people's part is still worse than murder, since it involves a principle that would have to make it impossible to generate again a state that has been overthrown.
>
> 2.193

It seems that fear of the revenant, the phantom king returning (Derrida compares *Hamlet*) is such that it creates the need to justify a willed killing by pronouncing it as punishment. A death sentence, then, is passed, from fear of the future. The spirit of punishment is paranoia, that the phantom may haunt, the spectre return. As in *Spectres of Marx*, the spectral is pervasive for Derrida. A murderer 'would like to identify death with nothingness'.[70] The impossibility of that shows in Derrida's writing about haunting. He opposes 'hauntology' to ontology, as the study of being, which assumes that something is 'there', in full presence. The ghost, in 'hauntology', is the unrecognized, the shadowy outside, what 'remains'. Hauntology shows that injustice remains. Fear of it engenders punishing, as a reaction formation, wanting to put the spectral out of consideration. As the Ghost in *Hamlet* has the power to look back at people, so the fear for those who murder or who would punish by the death penalty is that they may not be able to evade a returning look. The death penalty shows

---

[69] See 'Faith and Knowledge' (1996) in Gil Anidjar (ed.), *Jacques Derrida: Acts of Religion* (London: Routledge 2002), 80.
[70] Derrida, *Adieu to Emanuel Levinas*, trans. Pascale-Anne Brault and Michael Naas (Stanford: Stanford University Press 1999), 6.

a desire to evade the return of the repressed, by firm punishment. Killing is illogical, since that means the return of the look. What is feared, as so often in psychoanalysis, is what is desired. Derrida's interest in the revenant, as the repressed, which has accumulated power since it has lost its literal referent in death, is strangely anticipated by Kant. The death penalty aims to exorcise the spectre – whose effects are already felt, for if they were not, there would be no need of exorcism.

Derrida compares Kant with Robespierre, who started by opposing the 'cruel laws' – which Kant, in supporting the death penalty, supported. In the Revolution, 'the regicidal Robespierre' is 'faced with Kant as a reactionary, and a pitiless judge of the simulacrum of revolutionary justice' (2. 204). There seems to be a contest for which one is more cruel, and though we have seen Derrida linking cruelty with blood, he says it is difficult to know what cruelty is – for example, drawing on Reik, 'when we think we are less cruel when we abstain from cruelty, we risk being even more cruel' (2.204). Cruelty may not be something outside the law, but be its very principle, as it became for Robespierre. A law links ideal purity and cruelty, a point deducible from the law-giving Angelo in Shakespeare's *Measure for Measure*, who would have Claudio beheaded for getting a woman with child. For 'the idea is cruel' (2.205), cruelty meaning the elevation of moral feelings, and moral demands, and as the pursuit of the ideal, 'which is, by its nature, excessive ... there is no measure or moderation for cruelty' (2.205). That shows in Kant's inflexible morality, no less than Robespierre's. Such faith in virtue, which may be a reaction formation, debases the person to 'the rank of a ferocious beast whose thirst for blood cannot be quenched. Becoming cruel is the rigidifying or super-erecting effect of the puritanical or purifying excess of the moral law, a law that essentially reduces man to the stupidity of the beast' (2.206–7). All forms of fundamentalism, Christian, Jewish, Islamic, are in question. This sentence was first drafted in a week where Texas effectively banned abortion, complementing the hostility to women shown by Afghanistan's Taliban. The pun in 'supererecting' charges this fundamentalism as characteristically men against women, like much anti-abortionism.

Using Reik, this eighth session proposes confession, and not forgiveness, and not punishment, but flexibility (as something 'incalculable'), rather than the rigidity of correction, which is 'the imperious imperative of the superego' (2.206). That pursuit of the ideal makes Derrida ask if cruelty is what is proper to man. Not murder but the death penalty is relevant here, as an exercise in cruelty: which poses another question: is the death penalty what is proper to man?

(2.219). The last sections go from cruelty to blood, asking what would happen to the death penalty if blood no longer counted for anything symbolically – if sacrifice ceased to matter, for instance – and, reverting to Freud, considering decapitation as a substitute for castration (2.228), more primary than the death penalty as a punishment. If so, that means that there is no escaping from the sphere of substitution: blood standing for life, or thinking that killing can be retributive. Derrida's last section cites the *Ensayo sobre el Catolicismo et Liberalismo y el Socialismo Considerados en sus Principios Fundamentales* (1851) by the Spanish jurist Juan Donoso Cortés (1809–53) – an influence on Schmidt, and at the forefront in arguments about blood purity. Cortés says that 'he alone can inflict punishment for the one who may impose it for the other' (2.253), which means that punishment is carried out by a substitute, on behalf of the other (i.e. God) – on the assumption that this is not the end, that there is a last judgment beyond. An atheist state, then, cannot carry out law because of the finality of the death penalty: Catholicism, however, as an irrefutable theology permits the sovereignty of capital punishment, putting everything inside the dual spheres of imputation and substitution – guilt being imputed, the Atonement allowing substitution, substitution working itself out in 'bloody sacrifice'.

Derrida illustrates this via Abel and Cain (Genesis 4.1–16), quoting Cortés's lucid question: why 'the effusion of blood is here regarded either as a means of purification [Abel's sacrifice of a lamb] or as a crime. Why do all shed blood in one manner or the other?' (2.257). So the theologian asks. Blood is never shed in vain, whether in love (Christ's sacrifice) or in revenge (including capital punishment). On either side, blood must be shed. This sense of a law of substitution licensing the death penalty as bloody sacrifice, which implies a devaluation of lives since everything is substitutional, brings Derrida to his last questions. Does the loss of visibility of blood in culture (lethal injections replacing the guillotine) herald the end of capital punishment? It makes the cruelty less visible. Such a loss would mean for Cortés, as for Kant, the end of law itself. Which could only mean more bloodshed. The loss of law means loss of the ability to punish – which is what Freud, and Reik speaking for Freud, recommended.

Derrida's arguments about blood's visibility lose nothing when applied to hanging as opposed to guillotining. The classic text which defines a hanged man as either a scapegoat or as sacred, 'Cursed is everyone that hangeth on a tree' (Galatians 3.13), combines the image of the crucified bloody man, such as Christ, with the hanged man; and neither hanging – nor lethal injections – may be free from bloodshed. If absence of blood in modern modes of death means anything, it points to a squeamishness nonetheless parasitic on the language and symbolism of blood-letting. Historically, hanging was for the lower classes; but decapitation persisted in Britain till 1746 at least. The distinction between the two forms of execution did not hold in all European countries. In visual culture, images of decapitation – for example, of saints – ranked very high, above hanging: they often focused a sense of the injustice of the martrydom.

6

Decapitation and *A Tale of Two Cities*

> Even in the year one thousand seven hundred and eighty, the first letters written to you by your old love or by your little children, were but newly released from the horror of being ogled through the windows by the heads exposed on Temple Bar, with the insensate brutality and ferocity worthy of Abyssinia or Ashantee.
>
> *TTC* 2.1.52[1]

Derrida's theme of the visibility of punishment compares with this quotation from an early chapter of *A Tale of Two Cities*, Dickens expressing repugnance towards severed heads being exposed above Temple Bar, the City of London's ceremonial entrance-way. Dickens writes angrily, but with a sense of superiority to African primitivism – and colonialism is a subject of this chapter – but he could not have forgotten the detail which Dickens's editor notes, that a treaty signed by a British mission to the Ashanti was reneged on by the British governor of the Gold Coast, Sir Charles McCarthy, 'who in 1824 led a small force into Ashanti territory. The force was heavily defeated at the battle of Bonsaso, and McCarthy was killed, his skull being taken as a trophy and made into a drinking cup for the Ashanti king' (*TTS* 376, note).

Five things may be stressed about decapitation, four to be listed here, the fifth at the chapter's end: (a) more than hanging, decapitation suggests castration, a point in Freud's essay, 'Medusa's Head' (*SE* 18.273 – see also the dreams in *SE* 5. 366–7), and reinforced in representations of the beheading of Goliath by David (as by Donatello and Caravaggio), and of Judith beheading Holofernes (as by Donatello and Artemisia de Gentileschi); (b) decapitation gives a carnival of blood; (c) it stresses – as with the Ashanti – that the head is a trophy, a possession, a fetish, whether as illustrating state power, as at Temple Bar, or as the sign of one person's triumph over another, as with the execution of John the Baptist, as in

---

[1] *A Tale of Two Cities* appeared in weekly instalments in *All the Year Round* (30 April 1859–26 November 1859, followed by publication).

Caravaggio, as a present for Salome (Matthew 14: 3–12); (d) it conveys inexpressible suffering. Dickens describes Bradley Headstone (see Introduction), pursuing his rival, Eugene Wrayburn, at night:

> with the exhaustion of deferred hope and consuming hate and anger in his face, white-lipped, draggle-haired, seamed with jealousy and anger, and torturing himself with the conviction that he showed it all and they exulted in it, he went by them in the dark, like a haggard head suspended in the air, so completely did the force of his expression cancel his figure.
>
> OMF 3.10.534

Headstone is as if decapitated; his head walks around, and the separation between head and body dramatizes a psychic splitting which runs through execution, in those who command it, and who desire to witness such fragmentation, is complemented by the sense of suffering beyond anything else.

Such psychic splitting inheres in a novel full of introspection and inward secrecy, which undoes Poe's earlier criticism – made relative to *Barnaby Rudge* – that Dickens had no genius for mystery. This novel revises and rethinks much of *Barnaby Rudge*. Both open in 1775 and move to 1780. Carlyle begins his *The French Revolution* (1837) with the death of Louis XV in 1774. In 1775, the 'king with a large jaw and a queen with a fair face' of the novel's first page were Louis XVI and Marie Antoinette. 1775 saw the first fighting between the Americans and the British at Lexington (19 April 1775) in hostilities continuing to 1783; the American Revolution precedes the French. 1775 was associated with George Dance's rebuilt Newgate prison, begun in 1770, in use by 1780 and damaged in that year's Gordon Riots.

1780 sees Charles Darnay's trial for treason in London, and his release. His pro-Americanism is quoted against him at his trial from remarks made in 1775, when he wanted George Washington to gain almost as great a name in history as the then British king, George III (2.3.69). Darnay's trial puts him in danger of being hanged, drawn and quartered for treason (2.2.59), as historically happened to François Henri de la Motte at Tyburn in London on 27 July 1781, for the crime of giving British secrets to the French who were supporting the American War of Independence. The year 1780 concludes with Darnay rejecting his French aristocratic uncle, Monsieur the Marquis (Book the Second, Chapter 9).

The novel then winds back another twenty years (1.4.25) to the execution of Damiens – on 2 March 1757 (2.15.163). A like fate seems to be probable for the pre-Revolutionary peasant Gaspard, and it is alluded to in similar terms as that which would happen to Darnay in Britain, if convicted of treason. This *supplice* intersects Dickens with Foucault, describing the Damiens execution to indicate how the body in the *ancien régime* was the king's property (*DandP* 32–68). Mental torture, for Foucault, was the contrasting mode of punishment in the nineteenth century. The kidnapping of Dr Manette, and the Evrémondes' act of rape, is, significantly, dated to Christmas 1757, making it, memorably, an ugly instance of a Dickens 'Christmas Story'. Dr Manette, writing his condemnation of the Evrémondes in 1767, and released in 1775, narrates the 'almost eighteen years' (1.2.19) wherein he was buried in solitary confinement, starting from then. Such a punishment Godwin's *Enquiry Concerning Political Justice* (678) had criticized John Howard for, since he advocated it: it only produced 'madmen and idiots'. Solitary confinement is called being 'in secret' (see Book 3 chapter 1), and Dickens's *American Notes* record it as deeply horrifying. The novel's narrative ends in December 1793, or early 1794. Philip Collins thinks the novel was long in gestation, following interests which Dickens had long had – rather than resulting, predominantly, from acting Richard Wardour in 1857 in the play he had been involved with (to be discussed later): *The Frozen Deep*. The following novel, *Great Expectations*, whose span is 1800 to the early 1820s, aligns Newgate, criminals and the gallows – and secrecy, which in different ways, weaves itself into *A Tale of Two Cities*.[2]

In *Barnaby Rudge* and *A Tale of Two Cities* the 'crimes' are political – excepting Rudge's double murder, which is counterbalanced here by the Evrémonde brothers' double crime of rape and murder. *A Tale of Two Cities* opens by reprising statements about eighteenth-century torture in France, and anarchy in London and the uselessness of 'the hangman, ever busy, and ever worse than useless' (1.1.9), not least because working indiscriminately, in a way which implies torturing and inept violence working against violence, including street violence. Laziness in practising justice returns later, in this reading of the Black Act:

> Death is Nature's remedy for all things, and why not Legislation's? Accordingly the forger was put to Death; the utterer of a bad note was put to Death; the unlawful opener of a letter was put to Death; the purloiner of forty shillings and sixpence was put to Death; the holder of a horse at Tellson's who made off with it was put to Death; the coiner of a bad shilling was put to Death; the sounders of three-quarters of the notes in the whole gamut of Crime, were put to Death. Not that it did the least good in the way of prevention – it might have been worth

---

[2] Philip Collins, '*A Tale of Two Cities* and *Great Expectations*: Two Novels in Dickens's Career', *DSA* 2 (1972), 336–51, 378–80.

remarking that the fact was exactly the reverse – but it cleared off (as to this world) the trouble of each particular case, and left nothing else connected with it to be looked after.

2.1.52

The novel notes that hanging was then at Tyburn, making the Old Bailey 'a deadly inn-yard, from which pale travellers set out continually, in carts and coaches, on a violent passage into the other world, traversing some two miles and a half of public street and road, and shaming few good citizens, if any' (2.2.58).

Secrecy

The novel's second chapter, with Jarvis Lorry's terse message 'RECALLED TO LIFE' given to Jerry Cruncher, the 'resurrection man', is powerfully cryptic. Jerry returns to London, to Temple Bar. His entry into the city starts a third chapter, 'The Night Shadows', drawing on Bulwer and Poe, and implying that Dickens has learned from Poe's criticism. In this passage where the 'I''s identity is unattributable (but we will return to that question), secrecy triples identities: people are self-divided, and double, and they are how they appear to others. That seems to be echoed in the title: each person is a city twice over.

> A wonderful fact to reflect upon, that every human creature is constituted to be that profound secret and mystery to every other. A solemn consideration, when I enter a great city by night, that every one of those darkly clustered houses, encloses its own secret; that every room in every one of them encloses its own secret; that every beating heart in the hundreds of thousands of breasts there, is, in some of its imaginings, a secret to the heart nearest it! Something of the awfulness, even of Death itself, is referable to this. No more can I turn the leaves of this dear book that I loved, and vainly hope in time to read it all. No more can I look into the depths of this unfathomable water, wherein, as momentary lights glanced into it, I have had glimpses of buried treasure and other things submerged. It was appointed that the book should shut with a spring, for ever and ever, when I had read but a page. It was appointed that the water should be locked in an eternal frost, when the light was playing on its surface, and I stood in ignorance upon the shore. My friend is dead, my neighbour is dead, my love, the darling of my soul, is dead; it is the inexorable consolidation and perpetuation of the secret that was always in that individuality, and which I shall carry in mine to my life's end. In any of the burial-places of this city through which I pass, is

there a sleeper more inscrutable than its busy inhabitants are, in their innermost personality, to me, or than I am to them?

TTC 1.3.16

Secrecy and death inhere in individuality, whose inexorable power is imaged in a book snapping shut with machinic force, or water freezing over: these are also images of death. Allusions to the repressed or hidden, produce the word 'locked', and lead to the last sentence evoking cemeteries, like that in St Pancras churchyard, where the spy Roger Cly is buried – or rather, *not* buried, as Jerry Cruncher discovers, because the tomb's secret is that Cly has faked his death to facilitate his spying (2.14). Hence the ambiguity which makes the dead both inscrutable and busy. 'Busy inhabitants' refer to the sleepers in the tombs as well as to the inhabitants of the city who work in the small hours. With Cruncher, they are secretly raiding tombs to sell dead bodies to surgeons for dissection (as in *Four Stages of Cruelty*).

The paragraph anticipates the idea of solitary confinement, as a condition of life, but the writing is as if posthumous, for the third sentence on the awfulness of death, implies that the secrecy in the city is more intense than death, and the two following anaphorae ('No more ... It was appointed') apply to life and death equally. The sentence following 'My friend is dead' ends with an ellipsis, for that part beginning 'it is the inexorable' is incomplete, allowing the reading that the secret within the 'individual' is encrypted within the living 'I', who bears that death, that secrecy, while alive, as in the opening of 'The Man of the Crowd'. The 'burial-places' must be the darkly clustered houses of the first sentence, hence 'busy' makes the living and dead states indistinguishable. This writing makes the entrant to the city ghostly, shadowy, like the shadow Dickens envisaged going everywhere; the shadow being the not wholly alive (*Letters*, 5.622, to Forster, 7 October 1849).

Carlyle said of the Bastille prisoners: 'old *secrets* come to view; and long-buried Despair finds voice' (*FR* 1.5.7.152, my emphasis). Lorry is on 'secret service' (1.4.29). Darnay returns to France without telling his wife why; Carton's motives throughout are untold secrets. What passes between Manette and Darnay on his wedding morning remains untold. The novel is full of spying; a spy is a 'secret man' (3.8.289). Dickens is fascinated by the idea of a knowledge which a person has which is unknown to him or her. One dramatization of that comes with Darnay and Carton as virtual doubles; two comprising one person. That doubling parallels the Evrémonde twins, Darnay being the son of one of them, and criticizing both – seeing them as inseparable – when speaking to his surviving uncle, (2.9.117–18). The uncle has already praised secrecy, for 'Repression is the only lasting philosophy' (2.9.117).

With Dr Manette, 'no human intelligence could have read the mysteries of his mind in the scared blank wonder of his face' (1.6.48). He returns into social relationships through his daughter, and his life in Soho, but a night 'shadow' remains upon him, noticeable when he gives an 'intent' look to Darnay 'deepening into a frown of dislike and distrust, not even unmixed with fear' (2.4.77), a feeling revived when hearing of the unknown prisoner in the Tower who had written something in imprisonment in secret (2.6.97). His repression of his dislike of Darnay becomes lucid in his narrative, read out in the Revolutionary court, of being imprisoned, revealing the real history, the 'substance' behind the 'shadow' (title of 3.10). The 'shadow' is the fear created by realizing the Defarges have a will for revenge (3.3.258) on the imprisoned Darnay, intuited by Lucy and disavowed by Lorry. It recalls the chapter title, 'The Night Shadows', where shadows double (i.e. shadow) the night. The point is that substance and shadow are interchangeable, pointing to a knowledge which replaces the Doctor's shadowy present existence; again death and life seem interchangeable, questioning each other's reality.

Manette's hostility, unexplained for so long, shows the power of ambivalence. The loving father is vengeful; motives are double; his life comprises night shadows. He lacks conscious awareness of his past, though he keeps the shoemaker's bench and tools, and though Lucy thinks he has some theory about his past existence and his oppressors (2.6.92–3). How thin the partition is between what he knows, and has repressed, and his ability to think of that past and present as belonging to two different people, appears in the chapters giving the talking cure which Lorry practises on him after his nine days' derangement (2.8 and 2.9). Here, Lorry and he speak in third-person terms about his lapsing, regressing into another identity, as the mechanical maker of shoes. They act as though they were talking about other people; as if they were doubles talking about double behaviour, where it seems essential to keep one part of a person's life secret from him. There might, otherwise, be criminal tendencies understudying everything, needing repression. For criminality seems always to relate to double identities.[3] A criminal must have a double life; criminality assumes a pre-existent loss of borders, and identifying with another (who may be criminal).

One of the passengers in the Dover mail is assumed to have alighted for Chatham (2.3.70). That was, historically, associated with a specific spy, i.e. de la

---

[3] Albert D. Hutter, 'Nation and Generation in *A Tale of Two Cities*', *PMLA* 93 (1978), 448–62. See also his 'The Novelist as Resurrectionist: Dickens and the Dilemma of Death', *DSA* 12 (1983), 1–39.

Motte. Noticeably, however, Chatham was the place of Dickens's childhood, as if Dickens signed into the text his own identity as a spy or as treasonous. Charles Darnay connects with Charles Dickens through his initials CD, as Sydney Carton's name aligns him with Algernon Sidney (1622–83). A republican thinker and influence on Montesquieu, Sidney was sentenced for his part against the monarchy in the Rye House plot, by Judge Jeffreys, alongside an ancestor of the Lord John Russell to whom Dickens dedicates the novel. Carton works for Stryver, the lawyer who is compared to Jeffreys (2.5.83). It is as if the criminal and judge work together, as if needing each other. In draft, Sydney Carton's first name was Dick, which connects him with Dickens, while Dickens is also prominent through the name Richard Wardour, Carton's prototype. Darnay is the unconscious 'parricide' (2.15.163) whose aggression towards his uncle/father is fulfilled by the peasant Gaspard's revengeful wielding of the knife against him. Gaspard's part in the plot resembles, therefore, Mme Hortense in *Bleak House* killing on behalf of Lady Dedlock and Esther whose unconscious, or unstated, wishes Hortense fulfils. The act of murder accomplishes more than it knows consciously.

Carton and Darnay resemble each other, but that produces a sparring dialogue between them:

> 'Mr Darnay, let me ask you a question.... Do you think I like you?'
> 'Really, Mr Carton', returned the other, oddly disconcerted. 'I have not asked myself the question'.
> 'But ask yourself the question now'.
> 'You have acted as if you do; but I don't think you do'.
> '*I* don't think I do', said Carton. 'I begin to have a very good opinion of your understanding'.
>
> 2.4.80

The 'semblable' must reply; Carton forces the question, which may seem cruel because it is outside bourgeois manners, but he does not know whether he likes Darnay until Darnay answers the point. Darnay does so in a way which notes Carton's self-division between acts and thoughts. A moment later Carton, looking in the mirror, asks in soliloquy: 'Do you like the man?' – meaning Darnay; indicating that dislike is rooted in self-dislike. Darnay is as a mirror to Carton. Carton does not know whether he likes Darnay until Darnay answers the point, in a way which notes Carton's self-division.

Carton's dislike of Darnay – which, given the names, could add up to a dislike existing between two aspects of the same novelist – mirrors Manette's, not least because both dislikes are unconscious. Nor can Darnay, an innocent man yet thrice put on trial, as if everything insists that there is a fault in him, approve of himself. He feels guilty, and the trials are the Lacanian 'insistence [instance] of the letter [of the law] in the unconscious' (*Écrits* 412). Hence, though he has severed himself from his French past, his compulsive need to return to France (2.24), to assist those he felt he owed a moral duty. The extent of Darnay's masochism, his death drive, becomes apparent when considering how Dickens keys it into the historical pressure in Paris in August 1792 to dethrone the king, with the attacks on the Tuileries (10 August) and the loss of much life. This crisis moment was, historically, consequent upon the publication of the intimidatory Brunswick Manifesto (25 July 1792), which indicated that Louis and Marie Antoinette were corresponding with the enemy armies, and which led, on 19 August, to Prussia's invasion of France. The reasons for Darnay's going 'he did not discuss with himself' (2.24.234). Dickens reshapes what Poe had diagnosed as a deficient interest in mystery into a sense of the opaqueness of the self to itself. In his masochism Darnay is as self-divided as Carton, with whom that opaqueness shows in his refusal of a career – a legal one specifically – and his dissoluteness, part of the death drive. This latter implicitly rejects the optimism within Samuel Smiles's *Self Help*, a text of 1859, as well as the spirit of the then forthcoming *The Origin of Species* (1861). Carton's opacity to himself, so that he needs Darnay to tell him he does not like him, means that he twice frustrates the law to save Darnay, as if contemptuous of both law and man. A draft title for the novel was *Memory Carton*, for Stryver calls Carton 'Memory' (83). 'Carton' hardly had the sense of 'container' that it acquired later; 'carton' implies paper, and so writing; writing which, recalling the opening of 1.3, can hardly be read. If memory attaches to Carton, that is ironic, for Carton seems unconscious of what he knows. 'Memory' implies that he has an archive of an unforgettable past.

Violence and fascism

Darnay, returning to Paris, is confronted by the new machinery of the guillotine, while he is held 'in secret' in La Force. The events of August 1792 were followed by the September Massacres (2–6 September); carnival killings of prisoners.[4] The chapter 'The Grindstone', one of the most fascinating in Dickens, renders that

---

[4] See Eric Hazan, *A People's History of the French Revolution*, trans. David Fernbach (London: Verso 2014), 186–91.

violence. Lorry and Manette look through a window on men sharpening knives on the grindstone with grotesque 'false eyebrows and false moustaches' stuck on them. These Septembrists are 'beastly', and drunk, making 'dropping blood' and 'dropping wine' intermingle, like 'gore and fire', while each man has 'the smear of blood'. Men stripped to the waist have 'the stain all over their limbs and bodies; men in all sorts of rags, with the blood upon those rags, men devilishly set off with spoils of women's lace and silk and ribbon, with the stain dyeing those trifles through and through'. Thus transgendered, like Maenads, they rush off with:

> the same red hue ... red in their frenzied eyes; – eyes which any unbrutalised beholder would have given twenty years of life, to petrify with a well-directed gun. All this was seen in a moment, as the vision of a drowning man.
>
> 3.2.252

To Derrida's question 'what is blood?', which was answered via *Macbeth*, must be added another, 'what is wine?' For wine always supplements blood or is the image of it, as blood is supplemented by being made 'thick', or is made intoxicating by being given the character of wine. And wine *is* blood, as in the biblical image of judgment as treading the grapes of wrath, or in *Macbeth*, where drink allows Lady Macbeth to handle blood. Thus in 'The Wine Shop' chapter (1.5), the spilling of red wine anticipates, incentivises, the spilling of blood. Blood, semen, the sap of the grape and water are Dionysian. Liquids converge as obliterating discrete identity, smearing or staining it, and causing a profound reaction which is also fascination: abjection.[5] Hence the image of the drowning man in the quotation. The impact of this staining is to overwhelm, threatening identity, which must be compensated for by a reactive shooting, which responds to abject feelings which are fascist in their violent repudiation of the other, especially as that 'other' is defined in fantasies of liquids, as opposed to hard outlined male bodies, which define identity in terms of its separateness. The men enjoying blood have become women-like; the men looking on feel horror. Nakedness connects these revolutionaries to 'savages', a word in the text. Given the context of savagery, this looks imperialistic, fascist (though the term is anachronistic). A colonial discourse is at work, as it was with *The Perils of Certain English Prisoners*, Dickens's 1858 short story commenting on the Sepoy Revolution in India (*Christmas Stories* 171–256). Yet though Dickens's record is not good here, there is more to be said

---

[5] See the affinity here to Julia 'thesis about abjection, in *Powers of Horror*, and to Klaus Theweleit's *Male Fantasies*, where hatred of women relates to their identification with liquid, as opposed to hard masculinity. I explore it in my 'Monstrous Tyranny: Men of Blood: Dante and *Inferno* XII', *MLR* 98 (2003), 881–97.

about the intensity here. The arresting vision, or discovery, of a Dionysian sadism, lifting repression, including a secret sexual polymorphism, is a source of fascination, answered by an equal de-repression, an equal violence, expressed in the desire to shoot the men, 'petrifying' them in an absolute arrest. The carnival of violence, or theatre of cruelty, which Lorry and Manette see produces an answering violence in the narrating voice, in an action which recalls the power of the Medusa to paralyse/petrify. That was the killing force marking the stony Evrémonde chateau, seen in the chapter 'The Gorgon's Head' (2.9), wherein the old aristocrat is killed, 'petrified' by Gaspard (2.9.123). The Medusa was decapitated by Perseus, but what is decapitated retains the freezing, castrating potential, following Freud's logic. Violence is arrested and arrests, producing the stone head of Bradley Headstone's name, a primal figure for Dickens, as dead while alive.

The violence wanted to counter revolutionary violence is reactionary, criminal. It accepts a wish to lose twenty years of life, which associates it with a death drive. There is an absolute contradiction in the phrase 'unbrutalised beholder'. Is there any recognition that watching cruelty brutalizes? The point is obvious to Dickens from what he writes about executions, and his letters to the *Daily News*. But can a desire to pull a trigger be unbeastly? Shooting at the eyes – is that, in its orgiastic fervour, not equally sadistic, brutalizing the shooter – assuming there had not been a prior brutalizing? This shooting is an act of repression, desiring to blot out the vision of the shooter. (It is no coincidence that the novel opens at Shooter's Hill – the name not only evokes the hunting which the Black Act protected, it evokes cruelty.) Such shooting is not Benjamin's 'divine violence', it is more like reactionary violence. Dickens dramatizes an affectual state he can see no way out of save through utter negativity; the writing exceeds what a novelist might be expected to record. He knows that the revolutionary carnival is not causeless, and he is fascinated by the freedom it gives to the revolutionaries' bodies. This last point will hold us for the rest of the book.

Petrification is the name for shooting and blinding or killing, *and* seeing in a moment in a desire to freeze the action, to keep it in front of the fascinated gaze; while to fascinate retains the sense, as we have seen through Derrida, of castrating. In this complex of associations, where Dickens's language so exceeds conscious thought, neither blood nor violence nor cruelty are disowned, though they promote responding violence, arresting life, or holding life/death in an arrest, between these two. The novelist accepts his own complicity in violence and blood, acknowledging it in himself, not mastering the situation.

This scene is succeeded by another declaring the prisoners' indifference to others about to be put on trial, and killed:

The prisoners were far from insensible or unfeeling: their ways rose out of the conditions of the time. Similarly, though with a subtle difference, a species of fervour or intoxication, known without doubt, to have led some persons to brave the guillotine unnecessarily and to die by it, was not mere boastfulness, but a wild infection of the wildly shaken public mind. In seasons of pestilence, some of us will have a secret attraction to the disease – a terrible passing inclination to die of it. And all of us have like wonders hidden in our breasts, only needing circumstances to evoke them.

3.6.270–1

'Circumstances' reveal what is secret, 'hidden'. We have reverted to the concerns of the earlier chapter, "The Night Shadows", but instead of secrecy there appears an apparent boastfulness, called an 'infection', created by a kind of hysteria in the population in a time of disturbance.

This section includes the Bacchic, carnivalesque 'Carmagnole' (3.5) which the revolutionaries dance, in the December of 1793, during the Terror. There appears another surrender of limits, of the body, and of gender, which appals those outside its mass enthusiasm. In chapter 3.6, the 'infection' is the power of auto-suggestion; as people desire to die from pestilence, in a form of the death drive, so masochism drives people to the guillotine, like the 'terrible attraction' (2.24.233) – the death wish – which impelled Darnay back to France. Carton's acceptance of the guillotine for himself is obviously glanced at here, indeed it is being trailed, novelistically. His claiming the right to death is a masochism as intoxicated as the frenzy of the murderers killing the prisoners, though the text denies this in making him calm in his choice. The text, which speaks of people 'wildly shaken', as if hysterical, or in the condition of Macbeth, as he was when solicited by the witches, can barely acknowledge the logic of the connection. If Carton is a figure of intoxication, violent against himself, the text attempts to sublimate that, denying what it has affirmed. Nonetheless the novel's subject is the discovery of a mystery within identity, as already beyond death, which was seen in the opening paragraph of the novel's third chapter.

'I can devour thee'

The Jacobins dominated the Revolution by the autumn of 1793, after the defeat of the Girondins, producing the period usually named the Terror. David Andress quotes a Jacobin pronouncement of 5 September 1793:

It is time that equality bore its scythe above all heads. It is time to horrify all the conspirators. So legislators, place Terror on the order of the day! Let us be in revolution, because everywhere counter-revolution is being woven by our enemies. The blade of the law should hover over all the guilty.[6]

The guillotine is now the more primitive scythe. Daniel Stout notes how the French Revolution, including in *A Tale of Two Cities*, makes names numbers.[7] Carton is no. 23; the guillotine being the anonymising leveller, almost the state itself. When Carton asks the Woodsawyer, 'How goes the Republic?', he is answered:

> 'You mean the Guillotine. Not ill. Sixty-three today. We shall mount to a hundred soon. Samson [Henri Sanson] and his men complain, sometimes, of being exhausted. . . . Such a Barber . . .
> 'Go and see him when he has a good batch. Figure this to yourself, citizen; he shaved the sixty-three today, in less than two pipes!'
>
> 3.9.299

We hardly need note how the novel speaks for abolition: its stance was apparent in the lynching of Foulon (*TTC* 2.22, cp. *FR* 1.5.9. 158–9). Sanson the executioner wrote about *le délire de la mort* – a madness of death – which was produced by the guillotine and its power in people's lives: the opposite of the coolness intended in the machinery of death.[8]

Carton's query evokes the chapter 'Death' from volume 3 of *The French Revolution*, called 'The Guillotine'. Dickens quotes from it in relation to Mme Roland asking for pen and paper at the scaffold (*FR* 3.5.2. 261, *TTC* 3.15.360). The implicit question in 'Death' is answered: 'La Guillotine ne va pas mal'. *The Declaration of the Rights of Man* had minimized individual agency, making this

---

[6] David Andress, *The Terror: Civil War in the French Revolution* (London: Little, Brown 2005), 179. Historians' quarrels over the French Revolution include those over the status of the Terror, whether this was a unique moment, or, as the anti-Marxist François Furet in *Intepreting the French Revolution*, trans. Elborg Forster (Cambridge: Cambridge University Press 1981) asserted, inherent in 1789 itself, and with the 'pure democracy' which had been carried into the Revolution from Rousseau (making Jacobinism precede 1789). Sieyès, in *Qu'est-ce que le Tiers État?*, argued that 'the nobility was not part of the national will' (44); hence the nation had to be formed in opposition to the nobility. Furet sees the Revolution not as bourgeois, not democratic, but terrorist throughout implicitly, rather than in responding to events (e.g. war). He denies its defining status in terms of French history, opposing the Marxist historians Albert Soboul and Claude Mazauric. See Jack R. Censer, 'Historians Revisit the Terror – Again', *Journal of Social History* 48 (2014), 383–403. This includes discussion of Andress.
[7] Daniel Stout, 'Nothing Personal: The Decapitation of Character in *A Tale of Two Cities*', *Novel* 41 (2007), 29–52.
[8] Quoted, Julia Kristeva, *Visions Capitales* (Paris: Réunion des Musées Nationaux 1998), 105.

something on loan from the nation. 'Liberty, Equality, Fraternity or Death' – makes death 'the result of a commitment to a world without individuals' (Stout, 32, 33, *FR* 3.5.2.163, *TTC* 3.5.269). Death is inscribed in practices which have eliminated the individual, subsuming him or her into identification with past members of his class (Stout, 36). Carlyle notes the guillotine's 'speed of going' as

> an index of the general velocity of the Republic. The clanking of its huge axe, rising and falling there, in horrid systole-diastole, is portion of the whole enormous Life-movement and pulsation of the Sansculottic System.
>
> *FR* 3.4.6.147

It is the machine, too, for Dickens. Carlyle, attempting to total the number of executions, calls it 'a horrible sum of human lives' (3.7.6.237). Alfred Cobban estimates that, from March 1793 to 10 June 1794, 1,251 persons were executed in Paris, and, from 10 July to 27 July 1794, 1,376.[9]

Carlyle quotes the Girondin Pierre Victurien Vergniaud (1753–93), who was the twenty-second to be executed in a purge of the political party, the Girondins, in October 1793; one head per minute. So Carlyle notes at the end of the Book entitled 'Terror', whose subject is the destruction of Girondism. Carlyle ends with fleeing Girondists being found in a cornfield, their bodies half-eaten by dogs. Vergniaud pronounces the verdict: '[T]he Revolution, like Saturn, is devouring its own children' (*FR* 3.4.8.153). The Revolution, then, is Saturnine; a return to an old melancholic destructiveness, or, to interpret differently, the Revolution should be the opposite of Saturn, but actually repeats the destructiveness of the old order, as seen, for example, in the old Evrémondes.

Vergniaud's words apparently impacted upon Goya's *Saturn* (1820–3), one of fourteen so-called 'Black Paintings', though Goya had already produced a chalk drawing, *Saturn Devouring his Children*, in 1796–7, possibly from a Rubens in Madrid's Royal Collection.[10] To connect Revolutionary violence and war was Goya's subject with *Saturn*, as it must be for anyone considering modern terror. Goya had engaged with the disasters of war in contemplating both the French, a Revolutionary army but now an occupying force, in Spain from 1808 to 1814, and the guerrilla warfare against them. That warfare produced in Goya the painting *The Third of May 1808*, showing a Napoleonic firing squad – it had once been a Revolutionary force – shooting in reparation hunched prisoners, part of

---

[9] Alfred Cobban, *A History of Modern France Vol. 1: 1715–1799* (London: Penguin 1963), 238.
[10] On the influence of Vergniaud's words on Goya's 'Saturn' (1820–3), see Ronald Paulson, *Representations of Revolution (1789–1820)* (New Haven: Yale University Press 1983), 363–70.

a people's war, one of whom holds up his arms, Christ-like, protestingly.[11] The soldiers have a lamp in front of them, marking them off as Enlightenment figures: if so the worse for the reason which shoots the life and the vivid faces before it.[12] The eighty-two etchings comprising *The Disasters of War* burgeon with similar, even more summary and vicious, executions. Goya's Saturn, a reminder that sacrifice is offered to a god, recalls the undercurrent of the language of sacrifice in war and execution alike.

Paulson comments that Saturn has already eaten the head of the youth he holds and is devouring, giving another sense of decapitation. Paulson is not the only one to notice that the figure of Saturn seems to have been painted with an erection which increases the sexual/sadistic underpresence in whatever 'Revolution' represents, or whatever reaction induces revolution to become Saturn-like.[13] Nor is that foreign to Dickens. If Lucy was seen by Mr Lorry aged 2 (1.4.23), Charles Darnay was seen by his future father-in-law when he was 'a pretty boy' (3.10.317), and named by his mother who fears that, if no 'innocent atonement' is made for the crime of rape and murder, it will be required of the boy. Charles Darnay will be one of Saturn's children. Manette's statement written in 1767, recording a primal scene of rape and murder by brothers on a brother and sister, is read out in 1793 to the Revolutionary court, and Manette's denunciation of the Evrémonde family deliberately, however unconsciously, includes this attractive figure of the future as needing to be destroyed within Manette's desire for revenge. That, as it affects the future, is marked by excess; perhaps the little boy's appeal only fuels desire for vengeance. If that implication of a sexual undercurrrent is accepted, revenge, inseparable from revolution, is sexualized, which gives a reading of how the revolution devours its children which is the more surprising in terms of the chronology: Manette desiring revolution, the child Darnay becoming the victim of the revolutionary energies which emerge; Manette the old man reduced to craziness by the Revolution as he was by the *ancien régime*. Dickens braids together, and inverts, past and future, the past happening *before* the future, but narrated *after*; the past needing confrontation in the present, and constructing the future, which reconstitutes the past. Whereas *Barnaby Rudge* kept times separate, *A Tale of Two Cities* reveals that the past is in the present and future, and the future destroyed by the power of the past. That is what Saturn devouring his children means – consuming the future.

---

[11] Gwyn A. Williams, *Goya and the Impossible Revolution* (London: Penguin 1976), 1–13.

[12] On this painting, see Hugh Thomas, *Goya: The Third of May 1808* (London: Penguin 1972).

[13] Paulson, 363, 381. See Nigel Glendinning, 'The Strange Translation of Goya's "Black Paintings"', *The Burlington Magazine* 117 (1975), 464–77, and 479; reference 473.

In 'Redemption', the section in *Thus Spoke Zarathustra* which quotes the 'Anaximander fragment', Zarathustra argues that the best redemption would be freedom from the reactiveness of wanting to take revenge, and calling it punishment, a word which gives to revenge the sanctity of justice. That 'redemption' would mean freedom from the frustrated, anger, inseparable from *ressentiment*, at having to say 'it was' – that something bad has happened and gone into the past, and cannot be forgotten. The nihilism of the person (classed as a 'victim') desiring revenge for past injury produces the 'madness' which says 'this is itself justice, that law of time, that time must devour its children' (*Zarathustra* 2.20.120). There is a predisposition to want revenge, aka punishment, aka justice, as though justice only existed in awarding punishments. That equation Nietzsche has already theorized in another section of *Zarathustra* (2.7.86), 'On the Tarantulas', which stresses a poisonous moral purity in those who, in taking revenge, annihilate the future.

Revolutionary times unveil a cannibalistic principle which Goya unfolds, revealing the 'lowest, least blessed fact', Carlyle says, which 'necessitous mortals have ever based themselves [which] seems to be the primitive one of Cannibalism: That *I* can devour *Thee*'. This 'primitive Fact' is where we must start (1.2.7.44). Carlyle repeats an insistence on cannibalism (3.5.7.187). Thus *The Beast and the Sovereign* cites Hobbes, probably Carlyle's source: 'Man is a wolf to man' (*BS* 1.58). He then cites Lacan: '[M]an's ferocity towards his semblable exceeds everything animals are capable of, and carnivores themselves recoil in horror at the threat man poses to nature as a whole' (*Écrits* 120). Discussing this, and with the context of what he and Reik said about cannibalism, Derrida agrees with Lacan in 'opposing the hypothesis that there are such things as "criminal instincts" (*BS* 1.104), and that this eating, this cruelty, is practised on a 'semblable', a fellow:

> No experience has gone deeper than that of analysis in probing, in lived experience, the equivalence signaled to us by the pathetic call of Love: it is thyself that thou strikest, and the glacial deduction of Spirit: it is in the fight to the death for pure prestige that man gets himself recognised by man.
>
> *Écrits* 120, *BS* 1.105

Derrida notes the competitive violence of brothers with *Antigone*'s Eteocles and Polynices:

> [H]ow ... is a brother possible? How can one have two sons? How can one be the father of two phalli, erected one against the other? How can two beings of one sex cohabit in one family? ... Brothers are not possible in nature ... Two brothers, going head to head, can only kill themselves.
>
> *Glas* 175–6

Hence Cain and Abel; the brothers in *Hamlet*; hence *Totem and Taboo*, hence the 'semblables' of *A Tale of Two Cities* which include Darnay and Carton. Dickens can only resolve such phallic aggression through Carton's death drive which lets him take Darnay's place, and, being masochism, gains its own triumph in that. Carton goes to a suicidal death, though that insight is spoiled by a certain sentimentalism, which may be seen as a sublimation of his masochism, especially since on the scaffold he foresees so much which is uplifting, a cleaned-up Paris, and of his memory being held dear in the Darnay family.[14] He wins more 'prestige' than Darnay, in his proleptic musings, which makes Freud's point, that no one can imagine their own death.

If there is something of kitsch in Carton's death and his last words, that may relate to the novel's genealogy. It expanded from the sacrifical death of the play, *The Frozen Deep*, which derived from the aftermath of the expedition of 1845 under the command of Sir John Franklin (1786–1847), seeking for a north-west passage between the Atlantic and the Pacific. The crew was lost, as were Franklin's ships, *HMS Erebus* and *HMS Terror*. (Why such nihilistic names for such apparently benign explorations? The modern state reveals something about itself in this unconscious way.) An exploratory naval expedition, partly financed by Lady Franklin, was led by Francis Leopold McClintock in the *Fox*, and the findings published in *The Voyage of the Fox* (November 1859). Everything here was reacting to discussion which had been in the press and journals since 1854 when Dr John Rae reported to the Hudson Bay Company, on the authority of Inuits he had met, that Franklin's men had turned to cannibalism in their extremity.[15] McClintock did not report any evidence of cannibalism, but that may mean that he kept his opinions to himself.

Dickens's hostile reaction to Rae, in *Household Words*, spurred on by Franklin's widow, was a reaction formation.[16] The novelist who made Magwitch threaten Pip with the young man who would tear out his heart and liver (*GE* 1.6) was no stranger to fantasies of eating people. His reaction might have been compounded by what might have occurred on the *Medusa*, subject of the well-known painting,

---

[14] For defences of Carton's death as presented, see John Bowen, 'Counting On: *A Tale of Two Cities*', in Colin Jones, Josephine McDonagh and Jon Mee (eds.), *A Tale of Two Cities and the French Revolution* (Basingstoke: Palgrave Macmillan 2009), 104–25, and Jan-Melissa Schramm, 164–80.

[15] Andrew Moore, 'Sir Edwin Landseer's "Man Proposes: God Disposes": And the Fate of Franklin', *British Art Journal* 9 (2009), 32–7.

[16] 'The Lost Arctic Voyagers', (*HW* 2 December 1854), 361–5. See *Journalism* 2, 254–69, including Slater's discussion; James E. Marlow, 'The Fate of Sir John Franklin: Three Phases of Response in Victorian Periodicals', *Victorian Periodicals Review* 15 (1982), 2–11; John Kofron, 'Dickens, Collins, and the Influence of the Arctic', *DSA* 40 (2009), 81–93.

The Raft of the Medusa (Louvre, Paris, 1819), by Théodore Géricault, himself fascinated by painting guillotined heads, and by hanging, as in *Les supplices*' (in Rouen).[17] Géricault's painting, particularly a father/son grouping to its front left, was influenced by illustrations of an incident in Dante's *Inferno*: the execution-by-starvation of Ugolino and his four sons, imprisoned in a tower in Pisa (see Dante, *Inferno* 32.124–37, 33.1–90). Dante's narration gives the cryptic suggestion there that, at the end, the father tries to devour his dead children. Ugolino is seen gnawing into the nape of the neck of Ruggieri, who betrayed him; and Dante draws on this from a moment in Statius' account of war in Thebes: when Tydeus sees his dead foe Melanippus, he orders his head to be cut off:

> Taking it in his hand, he studied it
> Gloating to see it warm and the wild eyes
> Still wandering, unsure of death's firm grip ...
> ... And him [Pallas Athena] saw
> Drenched in the foul filth of the shattered brain,
> His jaws polluted with live human blood,
> Nor could friends wrench it from him.[18]

The associations of decapitation and cannibalism, eating the head, intimate that beheading has a further significance. They necessitate a reaction formation which refuses to acknowledge it because it seems literally too near the bone. Five years after the defensive *Household Words* article, Carton's decapitation reawakes and attempts to sublimate the fantasy of being cannibalized, when this had, actually, happened. Carton shows Dickens's willing surrender of power to compensate for a violence he feared and knew, and to which he gave coded expression.

Dickens showed himself blameable in the hot violence with which he turned on the Indians in the Sepoy Rebellion of 1857.[19] His reactionariness was attacked

---

[17] Nina Athanassoglou-Kallmyer, 'Géricault's Severed Heads and Limbs: The Politics and Aesthetics of the Scaffold', *Art Bulletin* 74 (1992), 599–618. See also Eitner, 107–206. I expand here on my '"Recalled to Life": Survival in Dickens and Dante', in Catherine Waters, Michael Hollington and John Jordan (eds.), *Imagining Italy: Victorian Writers and Travellers* (Newcastle-upon-Tyne: Cambridge Scholars Publishing 2010), 115–37.

[18] Statius, *Thebaid*, trans. A. D. Melville (Oxford: Oxford University Press 1992), 215.

[19] I discussed *The Perils of Certain English Prisoners* in *Dickens, Violence, and the Modern State: Dreams of the Scaffold*, 184–93; see also Mill's critique of Dickens on the Governor Eyre controversy, 171–3. See Lillian Nayder, 'Class Consciousness and the Indian Mutiny in Dickens's "The Perils of Certain English Prisoners"', *Studies in English Literature 1500–1900* 32 (1992), 689–705; Priti Joshi, 'Mutiny Echoes: India, Britons, and Charles Dickens's *A Tale of Two Cities*', *Nineteenth-Century Literature* 62 (2007), 48–87; Alex Tickell, '*The Perils of Certain English Prisoners*: Charles Dickens, Wilkie Collins, and the Limits of Colonial Government', *Nineteenth-Century Literature* 67 (2013), 457–89.

by John Stuart Mill, presenting himself as the more rigorous thinker, but ironies are never hard to find when people take the moral high ground, and so here. Mill, a Utilitarian, an abolitionist, who found a strange 'effeminacy' in the argument which thinks the loss of life worse than 'depriving [a man] of all that makes life desirable and valuable', retreated from complete abolitionism in 1868. He finds a reason, including deterrence, to hang criminals, 'when we can speak of "the irredeemable character of the offender"'. It is 'the most impressive form' of punishment, and the 'least cruel mode', 'less than life imprisonment with hard labour'. Mill thought miscarriages of justice were rare in England, and that it might be appropriate with a criminal 'solemnly to blot him out from the fellowship of mankind and from the catalogue of the living'.[20] Dickens can then afford to satirize both the abolitionist in *The Mystery of Edwin Drood* (16.183) and Mill's version of Utilitarianism. Mill makes Derrida's point about philosophy's inadequacy to discuss the death penalty, since it is committed to abstraction, and not to the concrete examples fiction requires. Mill's Utilitarianism can only 'blot' out – i.e. repress – the murderer from 'fellowship' – but what fellowship the murderer might be part of he cannot afford to acknowledge. Blotting out must happen because if the society which condemns recognized the murderer, it might learn something about its own constitution. Mill indicates, unconsciously, then, that the impulse to punish goes deeper than rational argument could support.

To the fascination with the morcellation of cannibalism we can add fascination with the fantasy of being torn to pieces, imminent in older forms of execution, and perpetuated in decapitation. Dickens began his 'public readings' of selections of his novels to audiences in 1858, telling a correspondent: 'I am the modern embodiment of the old Enchanters, whose Familiars tore them to pieces' (7 December 1857, *Letters* 8. 488). Being torn to pieces for this Orpheus, the Enchanter who is the victim of his own success, was no isolated image; he used it of acting in *The Frozen Deep* in 1857 ('I have been tearing myself to pieces'). He repeated it of acting the notoriously successful Sikes and Nancy episodes of *Oliver Twist* in 1868 – 'I shall tear myself to pieces.'[21] Malcolm Andrews, citing

---

[20] Quotations from James E. Crimmins, 'The Principles of Utilitarian Penal Law Reform in Beccaria, Bentham, and J. S. Mill', in Peter Karl Koritansky, *The Philosophy of Punishment and the History of Political Thought* (Columbia, MO: University of Missouri Press 2011), 131–71, see pp. 159, 160, 161. For Mill quotations, see *Collected Works*, ed. John M. Robson (Toronto: University of Toronto Press 1963–91), 28.266–72 (specifically 267, 269–70).

[21] Malcolm Andrews, *Charles Dickens and his Performing Selves: Dickens and the Public Readings* (Oxford: Oxford University Press 2006), 260. See Philip Collins (ed.), *Sikes and Nancy and Other Public Readings* (Oxford: Oxford University Press 1983).

evidence that these readings materially hastened his death, finds this self-description Dionysian. Allusion to the Enchanter, or to being torn to pieces, seems not specific or single; it may evoke Actaeon, or Don Quixote, victim of the enchanter Freston, in the adventure of the windmills (*Don Quixote* 1.1.8). It may evoke Goethe's poem 'Die Zauberlehrling' ('The Sorcerer's Apprentice'), where the spirits are too many for the hapless apprentice; behind that poem lies Faust, torn to pieces in Marlowe's *Doctor Faustus*. Macbeth, too, feels he is in danger of being shaken to pieces. For Lacan, the body in pieces – the *corps morcelé* – is the fantasy of fragmentation which the mirror stage works against, since it gives a fantasized unified identity to the narcissistic subject (*Écrits* 78). The mirror image protects against fear of becoming the body in pieces, but it produces an 'aggressivity' through the necessity of preserving that image which is paranoid.

Dickens reading of 'Sikes and Nancy' seems to activate, or fulfil, a desire for the scattering of his identity, by acting out murder and hanging. The author/reader identifies with both. If Sikes's death is accident, panic, fear of the crowd, and of being haunted by Nancy, then his dog's death, the dog being his 'Familiar' which he tried to put out of sight by drowning, seems to make his death suicidal. Acting shows the destructive action of the 'Familiars' – the demons, the spirits which are internal to the self, and perhaps external (even within the family). The readings repeat the murder and the suicide again and again, repetition being compulsive, part of the death drive. They bear within them something which is felt to be transgressive – pleasure in killing. To W. P. Frith, 16 November 1868, Dickens wrote, of the Sikes and Nancy reading, 'I have a vague sense of being "wanted" as I walk about the street' (*Letters* 12.221). This is Dickens as Eugene Aram, or the man of the crowd, or Jonas Chuzzlewit, or more, the dead man walking, recording entering a city by night in *A Tale of Two Cities* (1.3). This voice has the qualities of Carton, night-walker and melancholic, and posthumous from the beginning: the autobiographical passage standing outside chronological logic, as if the 'I' of Dickens has incorporated the dead Carton.

If Dickens records an impulse towards self-disintegration making him identify with the murdered, and with the fantasized sense of control, of sovereignty, that 'the Enchanter' embodies, murderer and murdered combine within one being. Awareness of the combination of opposites produces the most haunting writing of double states, which is part of Dickens's achievement throughout. The desire to disintegrate, a possible primary masochism, shows the difficulties involved in sustaining an identity, which is, as Freud or Lacan sees it, a paranoid structure, guarding itself against an otherness which would threaten it, with the power of the superego. The alternative to that identity formation means identifying with the violent fantasy, of the body in pieces, one which the suicide-terrorist seems to accept. Such a fantasy was inside the vision of the Septembrists.

7

On the USA: Violence and Terrorism

We reach the present day via a special case that Derrida mentions: the USA, which in 1972 suspended capital punishment – though, as it turned out, only temporarily – calling it 'unusual and cruel punishment' (*DP* 1.72).[1] William Schabas notes how abolition was promoted in the USA as a result of the Universal Declaration of Human Rights (1948). The death penalty could be seen as a human rights violation; for, like torture, 'an execution constitutes an extreme physical and mental assault on a person already rendered helpless by government authorities'.[2] Those states reintroducing the death penalty claimed that lethal injections removed the imputation that the death penalty was cruel and unusual, though this sounds disingenuous. While Europe dropped capital punishment, the last decades of the twentieth century onwards have seen a contrary acceleration in America.[3]

Two texts giving accounts of actual cases will be useful to concentrate on America: first Truman Capote's *In Cold Blood: A True Account of a Multiple Murder and its Consequences* (1966). Harper Lee worked alongside Capote, and the 'novel' was used, for its reconstruction of historical events by investigative journalism, by Norman Mailer in *The Executioner's Song* (1979). From there, we move to execution for terrorism, considering the Timothy McVeigh case, and terrorism itself, remembering especially 9/11, and America's 'war against terror', whose punitiveness included the CIA's execution of Osama bin Laden (2 May 2011), ordered by President Obama.

---

[1] On this, see Kelly Oliver, *Technologies of Life and Death: From Cloning to Capital Punishment* (New York: Fordham University Press 2013), 166–87.
[2] Eric Prokosch, 'The Death penalty versus Human Rights', in Roger Hood (ed.), *The Death Penalty: Beyond Abolition* (Strasbourg: Council of Europe 2004), 24.
[3] For contrasts between Europe and the USA on capital punishment, see Franklin E. Zimring, 'Postscript: The Peculiar Present of American Capital Punishment', in Stephen P. Garvey (ed.), *America's Death Penalty* (Durham, NC: Duke University Press 2003), 212–29.

In Cold Blood and *The Executioner's Song*

The Penguin edition of *In Cold Blood* prints on its front cover police shots of Dick Hickock and Perry Smith. Hickock was born in 1931 in Kansas City to respectable working-class parents who could not afford college for him. He had been married twice, with children. Having committed offences which had jailed him, he writes a statement (*In Cold Blood* 253–5), suggesting possible 'pedophiliac tendencies' towards girls. Perry Smith (b. 1928, Elko, Nevada), son of a Cherokee mother and an 'Irish cowboy' (120), was called a 'half-breed' (42, 263), making him a more heterogeneous force than Hickock. His statement to the court (250–3) tells of childhood abuse, feelings of inadequacy (bed-wetting), and assaults on traditional feelings of masculinity. They were executed on 14 April 1965 at Lansing State Prison near Leavenworth, Kansas, having murdered a family – Herbert and Bonnie Clutter, and their teenage children, Kenyon and Nancy, on 15 November 1959. The family, living 400 miles west of Kansas City, on a farm near Garden City, were Republican, Protestant, the apparent essence of white Middle America, save that Bonnie was clinically depressed.[4]

When in Lansing prison for other, unrelated offences, Hickock and Smith had been told by another prisoner, Floyd Wells, an ex-worker for Clutter, that Clutter possessed a safe. Robbery then was the motive for killing, but Hickock also wanted to rape Nancy, against Smith's wishes (261). Actually, Clutter possessed no safe and had no ready money, making the murders bloodily senseless. Smith says, 'there was even blood in my hair.' (We recall Chaucer's suicide, and Banquo's 'gory locks'.) For *OED*, 'in cold blood', which resonates with Derrida's question 'what is blood?', refers to an old, Galen-derived, physiology, which believed that actions could be performed without heating the blood. In Shakespeare, 'hot blood' and 'blood' are interchangeable, and it may be impossible to act in cold blood (*sang froid* – meaning coolness – is not the same idea). For if an action requires 'blood' at all, it requires the heat of passion. If Capote's title means that Smith killed the Clutters without cause and without passion, that is not the case,

---

[4] Truman Capote, *In Cold Blood* (London: Penguin 2017). Page references in text. On the text and the case, see Travis Linnemann, 'Capote's Ghosts: Violence, Media, and the Spectre of Suspicion', *The British Journal of Criminology* 55 (2015), 514–53. On the 'gay subtext', see Ralph F. Voss, *Truman Capote and the Legacy of In Cold Blood* (Tuscaloosa: Alabama University Press 2011), 100–21 especially, and Gerald Clarke, *Capote: A Biography* (London: Hamish Hamilton 1988). For Capote on capital punishment, see Voss, 122–49. Clarke quotes Kenneth Tynan, the British theatre critic, writing in *The Observer*, claiming that Capote could have done more to save Smith and Hickock, through an insanity plea (364–5); this is the sad corollary of the cold-blooded point that Capote needed their deaths to publish his book – Clarke: 'Tynan was right when he suggested that Capote did not want to save them' (365).

because although Hickock calls Smith 'a natural born killer' (51, 212) he is not: he has made up the story of having previously killed a black man to impress Hickock, and that pervades the conflicting desires in the murder. It makes Smith say 'it was something between me and Dick' (224) – an homoeroticism dividing the men as much as connecting them. The psychiatrist speaks of paranoia in Smith, and, in his killing, of a 'paranoid schizophrenic reaction' (273). Killing Clutter put him

> under a mental eclipse, deep inside a schizophrenic darkness, for it was not entirely a flesh and blood man he suddenly discovered himself destroying but a 'key figure in some traumatic configuration': his father? the orphanage nuns who had derided and beaten him? the hated Army sergeant? the parole officer who had ordered him to stay out of Kansas? One of them or all of them.
>
> 276–7

The novel's commentary associates with Willie-Jay, the chaplain's clerk, another prison ex-inmate, diagnosing Smith's 'flaw', as he calls it – i.e. his 'explosive emotional reaction out of all proportion to the occasion', and 'unreasonable anger at the sight of those who are happy or content' (41).

This language of what is proportionate partakes of the prevalent atmosphere which believes in the *lex talionis* (228, 278–80), so much so that Hickock says he is not against capital punishment:

> Revenge is all it is, but what's wrong with revenge? It's very important. If I was kin to the Clutters . . . I couldn't rest in peace till the ones responsible had taken that ride on the Big Swing.
>
> 308–9

Smith, however, says on the scaffold, 'I don't believe in capital punishment morally or legally', but he speaks the *lex talionis* language when reflecting that the Clutters had never hurt him 'like other people. Like people have all my life. Maybe it's just that the Clutters were the ones who had to pay for it' (277). In this contradiction, Smith is not marked by a sense of proportion, and is not rational; yet he calculates, and people must pay.

The last word on the two men comes from Alvin Dewey, who, 'like the majority of American law enforcement officials', which is what he is, 'was certain that capital punishment is a deterrent to violent crime':

> He never had much use for Hickock who seemed to him a small-time chiseller, who got out of his depth, empty and worthless. But Smith, though he was the true murderer, aroused another response, for Perry possessed a quality, the aura

of an exiled animal, a creature walking wounded, that the detective could not disregard.

313–14

This has a hint of Derrida's 'beast and the sovereign'. Smith as sovereign is like D. H. Lawrence's snake (in the eponymous poem) as discussed by Derrida in *The Beast and the Sovereign* (*BS* 2.236–49). Hickock is no 'great criminal' then, yet we may ponder on who is talking, and giving both verdicts, especially as Capote attended the hangings (Clarke, 354), though his book is silent about that. Is Dewey ventriloquizing what Capote feels? Capital punishment, like that personal assessment, happens 'in cold blood', and Dewey's response to Hickock's death seems cold-blooded enough. The men's poverty echoes Smith's diary entry: 'The rich never hang. Only the poor and friendless' (235); but Smith hints at something else, which is Capote's theme, 'that there are special, strange, gifted people in the world and they have to be treated with understanding' (quoted, Voss, 125). The novel wants to affirm that about Smith, though it is unclear from the text whether it believes there was any alterity about Hickock making him exceptional. Whether either was exceptional makes no difference; but if there is no place for the exception, there is something invalid in the system of justice, because that must assume that it can find a justice suitable for those who do not fit; for a society must accept the existence of the exception or misfit.

It seems that the subtext of murder is sexuality, though the novel does not say all it knows. While finding it easier to avow paedophilia in Hickock than on Smith as homosexual, the point remains that Dewey identifies with Smith, as, it seems, biographically, Capote did, even, possibly, having a sexual relationship with him when visiting him in prison.[5] If he did, at least there was no real withdrawal from what Smith represented, and Capote made an identification with criminality. If there is a disavowal of homosexuality in the writing, it knows, too, there is more to be said about Smith; there is a space for explanation which the novel must fill – as also with Hickock, who remains more opaque than Dewey/Capote allows.

If a prompting to criminality is guilt over insufficient masculinity, or comes from a feeling that masculinity must involve transgressive feeling, it is commented on tersely with reference to the wife, Bonnie Clutter, whose depression is modified by her escapes from home to Witchita, Kansas, for treatment and temporary employment. Yet 'she had liked it [being in Witchita] too well, so

---

[5] The possibility is discussed by Voss, 120; for the conditions of Capote's visits, see Clarke, 343–7.

much that it seemed to her unchristian and the sense of guilt she in consequence developed ultimately outweighed the experiment's therapeutic value' (26). The Protestantism which makes enjoyment sinful becomes her superego, and she must cling onto that guilt: hence the return to a worse guilt, called depression. The novelist who notes male deviance speaks in a feminist voice for Bonnie, just as Smith recognizes the possibility that she might have wanted her death, especially after the other shootings (225). Lacan translates the power of the Kantian imperative into psychoanalytic terms:

> [D]ispleasure is understood to provide a pretext for repressing desire, displeasure arising, as it does, along the pathway of desire's satisfaction: but displeasure is also understood to provide the form this very satisfaction takes in the return of the repressed.
>
> Similarly, pleasure doubles its aversion when it recognises the law, by supporting the desire to comply with it that constitutes defence.
>
> Écrits 663

If we understand 'displeasure' as frustration, exhaustion or suffering, it is that which prevents desire, as seeming preferable to that. It returns Bonnie to her unhappiness, from Witchita to Holcomb. However, such acceptance of 'displeasure' is misrecognized, as being satisfaction of desire itself, and repression ('defence') aids displeasure when desire (pleasure) sides with the law.

For the law is the secret subject: *In Cold Blood* notes its coldness, producing piety and hanging and disavowing its investment in blood. Kansas State abolished capital punishment in 1907, reintroduced it in 1935, and executed nine people between 1944 and 1954. The governor between 1957 and 1960 had been an abolitionist, and was defeated for reselection partly because of that (284–6). Desire for a deterrent is inseparable from the production of mistrust in Holcomb (5, 211–12), i.e. the sense that to people in Holcomb the murders seemed to hint at something concealed but nonetheless present in this most homogeneous of places, demanding explanations – saying the murderers could not have been acting alone – producing a paranoia not ultimately dissimilar to Smith's.

A few years later, the *Furman v. Georgia* case (1972) effectively ended capital punishment on the grounds of the Eighth Amendment forbidding 'cruel and unusual punishment' (*DP* 1.53). *Gregg v. Georgia* (1976) changed that legislation, permitting the State of Georgia to execute Troy Leon Gregg, who had shot and robbed two people who had given him a car ride. (Gregg was actually killed, in 1980, by being murdered after escaping from prison before execution.) The Eighth Amendment was seen to clash with the Fifth and Fourteenth Amendments, which did not make capital punishment unconstitutional. In 1972, that point had divided the Supreme Court, America's highest, whose nine members sit for life. *Gregg v. Georgia* had concluded that Gregg's death sentencing was not arbitrary or capricious because his trial was 'bifurcated' – i.e. it compelled mitigation/aggravating factors to be weighed separately from the pure abstraction of the guilty verdict: the man and his circumstances were not the subject of the verdict, and they failed to weigh sufficiently in any appeal against that abstract decision.

Capital punishment by lethal injection became the norm in the USA. Its resumption was marked with Gary Gilmore who opted, however, for the firing squad (Utah, 17 January 1977, the year when American's National Rifle Association (NRA) – founded in 1871, as one fall-out from the American Civil War – became less what it presented itself as being, a rifle club for hunting, than a political gun lobby, led by Harlon Carter). As part of the American 'New Right', the NRA insisted on a strong reading of the Second Amendment, giving individuals, not militias, the right to guns. Mailer memorializes Gilmore in *The Executioner's Song*, a text admirable in not objectifying him, unlike everything in the proceedings against him.[6] Unlike Gregg, Gilmore was not black – indeed Mailer notes his racism – coming from social deprivation which barely permitted him a chance. (The experiences in *The Executioner's Song* of Kathy Maynard, who tells her life in an interview (577–81), give an extraordinary sense, however, of how much humans can tolerate of the intolerable.)[7] Gilmore, born in 1940, with a father in prison (932), spent sixteen years in prison, then went through an intense on-off love affair with Nicole Baker, 19, twice divorced, with two children, and an ex-inmate of a mental hospital. They retained an intense love relationship through letters, and through suicide pacts at the time of Gilmore's two obviously pointless murders, committed within 48 hours of each other. He confessed and, asked why he had murdered, replied, 'Hey, I don't know. I don't have a reason' (288), though he acknowledged that he went in for compulsive behaviour (379, 380). The experts thought he had 'a personality disorder of the antisocial type'

---

[6] See Peggy Kamuf (translator for *The Death Penalty 1*), *Literature and the Remains of the Death Penalty* (New York: Fordham University Press 2019), 95–121; interesting analyses of texts following Derridean models.

[7] Norman Mailer, *The Executioner's Song* (London: Vintage 1979): page numbers in text. For the inadequacy of his defence, see Barbara Allen Babcock, 'Gary Gilmore's Lawyers', *Stanford Law Review* 32 (1980), 865–78. For the 'true life novel', see Robert M. Arlett, 'The Veiled Fist of a Master Executioner', *Crtiticism* 29 (1987), 215–32; Robert Merrill, 'Mailer's Sad Comedy: *The Executioner's Song*', *Texas Studies in Literature and Language* 34 (1992), 129–48.

(383). He waived his right to appeal, a fatal course since Utah had no automatic right of appeal against a death sentence.

The Executioner's Song's first half, 'Western Voices', gives Gilmore's life in Oregon and Utah – incidentally, the latter is currently one of the six American states with the highest suicide rates.[8] The second half, 'Eastern Voices', comments on the conflictual, and competing, post-sentencing discourses from New York and the East Coast, circulating from lawyers, medics and journalists, with different vested interests in the man, the sentence and what money could be made, especially for the journalist Lawrence Schiller who was buying exclusive rights to record people's recollections of Gilmore. These voices compelled postponement of the execution, and multiplied explanations for his behaviour. He gave several of these himself, post-sentence, all inadequate, often conforming to what was said about him: 'I was always capable of murder ... there's a side of me that I don't like. I can become totally devoid of feelings for others, unemotional. I know I'm doing something grossly fucking wrong. I can still go ahead and do it' (934). As Schiller's assistant, Barry Farrell, writes, speculating on a homosexual paedophilia in Gilmore, 'beware of understanding the man too quickly' (882). Perhaps the ability to don behavioural masks, which two people note as a Gilmore characteristic (673, 941) corresponds to a self-fashioning which was his only liberty.

Why the firing squad? An attraction to guns as American? Does fascination with murder and capital punishment create in the criminal the fantasy of being able to be present at the scene of his death? Such a fantasy, Elizabeth Rottenberg shows, activates, psychoanalytically, the attraction of the death penalty to judge and criminal alike. Derrida so discusses it (1.282). The fantasy is of control, even over the instant of death: hence Rottenberg quotes Gilmore giving his watch at his death to his girlfriend.[9] The fantasy might have activated Gilmore's desire to be shot, perhaps permitting, visually, the polarized situation of the state against the individual. Death by firing squad has been more reserved for enemies of the state, as with Brasillach: the last person thus executed in France, for instance, was Jean Bastien-Thiry – model for *The Day of the Jackal* – in 1963. The firing squad gives the simulacrum of dignity, as with Manet's pictures of the 'Emperor of Mexico'. Here, we see the Austrian Archduke Maximilian, executed on 19 June

---

[8] Anne Case and Angus Deaton, *Deaths of Despair and the Future of Capitalism* (Princeton: Princeton University Press 2020), 100.
[9] Elizabeth Rottenberg, 'Derrida and the Scene of Execution', in Kelly Oliver and Stephanie M. Straub (eds.), *Deconstructing the Death Penalty: Derrida's Seminars and the New Abolitionism* (New York: Fordham University Press 2018), 32–62.

1867, with two generals, Miguel Miramón and Tomás Mejía – the latter actually being shot – on either side. Manet shows six soldiers – plus one checking his rifle – shooting at point-blank range, the barrels of the guns seeming to connect with the victims. Behind the wall a group of Mexican peasants can be seen having scrambled up as if to see a bullfight.[10] The Mexican soldiers are dressed in, apparently, French uniforms, as if laying the blame for the execution on the colonial foreign policy of Napoleon III. Manet traces such shooting through the civil war and the fighting during the Commune (Adler, figs. 101, 102, 103, 104). He shows in Maximilian a gentlemanly innocence incapable of getting beyond his own illusions – relatedly, his wife Charlotte went mad in 1866, dying so in 1927. The soldier inspecting his gun shows 'the institutionalisation of death and violence endemic to modern society'.[11] If that suggests the surveillance of *Discipline and Punish*, then that is what the firing squad embodies, and what an army and modern warfare must include.

We have discussed Blanchot before the firing squad. *The Instant of my Death* ends with a meeting with André Malraux, to whom a similar near-death befell. The difference between these two near-deaths lies in Malraux seeing death as sacrifical, for the nation, and capable of mythicization.[12] Such mythicizing – of the nation, of state authority – had been practised by the Tsar in Dostoevsky's case; Lacoue-Labarthe (11–12) notes, from Bataille, that Manet's portrayal of the execution of Maximilian implies 'an absolute detachment'; he finds apathy, indifference, numbness in the picture. Manet, like Blanchot, will not mythicize the death sentence, but possibly the firing squad, more than other forms of execution, permits such myth-creating presentations of death as sacrifice. Hence Maximilian is supposed to have died praying 'that my blood which is about to be shed' will be 'for the good of the country'.[13] Did Gilmore's death imply a similar romanticism? Derrida cites Freud for people's disbelief in their own death: 'in the unconscious, everyone of us is convinced of his own immortality' (2.69–70).[14] Gilmore, like Eichmann, believed in reincarnation, which would illustrate

---

[10] Kathleen Adler, *Manet* (Oxford: Phaidon 1986), 110–18, see especially fig. 113 (the Mannheim version).

[11] Kristine Ibsen, 'Spectacle and Spectator in Edouard Manet's *Execution of Maximilian*', *Oxford Art Journal* 29 (2006), 213–26, 224.

[12] Leslie Hill, *Bataille Klossowski, Blanchot: Writing at the Limit* (Oxford: Oxford University Press 2001), 189–91.

[13] Juliet Wilson-Bareau, with John House and Douglas Johnson, *Manet: The Execution of Maximilian Painting, Politic and Censorship* (London: National Gallery 1992), 59.

[14] Freud, 'Thoughts for the Times on War and Death', *SE* 14.289. On the phantasm in Derrida, see Michael Naas, '"Comme si, comme ça": Phantasms of Self, State, and a Sovereign God', *Mosaic* 40 (2007), 1–26.

and strengthen that point. It is not possible to imagine not-being; which makes any such imagining life and death together what Derrida calls 'a fantasmatic virtuality' (*BS* 2.130, see also 2.157). The fantasm is a dream of almightiness, of sovereignty over life and death; it is how one would like to see reality, and there may be no other way to see it. That does not mean any less that the fantasm puts the self at the centre, as in all mythicizing practices and in the elevation of sacrifice.

Timothy McVeigh

Executions recommenced in the USA after Gilmore's shooting. An Anti-Drugs Abuse Act (1988) licensed injecting pentobarbital for some murders and for drug offences (the 'war on drugs' had been proclaimed in 1971). A recent report indicated how much states such as Arizona, Tennessee or Missouri were prepared to pay unknown sources for supplies of pentobarbital sodium salt, and midazolam, vecuronium bromide and potassium chloride – three drugs apparently used together – for executions.[15] The 1980s legislation was strengthened by the Violent Crime Control and Law Enforcement Act (1994).[16] Timothy McVeigh's bombing of the Alfred P. Murrah Federal Building in Oklahoma on April 1995, killing 168 people, came on the second anniversary of the FBI's assault on David Koresh's apocalyptic Branch Davidian sect at Waco, Texas. It prompted from the Republican-dominated American Congress an Anti-terrorism and Effective Death Penalty Act (1996). This, making it easier to remove aliens suspected of terrorism, and intensifying the dominion of federal law enforcement over state law, ensured that federal power could carry out the death penalty. It permitted McVeigh's execution (11 June 2001, aged 33), under the federal government legislation for what the press called 'the worst act of domestic terrorism ever carried out on American soil'.[17]

Terrorism becomes labelled not the act of the state, as in the French Revolution, but something committed by individuals against the state, its definition including

---

[15] Ed Pilkington, *The Guardian*, 10 April 2021. See *The Guardian*, 22 May 2022, for details of Arizona giving a prisoner a choice of cyanide gas or possibly faulty lethal injections – which made his lawyers try to argue for death by firing squad.
[16] Stuart Banner, *The Death Penalty: An American History* (Cambridge, MA: Harvard University Press 2002), 303 notes that, between 1987 and 1999, sixty-one inmates of death row were released on discovery of their innocence.
[17] Quoted, Stuart A. Wright, *Patriots, Politics, and the Oklahoma City Bombing* (Cambridge: Cambridge University Press 2007), 4. See also Wright's edited collection, *Armageddon in Waco: Critical Perspectives on the Branch Davidian Conflict* (Chicago: University of Chicago Press 1995).

killing innocent people, a practice enshrined in twentieth-century warfare. McVeigh's death was transmitted to an audience of 232 bomb survivors and relatives in Oklahoma City. His accomplice Terry Nichols was imprisoned, but the sociologist Stuart Wright's study of the bombing makes clear that there were others; that McVeigh was part of a 'Patriot movement', and that it is deeply oversimplifying to see him as the single 'great criminal', and his – perhaps any 'terrorism' – as a lone act.[18] Terrorism as a more solitary act appears with the teenagers Eric Harris and Dylan Klebold, shooting twelve students, a teacher and themselves at Columbine High School, Colorado (20 April 1999), in a planned paramilitary assault which was influenced by McVeigh, but was motivated by various forms of self-hatred and paranoid reactions to others, suicidal in character.[19]

Wright implies that this desire to singularize McVeigh was part of the policy of the NRA which wanted to distinguish itself from other far-right groups with whom McVeigh was associated. McVeigh, who had fought in the Gulf War, believed that the Waco siege, which had begun with the evidence of high-powered weaponry possessed in the compound, but which ended with some eighty dead in a fire caused either by FBI aggression or mass suicide, had shown the US government making war on Americans. As the rhetoric of the pro-gun lobby insisted, and as was proclaimed by protesters at Waco, 'A Man with a Gun is a Citizen. A Man without a Gun is a Subject' (Wright, 163). Hence the pressure for the 1996 change in the law.

McVeigh's attitude to the killings was curiously abstract. He told Wright in prison that it was not enough to bomb a building: 'there had to be a body count' (Wright, 5). The bombing – the terrorism – was, then, thought of as a war; there *had* to be body bags. Wright traces McVeigh's statement to the white supremacist James Ellison, saying in 1983: '[W]e need something with a large body count to make the government sit up and take notice' (quoted, Wright, 191). Terrorism has become like theatre and bodies are not specifically targeted; they are there for an audience to witness. In contrast to this, victims and their families are exhorted to find 'closure' in the execution of one person separated in his thinking from the reality of what he was involved in. The theatricality of McVeigh's execution, paralleling the desire to see body bags, contained the desire to diminish sharp divides within American society, of which he and his behaviour

---

[18] A point reinforced in Franco de Masi, *The Enigma of the Suicide Bomber: A Psychoanalytic Essay*, trans. Philip Slotkin (London: Karnac Books 2011), xii.
[19] See Ralph W. Larkin, *Comprehending Columbine* (Philadelphia: Temple University Press 2007).

were symptomatic. Capital punishment becomes an alibi for evading the exploration of these deeper conflicts, allowing the government to become more reactionary. In 2019, the US Department of Justice, under Attorney-General William Barr, directed the Federal Bureau of Prisons (Terre Haute, Indiana) to begin executions again after a lapse since 2003. From 14 July 2020 to 15 December 2020, ten people suffered the death penalty, including some *after* Donald Trump's defeat in the presidential election, one of Trump's parting gifts to the nation, alongside the gallows erected in the Mall in Washington DC on the occasion of the 6 January 2021 attack on the Capitol.[20]

Another fall-out from the Oklahoma bombing was Marsha Kight, the mother of one of those killed, lobbying for the Victim Rights Clarification Act (1997), to give legal standing to victims. Thus, a recent feature marking the death penalty in the US has been, since *Payne v. Tennessee* (1991), the admission of victim impact statements, offering another 'justification' for the death penalty: the harm done to families of the victims, so contributing to a new culture of revenge. Producing a 'victim culture', if that is what it is, has changed perceptions of criminality, producing a desire to increase punishment, especially when the criminal becomes more identified with the 'other'.

Terror and suicide

Three months after McVeigh's execution came the 9/11 attacks on New York and Washington DC. Suicide-killers replaced McVeigh's form of terrorism, in which he had no intention of being killed. People wanting to die makes the difference; we have here two forms of terrorism. This is a different world from Dickens, though he knew of the Orsini plot to blow up Napoleon III (14 January 1858). Dickens would have understood Capote and Mailer, but he could have had comparatively little sense of terrorism against the state, nor of the continuity between the licensing of state violence in the name of George W. Bush's 'war on terror', announced after 9/11, or the extent to which mass killings could go. He could not have visualized aerial bombings or war crimes or the genocides of the twentieth and twenty-first centuries. But this is Derrida's world.

---

[20] Austin Sarat, 'Trump is spending the last days of his presidency on a literal killing spree', *The Guardian*, 15 December 2020. For Lisa Montgomery's death, see *The Guardian*, 14 January 2021. The last men executed on Trump's watch were Corey Johnson, 14 January 2021, and Dustin Higgs, 16 January 2021: see BBC News online. See Sarah Churchwell, *The Observer*, 3 July 2022.

Genocidal wars, learning from imperialism and dwarfing 'terrorism' in the numbers destroyed, have prompted a responding terrorism. Modern terrorism is governmental *and* anti-governmental. The process, in its mutuality, illustrates Derrida's 'auto-immunisation', which, as a self-destructive drive, applies to the mentalities of the suicide-bombers, but hints that something in the US unconsciously attracted such aggression against itself, and which then allowed it to take the high ground as the victim (3,000 Americans died in the attacks of 11 September 2001, plus the suicide-terrorists). The most powerful country in the world exhibits Nietzschean *ressentiment*, representing itself as weaker than the aggressor, which has seized the initiative, challenging how the dominant capitalist form represents itself in spectacular form, in the symbolism of the *World* Trade Center towers (my italics). which were destroyed.[21] That more Marxist analysis, deriving from the arguments of the 'society of the spectacle' (Guy Debord), exceeds Derrida.

How does terror relate to a revolutionary act? For Žižek, the latter means jumping outside a revolutionary state into the sphere of contingency. This, which he calls an 'act', brings about the disappearance of the subject, within the *passage à l'acte*, which was discussed earlier with reference to Lacan. In this *passage* the subject suddenly flees the scene, going for the impossible and traumatic Real, rather than remaining inside the symbolic order.[22] The *passage à l'acte*, much more intense than its contrary, 'acting out', where the subject stages its affectual state, involves loss of ego, loss of self. Hence Slavoj Žižek argues:

> [A] revolution is achieved (not betrayed) when it 'eats its own children', the excess that was necessary to set it in motion. In other words, the ultimate revolutionary ethical stance is not that of simple devotion and fidelity to the Revolution, but, rather, that of willingly accepting the role of 'vanishing mediator', of the excessive executioner to be executed (as the 'traitor') so that the Revolution can achieve its ultimate goal.[23]

Žižek's 'vanishing mediator' is one whose individual agency does not survive a transition from one state to another, which he or she helps effect. There is something 'terroristic' within an authentic act, because the actor cannot survive

---

[21] Iain A. Boal, T. J. Clark, Joseph Matthews and Michael Watts, *Afflicted Powers: Capital and Spectacle in a New Age of War* (London: Verso 2005).

[22] See Jacques Lacan, *Anxiety: The Seminar of Jacques Lacan Book X*, ed. Jacques Alain-Miller, trans. A. R. Price (Cambridge: Polity Press 2018), 114–30.

[23] Quoted from Žižek, *The Ticklish Subject* (London: Verso 1999), 379 by Marc de Kesel, 'Act without Denial: Slavoj Žižek on Totalitarianism, Revolution, and Political Act', *Studies in East European Thought* 56 (2004), 299–334, quotation 321–2 (Žižek, 374–9).

the act, and is not the same at the end as at the beginning. The act is a jump into 'the Object (the Thing), i.e. into that which always already has dropped out from the Other (the symbolic order)' (De Kesel, 324). For, in summarizing Žižek's thought, De Kesel argues that 'the basis of politics will always be something radically excluded from it, and, speaking in the name of the excluded, politics must at the same time forever remain open to the excluded "Thing"'. This makes an act of terror like suicide a loss of self and of any position that the self might want to assume or has the language to assume. Žižek suggests that there are moments in Robespierre where his position is like the *passage à l'acte*.[24] When Žižek cites the 'revolution devouring its children', he takes that positively, meaning that the act finds its subject at the end of the process. How it finishes is not how it starts. Its onwards motion entails the loss of what was expected or wanted at the beginning. Though criticizing Robespierre, Žižek insists that a left politics cannot refuse a history which includes revolutionary terror, because 'that which produces the general good is always terrible' (Saint-Just, quoted, Žižek, 160), or, as Robespierre asked, 'Citizens, do you want a revolution without a revolution?' (Ducange, 43, Žižek, 161).

Remembering Benjamin's 'divine violence', Žižek says its 'motto' must be '*fiat iustitia, pereat mundus*' (let justice be, let the world perish). He cites Robespierre's idealism in his last speech, quoting from his stated 'deep horror of tyranny' and asserts that 'it does exist':

> that compassionate zeal for the oppressed, that sacred love for the homeland, that even more sublime and holy love for humanity, without which a great revolution is just a noisy crime that destroys another crime ... that generous ambition to establish here on earth the world's first republic.
>
> Ducange, 159–60

Yet Robespierre's unqualified adjectives ignore the unconscious which disturbs all purity. The death penalty is being justified in terms of doing good – but to whom? Žižek validates Robespierre by saying that 'love without cruelty is powerless, cruelty without love is blind',[25] but these absolutist statements are made to justify violence in terms of doing good. A non-Nietzscheanism in Žižek declares:

---

[24] Slavoj Žižek, *In Defence of Lost Causes* (London: Verso 2017), 157–210.
[25] Žižek, *Violence*, 173.

> [I]t is through *justice*, the point of non-distinction between justice and vengeance, that the 'people', the anonymous part of no-part [i.e. the remainder, those who have neither names nor papers] imposes its terror and makes other parts pay the price – Judgment Day for the long history of oppression, exploitation, suffering.
>
> *In Defence of Lost Causes* 142

The Genealogy of Morals does not so elide justice and vengeance. Justice can never be self-evident, but is likely to tip into the injustice and *ressentiment* of revenge, including the death penalty. Vengeance, while not disowning that name, presents itself as justice, on the assumption of absolute equality with the Terror, or the guillotine, as that presented itself historically. If justice and revenge *can* be elided, that is because justice was always, secretly, revenge, because there has always been a previous history of injustice, and justice can never slice through things and pretend that the past is all evened up in a single act ambiguously named justice or revenge. No act can be one of purity, which is what terror, especially revolutionary Terror, or capital punishment pretends to be, though perhaps not even that, sometimes.[26]

Considering the suicide-terrorists of 11 September 2001, and the deaths and destruction caused, Alain Badiou finds in operation the 'disjunctive synthesis of two nihilisms' – one, that of advanced American capitalism, showing its hand in retaliation: 'striking blindly to demonstrate one's strike capacity', while, with the 'terrorists',

> nothing speaks louder than the silence, the terrible silence of the authors and planners of this crime. For with affirmative, liberating, non-nihilistic political violence not only is responsibility always claimed, but its essence is found in claiming responsibility.

Here, however, 'the act remains unnamed and anonymous, just like the culprits, this being 'the infallible sign of a type of fascist nihilism'. He calls the American side

> nihilistic in its extensive form, the market having become worldwide; nihilistic in its fetishization of the formalism of communication, and nihilist in its extreme political poverty, that is to say, in the absence of any project other than its

---

[26] Jean Paulhan, *The Flowers of Tarbes or Terror in Literature*, trans. Michael Syrotinski (Urbana: University of Illinois Press 2006) discusses the impossibility of literature being 'terrorist'; it is always inseparable from tradition. Blanchot's sense of its possible purity, which is glanced at in 'Literature and the Right to Death', is criticized by Derrida for its totalitarian possibilities in the *Death Penalty* seminar 1, 111–20.

perpetuation of American hegemony and of vassalage, made as comfortable as possible, for the others.[27]

Derrida supports the Americans more, finding that bin Laden's terrorism, given its fundamentalism, offers no future, and so gives his preference for the side attacked in 11 September, which he says does so offer a future. But that pro-American position looks complacent, and that terrorism *did* have an agenda (e.g. in relation to the Middle East).[28] Derrida says the two sides are not separate; the conditions and opportunities for terrorism were manufactured in the United States; both shared in 'self-destructive, quasi-suicidal, auto-immunitary processes' (115).[29] The affinity may be affirmed since both the USA and the Islamic sources of 'terrorism' have theological tendencies, which make them see bodies in limiting ways. But in addition, there is the sense of the body as caught up in global networks of information, which cause estrangement within those religious groups, and a sense that autonomy, especially over the body, has been lost. Hence terrorism conventionally understood takes corporeal revenge against 'the decorporealising and expropriating machine':

> What is referred to as 'killings' and 'atrocities' – words never used in 'clean' or 'proper' wars ... is here supplanted by tortures, mutilations, and beheadings of all sorts. What is involved is always vengeance, often declared as sexual revenge: rapes, mutilated genitals or severed hands, corpses exhibited, heads paraded.
> 'Faith and Knowledge', 88

Terrorism is inseparable from – grows with – war, and other forms of violence.[30] But acts of suicide-terrorism are usually less programmed, or financed, than in '9/11'; they are acts of desperation where the first question to be asked is whether the bomber acted alone, or as part of a concealed group. Rejecting the

---

[27] Alain Badiou, *Infinite Thought: Truth and the Return to Philosophy*, trans. Oliver Feltham and Justin Clements (London: Continuum 2005), 119–20.

[28] Giovanna Borradori, *Philosophy in a Time of Terror: Dialogues with Jörgen Habermas and Jacques Derrida* (Chicago: University of Chicago Press 2005), 113–14. Michel Rosenfeld, 'Derrida's Ethical Turn: The Case of Terrorism', in Peter Goodrich, Florian Hoffmann, Michel Rosenfeld and Cornelia Vismann (eds.), *Derrida and Legal Philosophy* (London: Palgrave Macmillan 2008), 71–98.

[29] Marc Redfield, 'Virtual Traumas: The Idiom of 9/11', *Diacritics* 37 (2007) 54–80 instances Derrida finding three versions of auto-immunity in 9/11: (1) a 'quasi-suicidal' activity working in 'all processes of capitalisation and technologisation': 'the threat comes from the "inside": the terrorists exploited the technology of the superpower and guarantor of world order, in attacking the symbolic "head" of that order; (2) the threat, though a Cold War legacy, comes from the "future" as the traumatic possibility of a worse disaster to come; and (3) the threat is exacerbated by efforts to defend against it' (77). Compare Martin McQuillan, 'Introduction' to *Deconstruction After 9/11* (London: Routledge 2009), 10–11.

[30] See Borradori, 110 (and discussion 91–110).

characterization of the suicide-terrorist in terms of theological motivation, and including such other terrorist incidents as the Columbine shootings of 1999, Talal Asad in *On Suicide Bombing* analysed them in terms of suicidal desperation, and of warfare where the body is expected to die anyway. The horror that others feel at this is not at 'dying and killing (or killing by dying), but from the violent appearance of something that is normally disregarded in secular modernity: the limitless pursuit of freedom, the illusion of an uncoerced interiority that can withstand the force of institutional disciplines' (Asad, 91). The terrorist brings out something which is repressed in ordinary life (the horror felt at the Septembrist 'terrorists' in *A Tale of Two Cities* is referable to this), and has gone beyond institutional disciplines whose 'biopower' is seen as a repression of the body in bringing the body back, if only in the terroristic act of suicide in front of someone else, which is horrific, and especially for the witnesses.

Asad continues that the assumption that 'the meaning of life is death' – that death is the significant action, and the one prevailing over others – dominates the suicide terrorist, who is both criminal, and agent of law in killing himself, exerting crime and punishment together in the act. This defeats attempts to judge the case by normal liberal standards which would separate these two. The suicide-terrorist takes over the work of violence which the state claims for itself. To this Asad adds another point, which disallows thinking of the suicide-terrorist as an exception to the principles by which the modern state runs its affairs. The first two sentences here rely on Benjamin's 'Critique of Violence':

> Liberalism, of course, disapproves of the violent exercise of freedom outside the frame of law. But the law is founded by and continuously depends on coercive violence. If modern war seeks to found a free political community with its own law, can one say that suicide terrorism (like a suicidal nuclear strike) belongs, in this sense, to liberalism?
>
> 91–2

The double action of the suicide-terrorist – killing, and punishing killing – brings out the dichotomy in the state, which also does these things, but which, by keeping these actions apart, represses its share in violence.

To Asad's sobering judgment we may add that capital punishment in the USA is inseparable from the violence characterizing some egregious forms of fundamentalist 'Islamic' terrorism (Asad gives many reasons justifying the scare quotes here, and we may think of some of the tortures inflicted by the Ku Klux Klan, to which he does refer, as terrorist activities). A return of violence in both blocks of power – the USA and 'radical' Islam – may mark a fantasy, which involves nostalgia for the directness of the body, and its powers of agency, which globalization is felt to have expropriated and nullified. Nostalgia, however, is always unreal: definitionally, it claims a past which never existed. Derrida's last quoted point from 'Faith and Knowledge', quoted above, holds there: the attempt to claim agency is violent. Officially practised, capital punishment may resemble the act of terrorism, and neither are separate from revenge.

In Conclusion

Dickens cannot be contained in the nineteenth century, and while many novelists have done more specialist work than he, his oeuvre challenges comparison with any other attempt to write modern life, its affiliations being with Shakespeare, Nietzsche and Freud, and writers of a modernist Marxism. A Venn diagram would connect these names with Derrida, most self-conscious of (anti-) philosophers, and make the comparison which this book has attempted inevitable. This conclusion, without revisiting material already discussed, considers the problems that these two great writers are held by, and which make abolition impossible.

'New cruelty'

'Everything he did was bold and audacious and cruel and greedy, and I am really very very sorry', finished Miss Marple, looking as fierce as a fluffy old lady can look, 'that they have abolished capital punishment because I do feel that if there is anyone who ought to hang, it's Dr Quimper.'

'Hear hear', said Inspector Craddock.[1]

Though the death penalty has been abolished in many countries, national ideologies – which Dickens satirized, outstandingly with Mr Podsnap's contempt for what is 'not English', in the high tide of Britain's imperial rule (*OMF* 1.11.137) – keep it alive as a fantasy. It is refreshed for us through 'nice' detective fiction, like that of Agatha Christie (1890–1976), still popular, especially through adaptations of her detective novels and plays, offering simple solutions to fictionalized problems, proposing that one person is to blame for a societal issue.

---

[1] Agatha Christie, *4.50 from Paddington* (London: the Agatha Christie Collection: AC Publishing 1949), 222.

Fluffy old ladies – e.g. Miss Marple, of the fantasizd village of St Mary Mead – sanitize by their apparent harmlessness what the death penalty means, and her word 'cruel' prevents the reader seeing the cruelty of what she says she wants. And should any law enforcement agency be so openly up for violence as opposed to justice in the law courts, as Inspector Craddock, taking a lead from the amateur detective? Many unconscious attitudes (the very Q of the murderer's name insinuates villainy, or queerness) get fed in via such gentle-violent utterances.

Given 1949 as the date of *4.50 from Paddington*, Miss Marple was referring to the Labour government's attempt, under Home Secretary James Chuter Ede, to abolish the death penalty. The House of Lords prevented it, though it stopped whipping in prisons. Christie's fluffy disinformation was strangling abolition in the cradle. 65 per cent of the population were then against abolition, though moves towards that had resumed after 1868, with the Humanitarian League, which also campaigned against bloodsports, and the Howard League for Penal Reform (1921).[2] The British government shot 327 men for desertion during World War One: abolition of this practice was led by Labour MP Ernest Thurtle.[3] In 1934 the Labour Party committed itself to total abolition; failure after 1945 meant Clement Attlee (Prime Minister) creating a Royal Commission to investigate abolition. Nonetheless, inertia meant that the National Campaign for the Abolition of Capital Punishment needed relaunching in August 1955 after the hanging of the last of fifteen women in the twentieth century, Ruth Ellis (13 July 1955, Holloway Prison). The Homicide Act, restricting the death penalty and admitting diminished responsibility as a defence, came in 1957, and was in abeyance after Sydney Silverman (1895-1968)'s November 1965 Private Members' Bill.[4] Abolition in the UK followed in December 1969.

Agatha Christie's agenda is nostalgic, evoking a day when murderers were safely executed, and the influence she has had on a certain conservative demographic illustrates the power of manipulation of public feelings. Unfortunately, the gallows *can* be brought back, as happened in a rape/murder

---

[2] James B. Christoph, *Capital Punishment and British Politics: The British Movement to Abolish the Death Penalty 1945-1957* (London: George Allen & Unwin 1962), 35-75.

[3] See Anthony Babington, *For the Sake of Example: Capital Courts-Martial 1914-1920* (London: Leo Cooper 1993); Julian Putkowski and Julian Sykes, *Shot at Dawn* (Barnsley: Wharncliffe Publishing 1989); Gerard Oram, *Worthless Men: Race, Eugenics. and the Death Penalty in the British Army in the First World War* (London: Francis Boutle 1998).

[4] See Jonathan Goodman and Patrick Pringle, *The Trial of Ruth Ellis* (Newton Abbot: David & Charles 1974) and Emrys Hughes, *Sydney Silverman: The Rebel in Parliament* (London: Charles Skilton 1969), 95-112, 144-56, 171-82.

case in Delhi, which became international news, and showed *ressentiment* feeding punishment and crime and nationalism alike. On 20 March 2020, at 5.30 a.m., four men were hanged in Tihar Jail, Delhi: Mukesh Singh, 32, Arkshay Singh Thakur, 31, Pauran Gupta, 25, a fruit seller, and Vinay Sharma, 26, a gym instructor, convicted of rape, with murder added later. Mohammed Afroz, 17, from Uttar Pradesh, was classed as a juvenile, and sentenced to three years in a remand home. Another, Ram Singh, the brother of Mukesh, who was 23 in 2012, from Rajasthan, hanged himself in prison on 11 March 2013 in questionable circumstances.[5] Mukesh Singh, Vinay Sharma and Ram Singh lived in the Ravi Das slum in Delhi, among many outsiders to Delhi.

Mukesh Singh had been the bus driver on 16 December 2012, when Jyoti Singh Pandey, a physiotherapist intern, was raped on the private bus which she and her male friend, after a cinema visit, had been invited onto by these men, as though the bus was going towards their destination. The men, alcohol-fuelled, were joyriding. The friend, Awindra Pratap Pandey, was also attacked, and both were thrown off the bus. Jyoti Singh, whose name was withheld, and given as 'Nirbhaya' ('fearless') died of her injuries – including hideous penetration with iron rods – in a Singapore hospital, on 29 December. Protests, and national and international press coverage, commented on India's casual frequency of rape and degradation of women, and its selective reporting – in India, obviously, with the rape of Dalits.[6] There were calls for castration (as Kant had recommended),[7] and capital punishment, as with the woman's parents, though many women activists spoke against the death penalty, which in India is reserved only for 'the rarest of rare cases'. Convicted in September 2013, the subsequent time was spent in appeals, each considered separately and sequentially. India's law was changed in 2013 to allow these executions.[8]

On 27 November 2019, near Hyderabad, a 27-year-old veterinarian was raped and murdered. A tyre of her bike, parked at a highway toll plaza, from which she took a bus to work, had been deflated; the men offered to help, dragged her off, and afterwards burned her body in the underpass of a national highway. The case

---

[5] 'Profile: Delhi rape accused: Ram Singh', *BBC News*, 11 March 2013.
[6] Anand Teltumbde, 'Delhi Gang Rape Case: Some Uncomfortable Questions', *Economic and Political Weekly*, 9 February 2013, 10–11. For the demonization of the gang as migrants from 'medieval' villages, see Poulami Roychowdhury, '"The Delhi Gang Rape": The Making of International Causes', *Feminist Studies* 39 (2013), 282–92.
[7] B. Sharon Byrd, 'Kant's Theory of Punishment: Deterrence in Its Threat, Retribution in Its Execution', *Law and Philosophy* 8 (1989), 151–200, 152.
[8] *Indian Express*, 21 March 2020; *The Guardian*, 20 March 2020.

aroused agitation for its similarity to the Delhi case, and protesters gathered outside the prison. Four men accused of this rape were arrested and taken from Cherlapally prison on 6 December by ten members of the Telangana police to the crime scene in the early hours of the morning, apparently to look for clues. In what the police called an 'encounter', they were shot dead at 6.30 a.m. The *Indian Express* reported that the family of the woman thanked the police and the government, the father saying, 'My daughter's soul must be at peace now', while crowds at the scene praised a 'quick delivery of justice ... justice is done ... we are very happy that justice has been delivered to the victim's family without wasting much time'.[9] The newspaper added how poor, corrupt policing, and legal delays, produced vigilante reactions from the public, and, since many politicians supported the police, that 'India's political class is choosing to whip up a toxic primal anger that never lies too far beneath this grossly unequal society'.[10] *Ressentiment* indeed, created by playing on a sense of chaos which has been created and manipulated. Legal delays, populist politicians, police corruption, and people's sense that justice is not being done accelerated this police violence/murder. Victimhood makes voices heard which have been silenced, as with violence against women, but is also used by atavistic voices to force justice's hand.

Rape focuses attention on masculinity, whose need for display of power must have exceeded sexual desire, for the men were not specifically looking for a sexual opportunity. Gang rape, especially within India's neoliberalism, may be a way wherein disempowered males feel they are not 'losers'. It has something of a reaction-formation quality. The BBC reported Mukesh Singh saying, '[A] decent girl won't roam around at night. A girl is far more responsible for rape than a boy. Housework and housekeeping is for girls, not roaming in discos and bars doing wrong things, wearing wrong clothes. About 20% of girls are good.'[11] Such a perception makes rape a blow struck at the globalizing modernity which excludes these men, who feel that some women, like the intern, have done better than them.[12] Rape then justifies itself as cleaning up the neighbourhood, so reflecting back onto the conditions of crowded slum-living, as well as being nostalgia for non-existent male power.[13] Hence hatred of women, whom slum

---

[9] *Indian Express*, 7 December 2019.
[10] 'Crime as Punishment', Editorial, *Indian Express*, 7 December 2019.
[11] 'Delhi Rapist says victim shouldn't have fought back', *BBC News*, 3 March 2015. See also 'Profiles: Who were the Delhi gang rape convicts?', *BBC News*, 20 March 2020.
[12] On sexual harassment of women, see Jacqueline Rose, *On Violence and On Violence Against Women* (London: Faber & Faber 2021). The classic study for rape as men controlling women is Susan Brownmiller, *Against our Will: Men, Women and Rape* (New York: Simon & Shuster 1975).
[13] For rape and hate crime, see Mark Austin Walters and Jessica Tumath, 'Gender "Hostility", Rape, and the Hate Crime Paradigm', *The Modern Law Review* 77 (2014), 563–96.

conditions degrade worse than men, and hatred of women, perhaps originating from fear, since only 20 per cent are declared 'good', i.e. controllable, or unmotivated by their own sexual feelings. As Mukesh Singh continued, 'people' 'had a right to teach them the lesson', and the woman should have put up with it. 'When being raped, she shouldn't fight back. She should just be silent and allow the rape. Then they'd have dropped her off after "doing her", and only hit the boy.' Further:

> [T]he death penalty will make things even more dangerous for girls. Now, when they rape, they won't leave the girl like we did. They will kill her. Before, they would rape and say, 'Leave her, she won't tell anyone'. Now when they rape, especially the criminal types, they will just kill the girl.

There may be discerned a rapport – identification almost – which the criminal wants with the victim. Neither tells, or both die. It supports Camus's footnote: '[I]t is possible to read every week in the papers of criminals who originally hesitated between killing themselves and killing others' (Camus, 191).[14] That the death penalty excites a harder punishing of the victim comes from Dickens's third public letter. The woman is made instrumental in a contest of forms of violence, inside male–male rivalry, or hatred, producing violence towards the male friend. Guilt, and inadequacy, produces the impulse to become the 'superego' which by violating pretends it punishes. If Ram Singh was murdered in prison, that might have been a Hyderabad-like 'encounter', displaying male violence coming from a sense of guilt, expressed in the 'narcissism of minor differences'. (Freud's phrase, SE 11.199). If gang violence succeeded gang rape, this male–male solidarity, if not homoeroticism, implies that the assailant finds validity not from the victim (the frustration inside rape is that there is no question of gaining the desire of the other) but other males.

If Mukesh Singh said what was reported, rape becomes a vigilante act, policing women's sexuality by teaching them, followed by police vigilantism; policemen have a track record in raping and killing women. Capital punishment becomes state vigilantism, which public pressure makes weakness disguised as strength, confirming Judith Butler, that there can be no mere instrumental form of violence not prompting a further culture of violence: '[T]he use of violence only makes the world a more violent place, by bringing more violence into the world.'[15] Such punishment is a confession of helplessness. Easier to hang people than to

---

[14] For Camus and the Delhi case, see Manash Bhattacharjee, 'The Imperturbable Machine: Albert Camus on Capital Punishment', *Economic and Political Weekly* 48 (23 February 2013), 10–12.
[15] Judith Butler, *The Force of Non-Violence: An Ethico-Political Bind* (London: Verso 2020), 20.

accept that they have come from totally miserable conditions, meaning that to leave them alone is almost punishment enough. No one will clear up the misery of the slums, which is where any concept of remedial action must begin. We recall Mr Jaggers's comments about children only growing up to be hanged – and who considers alternatives to prison?[16] Tabloid journalism, building a fantasized national consensus whose concomitant is heteronormative masculinity, would rather reveal the names of those who are given new identities or encourage throwing away the prison key.

Vigilantism, combined with a sense that the nation is defined by protective white males who compensate for their lack of productive power in the community by the assertion of masculinity with gun possession, is promoted by America's NRA.[17] The ideology which shoots to defend white people against fantasized threats from blacks or Latinos enables America's capital punishments. Shooting – of animals or people – gives the illusion of control (hunting gives the fantasy of winning a war). Crime and punishment follows a pattern of repetition, repetition denying an origin for events. The uncanny prevalence of repetition means that, for Derrida, it launches castration fears, out of a sense of a loss of autonomy, an inability to do things differently.[18]

In 2015, Western media published images of beheadings of Western hostages – carried out by ISIS (the Islamic State of Iraq and Syria), a group which became prominent with the Iraqi Abu Bakr al-B'aghdadi (1971–2019) being proclaimed a caliph (the supreme ruler in Islam) in June 2014. ISIS, self-replacing al-Quaeda, moved into Syria in 2013, targeting and 'purifying' other Muslim groups. The punishment normally carried out by the state as an act of terror has been commandeered by the terrorist, whose role is to punish. The Kuwaiti-born, London-educated Mohammed Emwazi (b. 1988 – killed in a US airstrike in November 2015), called 'Jihadi John' by the *Spectator*, was the ISIS executioner, and the beheading image shows what is implicit from the 'great criminal' through to the suicide-terrorist: capital punishment is being ironized when terrorism gets its revenge in first, and attempts to be original, autonomous. But repetition follows. The 'war on terror' whose language means that rules of warfare and international law need not be respected, since no definable 'war' is happening,

---

[16] See Andrew Coyle, 'Replacing the Death Penalty: The Vexed Question of Alternative Sanctions', in Peter Hodgkinson and William A. Schabas (eds.), *Capital Punishment: Strategies for Abolition* (Cambridge: Cambridge University Press 2004), 92–115.

[17] Jennifer Carson, *Citizen-Protectors: The Everyday Politics of Guns in an Age of Decline* (Oxford: Oxford University Press 2015), 163–71.

[18] Derrida, *Dissemination*, trans. Barbara Johnson (Chicago: University of Chicago Press 1981), 220, 272.

was reinforced by the language of 'the axis of evil' (so George W. Bush), attempting to co-opt the sanctions of sacredness and theology. 'Evil', however, is the rhetoric of ISIS taking on 'the West', especially its 'liberal' sexual values. Beyond formal differences between these cultures, they share much, as with their mutual belief in punishment by execution.

The Delhi rapists showed extreme cruelty, and if murder's 'justification' is the attempt to assert identity, securing that over the other's body, however cruelly, the attempt to assert sovereignty must learn that 'the one who kills is *always* his victim's inferior'.[19] Nabakov's point bears out much in Dickens's examples of where it is 'better to be Abel than Cain' (*OMF* 685). Derrida names psychoanalysis that which should be 'turned toward what is most *proper* to psychical cruelty'. He notes that, for Freud, cruelty has neither a contrary term nor an end.[20] Derrida notes, however, a 'new cruelty' ('Faith and Knowledge', 89), emanating from 'targeted killings' and 'surgical strikes' (a phrase which echoes the last plate of *Four Stages of Cruelty*) in drone strikes, i.e. from unmanned aerial vehicles (UAVs). Such drones create terror in the target populations, e.g. Pakistan, Afghanistan, Yemen, Iraq and Somalia. Terror and hyper-cruelty go together, the latter exceeding any scale a body could deal with, erasing all possibility of contending against it. But it is an incitement to older forms of cruelty in terrorism, for instance, where the body is again the focus, and on display.

That point shows, for Dickens, in how he writes about the Septembrists. Fascination with their bodies, which is exceptional in him, and more weighty because of that, comes from knowing that they speak for a new, direct assertion of, or fighting for, power. Dickens's debt to *Macbeth* has often been noticed, and has been a leitmotif throughout this book because the play shows the same fascination with blood and reaction against it, and identification with excess, if not madness, which Dickens's texts also have. Dickens seems prescient in seeing that the power and excess the terrorists claim is in proportion to the extent that modernity dispropriates, delegitimizes, the body, a point Chapter VI stressed.

The power desired contrasts with drone warfare-at-a-distance, which cynically destroys bodies without affecting the sovereign state, America, whose nihilism, even while affecting to honour human rights, is thus demonstrated. The

---

[19] Vladimir Nabokov, *Pale Fire* (London: Penguin 1973), 185.
[20] Derrida, 'Psychoanalysis Searches the States of its Soul: The Impossible Beyond of a Sovereign Cruelty', in *Without Alibi*, trans. Peggy Kamuf (Stanford: Stanford University Press 2002), 240. See Elisabeth Weber, 'Ages of Cruelty: Jacques Derrida, Fethi Benslama, and their Challenges to Psychoanalysis', *Mosaic* 48 (2015), 1–27.

USA is not unique here, however egregious an example it seems to be. 'New cruelty' is non-carnivalesque, unlike the old cruel forms described in *The Genealogy of Morals* (2.3). It condemns its subjects to – to say the least – disciplinary coldness, and to the knowledge that people do not count, being, rather that euphemism, 'collateral damage'. Injury and injustice, after all, share a common root.

None of that cruelty, institutionalizing punishment as having to be meted out, and thus preserving the negativity and *ressentiment* of the ethos of revenge which Nietzsche discusses, would be possible without upholding the existence of the nation state. This is the obstacle which Derrida considers insuperable, preventing the abolition of the death penalty. The nation state, which multinational capitalism needs, is the force which upholds *ressentiment*, contending for a justice which claims that it must have it in its most favoured and lasting mode. The state must claim the right to award death to those who are inside it but are deemed non-conformable to it, or to those who are judged outside its interests, a threat to it. Execution comes about either via the 'new cruelty' of modern warfare which destroys bodies indiscriminately, with no regard to individuals, or by the anachronistic force of individual capital punishment. Here the old cruelty still persists, showing up an obscenity within state power.

Index

Adorno, Theodor 124
Agamben, Giorgio 102
Ainsworth, W.H. (William Harrison, 1805–82) 3, 31–2, 58
American abolitionists (c.19) 15–16
Anaximander fragment 103–4, 108, 167
Andress, David 77, 163–4
Anidjar, Gil 59, 136, 137, 149
Antal, Frederick 62
Antigone (Sophocles) 106, 113, 167–8
Arasse, Daniel 127–8
Arendt, Hannah 119–25, 147
Asad, Talal 11, 188–9
auto-immunity 149, 184, 187

Badinter, Robert xiii, 22, 115
Badiou, Alain 186–7
Bataille, Georges (1897–1962) 101, 131, 180
Baudelaire, Charles (1821–67) xi, 62, 87
Beauvoir, Simone de (1908–86) 119–25
Beccaria, Cesare (1738–94) 4, 15, 29, 33, 50, 114, 119, 129, 147, 170
Benjamin, Walter xi, xii, 8–10, 81, 85, 86, 88, 104–8, 124, 136–7, 143, 162, 185, 188
Bentham, Jeremy 29, 170
Bible 5–6, 124, 135, 136–9, 151
biopolitics and biopower 102, 113, 124, 188
Black Act 30, 110, 155, 162
Blake, William (1757–1827) 75, 111, 126
Blanchot, Maurice (1907–2003) xi, 18, 75, 96–7, 101, 103, 108, 112, 113, 116, 117, 132–3, 180, 186
blood 65, 125, 126, 127, 135–42, 151, 174
Boswell, James (1740–95) 27–8
Brasillach, Robert (1909–45) 120–5, 179
Bright, John (1811–89) 43, 45, 46
Bulwer, Edward George Earle Bulwer-Lytton, Ist Baron Lytton (1803–73) 2, 4, 32, 78, 84–5, 87, 94, 97, 156, 171

Burke, Edmund (1729–97) 80–1, 126–7
Butler, Judith 121, 195

Calcraft, William (hangman, 1800–79) 39, 45, 74
Camus, Albert (1913–60) 119, 134, 135, 195
Capote, Truman (1924–84), *In Cold Blood* 173–7, 183
Carlyle, Thomas (1795–1881) xii–xiii, 39, 85, 126–7, 154, 157, 164, 165, 167
Chaucer, Geoffrey (1340–1400) 137, 174
Chittick, Kathryn 31, 67
Cixous, Hélène 17
Christie, Agatha 191–2
Cobban, Alfred 165
Cobden, Richard (1804–65) 43, 45, 46
Collins, Philip xi, 35, 41, 155
Collins, William Wilkie (1824–89) 12, 40, 41, 49, 155, 169
  The Frozen Deep (play, with Dickens) 155, 168, 170
Columbine High School shooting 192, 188
Cortes, Juan Donoso 151
Courvoisier, François Benjamin (d. 1840) 30–1, 35, 36
Cromwell, Oliver (1599–1658) 127
cruelty 55, 59, 93, 115, 117, 119, 137, 150, 192, 197

Dante Alighieri (1265–1321) 169
Davis, Angela 18
De Maistre, Joseph 125–6
De Quincey, Thomas (1785–1859) 2, 9
Debord, Guy 184
Defoe, Daniel (1660–1731) 56, 111
Delhi rape case 193–6, 197
Derrida, Jacques x–xii, 7, 8, 10, 14–23, 29, 47, 59, 82, 93, 101–12, 138, 147, 149
  The Beast and the Sovereign 102, 108–12, 122, 167, 176, 181

The Death Penalty 47, 59, 113–19, 125–35, 142–52, 173, 179, 180, 186
Dissemination 196
'Faith and Knowledge' 59, 189, 197; *see also* autoimmunity
Force of Law 104–8
Glas 106, 167–8
Dews, Peter 59, 124
Dickens, Charles
  American Notes 77, 155
  Barnaby Rudge 11, 31, 45, 47, 50, 67–76, 85–6, 154, 155, 166
  Bleak House 41, 68, 76, 92, 94–8, 101, 129, 133
  A Christmas Carol (*Christmas Books*) 116
  David Copperfield 11, 77
  'The Demeanour of Murderers' 12–13
  'The Finishing Schoolmaster' 74
  Great Expectations 10, 12, 22–3, 38, 58, 60, 73, 155, 168, 196
  Hard Times 37
  'Hunted Down' 32
  'In and Out of Jail' (with Henry Morley and W.H. Wills) 98
  Little Dorrit 10, 30, 56, 60, 90, 116
  Martin Chuzzlewit 94
  Master Humphrey's Clock 76, 87
  The Mystery of Edwin Drood 170
  The Old Curiosity Shop 85
  Oliver Twist 8, 10, 11, 18, 32, 33, 46, 52, 64, 69, 84, 86, 117, 139, 170, 171
  ''On Duty with Inspector Field' 95–7
  Our Mutual Friend 13–14, 18, 20, 154, 162, 191, 197
  'The Perils of Certain English Prisoners' 161, 169
  'Pet Prisoners' 97
  Pictures from Italy 38
  Sketches by Boz 55, 76, 87
  A Tale of Two Cities 11, 41, 98, 107, 114, 153–72, 188, 197
  'A Visit to Newgate' 11
  'A Walk in a Workhouse' 97
Différance 92, 101, 104, 112
Dostoevsky, Fyodor (1821–81) xiii, 114, 126, 131, 180.
Duras, Marguerite 18

Egan, Pierce (1772–1849) 3, 42
Eichmann, Adolf 120–5
Eldon, Lord (John Scott, 1st Earl of Eldon 1751–1838) 39
Ellis, Ruth 40, 192
Ely 75–6
Evans, Richard J. 135
Evans, Timothy 19
evil, radical evil and the banality of evil 59, 109, 121–2, 124, 197
Ewart, William 30, 41

fascination 75, 89, 115–19
fascism 160–72, 186
Fauntleroy, Henry 2–4, 6, 30
Felman, Shoshana 120–1
Field, Charles, Inspector 12, 94–5, 97
Fielding, Henry 44, 48, 49–66, 80
  Amelia 63, 64
  A Clear State of the Case of Elizabeth Canning 63–4
  The Covent Garden Journal 53, 64
  An Enquiry into the Late Increase of Robbers 50–3, 57, 72
  Examples of the Interposition of Providence in the Detection and Punishment of Murder 64
  Jonathan Wild 55–7, 64, 65
  Tom Jones 48, 53, 64
  A True State of the Case of Bosavern Penlez 63, 65
  A Voyage to Lisbon 55
Fielding, Sir John 50
Fielding, K.J 18
Forster, John (1812–76) 68, 77
Foucault, Michel xi, xii, 10, 18–21, 46, 47, 51, 82, 96, 101, 102–3, 113, 114–15, 128, 135, 155, 180
Franklin, Sir John 168–9
French Revolution 30, 51, 77, 78, 102, 125–9, 146, 147–9, 153–72
Freud, Sigmund (1858–1939) 5–8, 13, 14, 34, 37, 61, 89, 110, 111, 117, 118, 134, 143, 151, 153, 162, 168, 172, 180, 196
fundamentalism 150, 187

Garrick, David (1717–79) 52
Gatrell, V.A.C. 33–4, 75

Gay, John (1685–1732) 55, 56
Gearhart, Suzanne 19
Géricault, Théodore (1791–1824) 61, 169
Gilpin, Charles (abolitionist) 43
Glover, Edward 116
Godwin, William (1756–1836) 2, 30, 33, 76–84, 91
   Caleb Williams 77–84, 85, 88, 92, 93, 147
   Enquiry Concerning Political Justice 78, 147, 155
   Fleetwood 77, 78
Goethe, Johann Wolfgang von (1749–1832) 77, 85, 104, 171
Goya (Francisco José de Goya y Lucientes, 1746–1828) 165–7
'great criminal' xii, 3, 6, 8, 9, 10, 13, 14, 17, 18, 22, 40, 84, 104, 107, 121, 131, 143, 176, 182, 196
Grey, Sir George, 2nd Baronet, Whig M.P. 1799–1882) 41
guillotine, the xii, 9, 59, 62, 115, 116, 118, 125–31, 134, 147, 151, 160, 163, 164, 165, 169, 186

Hastings, Warren (1732–1818) 80–1
Hazlitt, William (1778–1830) 18, 78
Hegel, Georg Friedrich Wilhelm 97, 101, 106, 113, 147–8
Heidegger, Martin 102, 103–5, 111
highwaymen 32, 60, 84, 95
Hobbes, Thomas (1588–1679) 29, 109, 110, 167
Hogarth, William x, xv, 27, 38, 47, 49–66, 74, 84, 86, 111
   Four Stages of Cruelty 55, 57–62, 65, 110, 157, 197
   Gin Lane 59
   The Harlot's Progress 57
   Industry and Idleness 58–9, 84
   Sarah Malcolm 57–9
Holcroft, Thomas (1745–1809) 79
Hölderlin, Friedrich (1770–1843) 108
Hollingsworth, Keith 4
Hood, Roger 16
Hood, Thomas (1799–1845) 12, 94
Howells, Christina 145
hunting 30, 46, 87, 136, 162, 178, 196
Hugo, Victor 19, 29, 113, 125–9
Hutter, Albert D. 158

Il y a 75
ipseity 98, 101, 103
Ireland, John 58

Jacobean (and Elizabethan) drama 65, 66, 84
Jerrold, Douglas 32, 43–5
Johnson, Barbara 93, 196
Johnson, Dr Samuel 27–8
justice 8, 17, 18, 20, 22, 28, 29, 36, 39, 45, 52, 56, 63, 66, 101–12, 123, 124, 125, 139, 143, 144, 148, 150, 156, 167, 170, 176, 185, 186, 192, 194, 198

Kafka, Franz (1883–1924) 132–4
Kamuf, Peggy 103, 113, 178, 197
Kant, Immanuel (1724–1804) 53, 59, 106, 110, 118–19, 121, 124, 143–4, 146, 149, 150, 177, 193
Kierkegaard, Søren (1813–55) 106
Kofman, Sarah 17
Kristeva, Julia 17–18, 121
   and abjection 160, 164

Labour Party, UK 191–2
Lacan, Jacques 22–3, 83, 93, 109–11, 119, 132, 160, 167, 171, 177, 184
Lacenaire, Pierre François 9
Lacoue-Labarthe, Philippe 133, 180
Lamb, Charles (1775–1834) 1–6, 8, 11, 17, 79
Langland, William (c.1332–86) 27
Le Bon, Gustave (1841–1931) 87, 89
Leavis, F.R 63
   and Q.D. Leavis 22
Leech, John (1817–64) 42
Levinas, Emmanuel 75, 96, 101, 107, 149
lex talionis 36, 59, 61, 119, 143, 144, 145, 146, 175
Lillo, George (1691–1739) 58
Linebaugh, Peter 27, 61, 63, 70

Mabbott, Thomas 87
Macaulay, Thomas Babington, 1st Baron Macaulay 1800–59) 39
McVeigh, Timothy 181–3
madness 7, 67, 68, 70, 79, 103, 106, 113, 127, 134, 164, 167, 197
Magnet, Myron 31, 72

Mailer, Norman, *The Executioner's Song* 178–81
Malraux, André 180
Manet, Edouard 179–80
Manning, Frederick and Maria 41–7, 74, 96
Marcus, Steven 67
Melville, Herman 107
Mencken, H.L. (Henry Louis, 1880–1956) 15
Meredith, Sir William 69, 70–1
metaphysics of presence 101–4, 106
Mill, John Stuart (1806–73) 29, 170
Milnes, Richard Monckton 30–1
Mitterand, François 22, 115
Montesquieu, Charles Louis de Secondat, Baron de la Brède et de Montesquieu (1689–1755) 29, 129, 159
Motte, François de la 154, 158–9
Mummelstein, Benjamin (1905–89) 122
Myers, F.W. (Frederic William Henry 1843–1901) 89

Nabakov, Vladimir 197
Nietzsche, Friedrich (1844–1900) xi, 6–10, 20–1, 82, 101, 103, 113, 118, 119, 138, 145, 167, 184, 185–6, 191, 198

Oliver, Kelly 18, 104, 145, 173, 179

Palmer, William 12, 13, 41, 95
Paulhan, Jean 186
Paulson, Ronald 57–9, 61, 63, 127, 166–6
Peel, Sir Robert (1788–1950) 34
picaro, the 84
Poe, Edgar Allan x, 11, 15–16, 67–98, 154, 156, 160
  Eureka 91
  'The Man of the Crowd' 76, 86–94, 157
  'The Masque of the Red Death' 86
  'The Murders in the Rue Morgue' 90, 94
  'The Purloined Letter' 90
Preston, John 49
Punch 42–3, 47

Radzinowicz, Leon 9, 51
Raleigh, Sir Walter (1552–1618) 140
rape xiv, 144, 155, 166, 174, 187, 192–5

reaction formation 145, 149, 150, 168, 169, 194
Reik, Theodor 144–51, 167
revenge 7, 17, 20, 31, 64–6, 77, 84, 92, 93, 119, 120, 123, 138, 143–5, 151, 158, 159, 166, 167, 175, 183, 186, 187, 189
Reynolds, John (1588–1655) 64–5, 84
Robespierre, Maximilien François Marie, Isidore de, 1758–94) xii, 39, 114, 127, 146, 147, 148, 149, 150, 185
Romilly, Samuel 9, 33, 38, 69
Rose, Jacqueline 40, 194
Rudé, George 85, 87

Sade, Donatien Alphonse François, Marquis de Sade (1740–1814) 119, 127
Sarat, Austin 16, 183
Schabas, William 16, 173, 196
Schmitt, Carl 109, 113, 114, 151
Scurr, Ruth 148, 149
Shakespeare, William
  Coriolanus 142
  Hamlet 5–6, 7, 77, 80, 82, 130, 138, 142, 149
  I Henry IV 1, 66
  3 Henry VI 82
  King Lear 60–1, 109
  Macbeth 2, 7, 9, 39, 41, 44, 52, 61, 75, 77, 92, 121, 138–42, 161, 163, 171, 174
  Measure for Measure 150
  Othello 82, 115, 121, 136
  Richard the Third 80, 121
  Romeo and Juliet 58
Shelley, Percy Bysshe (1792–1822) 19
Sheppard, Jack (1702–24) 3, 31, 32, 56, 59, 83, 84
Sidney, Algernon 127, 159
Simmel, Georg 88
Slater, Michael xiv, 45, 95, 168
Sorel, Georges (1847–1922) 89
spectres, and 'hauntology' 59, 101, 103, 117, 149, 150, 180
Spierenburg, Pieter 34
Stout, Daniel 164
Swift, Jonathan 54–6, 118

Tambling, Jeremy xi, 16, 29, 62, 94, 117, 161, 169

Tarde, Gabriel 89
Terror 51, 79, 83, 96, 147–8, 163–4, 173, 181–9, 196–8
Thackeray, William Makepeace 30–1
Theweleit, Klaus 161
Thurtell, William 1, 4, 12, 34, 38
Trilling, Lionel xi
Troppmann, Jean-Baptiste 129–31, 132
Turgenev, Ivan (1818–83) 129–31
Tynan, Kenneth 174

United States of America 15, 16, 18, 21, 173–84, 186, 187, 196, 197
Utilitarianism 7, 10, 16, 17, 18, 29, 50, 98, 110, 111, 119, 124, 170
see also Bentham; Mill

Vergès, Jacques 21–2
victimhood 17, 120, 145, 167, 183, 194

Vidocq, Eugène François (1775–1857) 91
Voss, Ralph F. 174, 176

Waco, Texas 181–2
Wainewright, Thomas (1794–1847) 32
Ward, Ned (Edward) 44
war (in Iraq, Syria, Ethiopia, Ukraine, Yemen) and 'war against terror' xiii–xiv, 112, 122, 165–6, 180–3, 188, 196–8
Welsh, Alexander 49
Wild, Jonathan 3, 54, 55–6, 61, 81
Wilson, Edmund 11
Wollstonecraft, Mary (1759–97) 127
Wordsworth, William (1770–1850) 33, 67
Wright, Stuart A. 181, 182
Wyatt, Sir Thomas (1503–42) 140–1

Zirker, Malvin R. 65, 73
Žižek, Slavoj 147, 194

www.ingramcontent.com/pod-product-compliance
Lightning Source LLC
Chambersburg PA
CBHW052112300426
44116CB00010B/1636